English Language Teaching

English Language Teaching

Edited by
MEENAKSHI RAMAN

PUBLISHERS & DISTRIBUTORS (P) LTD

Published by

ATLANTIC

PUBLISHERS & DISTRIBUTORS (P) LTD

7/22, Ansari Road, Darya Ganj,
New Delhi-110002
Phones : +91-11-40775252, 23273880, 23275880, 23280451
Fax : +91-11-23285873
Web : www.atlanticbooks.com
E-mail : orders@atlanticbooks.com

Branch Office
5, Nallathambi Street, Wallajah Road,
Chennai-600002
Phones : +91-44-64611085, 32413319
E-mail : chennai@atlanticbooks.com

Printed in India at Nice Printing Press, A-33/3A, Site-IV, Industrial Area, Sahibabad, Ghaziabad, U.P.

PREFACE

For many decades, teaching English whether for the beginners or for the advanced learners has been a challenging pursuit for the teachers of English. Though technology has opened innumerable avenues for teaching English using various modern techniques, teaching in the traditional classroom set up still has its own charm. Keeping in view the needs of the teachers and learners of English who also actively involve themselves in research, we have brought out this volume on English Language Teaching.

The insightful papers included in this volume speak on the multifarious aspects of English Language Teaching and provide adequate coverage on the theoretical as well as the practical domains in the field of ELT.

Usha Manjunath and Kathyayani Venkatesh review the major methods in English Language Development (ELD) that are found useful in a bilingual context, specifically with the experiences gained from educating Spanish children in U.S. schools. Their paper identifies major issues in ELD in India and looks at what we as educators can learn from the American experience.

Meenakshi Raman accentuates the idea that news media, both print and visual, use language extensively and play a crucial role in communicating various types of information to people across diverse cultural settings. In her paper she discusses the advantages and the methodology to be adopted for viewing, reading and analyzing the news items in ELT classrooms.

Mehmet Celik provides a framework of English intonation for the teaching of English as a second/foreign language. The framework proposed is primarily based on what is most salient in the more recent scholarly studies of intonation phenomena, and secondarily, on what can be teachable. The paper will be of immense help to the teachers of English as the author's own experience in the teaching of the phenomena has been brought out.

Emphasis in teaching of reading has shifted from teaching it as a passive skill to demanding active participation from the student readers. Malavika Sharma argues that readers must bring meaning to print rather than expect to receive. Besides, she discusses the strategies of teaching reading comprehension.

Krishna Mohan and Meera Banerji have made an attempt to provide a fresh taxonomy of ELT. In this paper they suggest that the principles and concerns of ESP should shape the ELT course design at the university level in India.

Mimi Singh Sandhu emphasizes the need for the learners to feel the language while learning. She suggests that a dynamic approach can be adopted for teaching the students at the college level through accent and intonation levels.

Keeping in mind the increasing importance given these days to Distance Learning, Pushp Lata in her paper, emphasizes the student-centred approach in designing teaching material and curricula for teaching of English to the distance learners.

Sangeeta Sharma demonstrates how subtlety of language can be adeptly and judiciously used by the copy writer in creating advertisements and thereby can be easily used in ELT classrooms.

Huang, Shih-Jen and Liu, Hsiao-Fang address issues such as (i) the similarities and differences of language teaching and learning between a traditional classroom and a multimedia language lab under the communicative framework, (ii) changes in the roles of teachers and students when they are in a different teaching environment from traditional classroom, and (iii) the implications of the Communicative Language Teaching Approach in a multimedia computer language laboratory.

Alessandro Monti discusses the lexical migrancy leading to the emergence of a literary language grounded on disjunctive sequences of lexical diaspora. The paper lays bare what is "untranslatable" in this aesthetics of exchange which makes the gap going beyond the mere severance of continuity and does transcend the blessed proliferation of cross-cultural texts.

Gerd Rohmann demonstrates Aldous Huxley's early journalism and brings to light an important idea that a critic really speaks only of himself and is only interested in what he reveals about himself.

N.D.R. Chandra, keeping pace with the technology-driven world of today, discusses the immense impact of the Cyber Age on the English. He emphasizes the need for teachers and educationists to evolve a cultural literary canon considering local, national, economic and global demands.

Mihaela Mudure has presented a paper from the perspective of comparative multiculturalism. The author firmly believes that there is no monocultural society, that all societies are multicultural, characterized by ethnic and cultural diversity.

Sivasish Biswas in her paper 'A Quest for Meaning' argues that readers interpret a text, because they try to understand and make some meaning, or order their experiences. Thus meaning is constantly created and recreated—it is a perpetual quest.

In his paper, Shailendra Kr. Mukul elaborates how to use language with different people in different situations and stresses the importance of communication approach to language learning. The paper highlights that acquiring communicative competence is much morphology, syntax and phonology of a language.

Jaydeep Sarangi focuses on the role of classroom teacher in ELT in India as ours is a multi-lingual country. He highlights the fact that learners come from different socio-linguistic backgrounds and pluralism is a hallmark of ELT in India.

Ghanshyam and Kushwaha discuss the concerns of National curriculum framework to meet the changing societal needs and demands and how these are directly and indirectly influenced by language teaching. The paper brings forward the authors' belief that drama in the class of ESL can play vital role in meeting these demands.

Smita Jha argues that Pidgins and Creoles are not the deformed/distorted versions of other languages or media of expression in their own right. Rather, they are the necessary steps in the evolution of languages.

Harekrishna Pradhan, in his scholarly paper proposes a model of stylistics incorporating an eleven-component framework drawn from the various schools of Linguistics and Linguistics Criticism including Discourse Analysis, Pragmatics and Text Linguistics as well as Traditional rhetoric. The author demonstrates this model by applying the framework to Orwell's *Nineteen Eighty-Four.*

All the contributors to this Volume are teachers engaged in teaching, research and production of materials. I thank each one of them for contributing scholarly papers.

My special thanks to all faculty members of the Languages Group, BITS, Pilani for giving me their valuable suggestions in editing this Volume.

Mere thanks in a few words will be highly inadequate to express my sincere gratitude to Dr K.R. Gupta, Chairman, M/s Atlantic Publishers and Distributors who has entrusted me with the responsibility of editing this Volume on ELT. I also thank him and his organization for seeing the book through the press.

MEENAKSHI RAMAN
Editor

CONTENTS

1

English Language Development and Academic Performance in a Multi-linguistic Context

USHA MANJUNATH and KATHYAYANI VENKATESH

The importance of English language learning cannot be overstressed. It is the official language of 63 countries and unofficial second language in many countries. Nearly one billion people around the world have some knowledge of English, either as a native language or as a second/foreign language. Except for certain regions in the world, English is the predominant language of international commerce. Proficiency of English language in the job market has not only become more crucial with globalization of trade but has opened up new jobs themselves with advances in telecommunication technology. Many countries in the Indian Subcontinent use English as an important tool in higher education, administration and mass media. Presently it is taught in almost every country on earth.

English language learning/teaching for educational purposes are fraught with difficult challenges in many countries like India and the United States of America. The latter as a nation of immigrants represents cultural and linguistic diversity. It can be viewed as a mixture of distinct cultures and tongues. Though much more complex, India's linguistic situation can be compared to that of U.S.A. The various states of India have their own languages apart from the National Language (Hindi). National Policy on Language Education in India recommends teaching of three languages through schooling and for functional purposes, English chosen as one among those three in many situations.

In general, children's educational success can be best achieved when academic instructions are given in the mother tongue (primary language or L1). Previously in the U.S., schools were designed to educate students whose native language was English. Others whose language was not English were expected to succeed just by being exposed to English. However, the increasing population of ethnic minority students has challenged the educators to change the basic assumption regarding schooling. There is a need to provide quality education to these students. India on the other hand has had English as a Second or Foreign Language at various levels of schooling for nearly three centuries because of its history of British colonization. In fact many of the professional and technical education in India are provided in English. This has proved to be an advantage to Indian Information Technology professionals in the business world. The last four decades has also seen more and more parents opting English as a medium of instruction even at elementary school level for their children. Thus the focus is not only on schooling (teaching academics) but also on teaching the language (English) so that the children from other language background can benefit from academic instruction. This paper reviews major methods in English Language Development that are found useful in a bilingual context, specifically with the experience gained from educating Spanish children in U.S. schools. The last section identifies the major issues with ELD in India and looks at what we as educators can learn from the American experience.

English Language Development

Before going into details of English Language Development (ELD) it is necessary to be familiar with language acquisition and its stages. Language acquisition goes through the following stages: Pre-Production (silent period), Early Production, Speech Emergence, Intermediate Fluency and finally towards Advanced Fluency. Basic Interpersonal Communication Skill (BICS) level is one in which the child will be able to communicate basic needs and wants, can carry on basic interpersonal conversation. This process takes about 1 to 3 years to develop. But BICS is not sufficient to facilitate academic success. On the other hand, Cognitive Academic Language Proficiency (CALP) is the ability to communicate ideas and thoughts with clarity and efficiency. It is the ability to carry on advanced interpersonal conversation. It takes about 6 to 7 years (or longer) to develop and is essential for academic success. The BICS develops in the initial period of language acquisition (up to intermediate level) and the CALP starts from early advanced level and continues to develop.

With this background let us examine the methods of English Language Development and how the educators teach the language as well as the academic content. Language acquisition research stresses the importance of language in providing the cognitive foundation for instruction. Language and academic development is better achieved by including the student's primary language. Mere emphasis on grammar, spelling and accurate pronunciation is not the primary purpose of language instruction. Accent is not the indicator of fluency in a language. Language is not merely learned from drills and worksheets but from active process seeking meaning. It is best achieved through direct engagement and experience.

The focus of ELD methods have shifted from Grammar based approaches to communicative approaches and Academic Content based approaches. The communicative approaches include the Natural Approach and Total Physical Response. Their main focus is Language Acquisition. Current ELD approaches aim at language development as well as academic content instruction. Language Experience Approach on the other hand focuses on Literacy Development. A well-balanced ELD programme will utilize activities or lessons that are content-based, literacy and literature-based as well as communication-based.

Methods of English Language Teaching

All the methods discussed above can be divided into broadly into three categories:

1. Instructions for Language Development which includes the Natural Approach, Total Physical Response and Content-based ESL.

Natural Approach is similar to the way in which a child naturally acquires first language within the home and community. The acquisition of second language is similar to first language acquisition. The following basic principles are important in this approach—Comprehension precedes production; Production emerges in stages; the activities play a central role and must be meaningful. The teacher is required to provide comprehensive input and opportunity to interact in a language rich environment. Speech is secondary and during speech emergence the errors are not corrected.

Total physical response is also based on the way in which the child acquires the first language. It can be engaging as it involves body movements. Basic principles of this approach are—Listening precedes Speaking; Understanding is developed through the use of body movements; and Speaking is never forced. The teacher gives commands and models the action. This is repeated until the students respond easily. Gradually the modelling is faded and students learn to respond to verbal directions. The complexity of commands is increased gradually.

2. Literacy Instruction for English learners which includes the Language Experience Approach (LEA).

The Language Experience Approach is designed to extend oral language development naturally into reading and writing using the student's language. The assumption being that the natural developmental processes that children undergo in learning their first language (oral and written) also occur in second language acquisition. In reading, the natural processes include using the knowledge of sound/symbol relationship (grapho-phonics), word order and grammar (syntax) and meaning (semantics) to predict and confirm the meaning and structure.

Classrooms supporting this approach share the following features: Students are engaged in meaningful activities and also use their knowledge of topics from the text that are familiar to them. Instruction is cognitively demanding. However it is scaffolded to ensure student's success. Scaffolding is to provide temporary support by capable person to help the students understand the new concepts and skills. Gradually the scaffolding is reduced. Learning is organized into topics and themes in such a way that the students can build on previously learnt concepts/vocabulary, grammatical structures and academic skills. Flexible grouping of students is carried out during learning. Immersion techniques are used wherein students are provided with a print rich environment.

3. Instruction for Academic/Content Development which includes Primary Language Instruction, Specially Designed Academic Instruction in English (SDAIE)/Sheltered English, Cognitive Academic Language Learning Approach (CALLA), Mainstream (grade/class level) Classroom Instruction and Computer Assisted Language teaching.

Primary Language Instruction is reported to be the most effective method for developing language and literacy in both primary and second languages (L1 and L2). ELD is built into the curriculum. The training programme includes daily systematic ELD, academic instruction through L1. This is suitable for students in earliest stages of Language Acquisition.

SDAIE/Sheltered English includes ELD with high intensity English with at least 75% instruction in English and continued L1 support (not to exceed 25% of the instruction time). This is suitable for students with Intermediate Fluency in English. Teachers can make use of cooperative learning, audiovisual media, multicultural sources and grouping of students to benefit and motivate. It has been reported that the mainstream students also benefit from this technique.

CALLA is designed to promote acquisition of academic language proficiency. It focuses on explicit instruction of learning strategies. It integrates content, Language and strategies (which the students apply and use on their own to help them learn). Strategies involve metacognitive (to plan, monitor and evaluate learning), cognitive (to interact with the materials and apply to specific to learning task) and social-affective (to interact with others). Such strategies help avoid trial and error learning and to correct their mistakes.

Mainstream (grade/class level) classroom instruction is the goal for English learners. The goal is fluent English proficiency and mastery of grade level content. This in turn incorporates ELD, SDAIE and all instructions in English. Students with advanced proficiency who no longer need additional language support can be the appropriate candidates for such an approach.

ELD and Academic Performance

Having reviewed some important methods currently practised in the U.S. let us examine how these programmes are implemented to maximize academic performance. In schools at present with Spanish speaking students, Transitional Bilingual Instruction (TBI), Sheltered English Immersion Programme (SEI) and Sheltered English Mainstream (SEM) are the three major programmes followed. The usual practice is to enroll children typically for one year in the appropriate programme (which may last longer depending on the student needs). Then evaluate them at the end of one year. The evaluation is based on a battery of tests such as language proficiency test (California English Language Development Test—CELDT), Teacher observation (Student Oral Language Observation Matrix) and Standardized test scores, Reading and Writing Proficiency Testing. Based on their progress students are moved to different programmes. Transitional Bilingual Instruction programme can range from Submersion (with least support from L1) to Dual Language Instruction (includes academic instruction in L1 for as long as possible along with L2/English for part of the school day, *i.e.* most support from L1). Usually students are in these programmes for a period of 3 to 4 years and then mainstreamed. Studies have shown that traditional ESL programmes students benefit initially. But in the long run (by 12th grade) their achievement levels are not high as those trained using two-way bilingual programmes (Dual Immersion Programme). The latter group continues to show enhanced performance and the students tend to stay at the top. Such studies highlight the fact that language complements learning and that performance of bilingual students can even surpass that of monolinguals. Some educatcrs in the U.S. are beginning to view bilinguals as an asset in education than a problem.

Strategies for Teaching English Language Learners

Classroom is a home for the language of students and the teacher is stimulating the language experience. In a class promoting ELD, primary language is welcome with focus still aimed at ELD. Developing proficiency in English is a multifaceted task. Students should be able to use their listening skills to gain information. They must make use of speaking to demonstrate their knowledge. They should use reading and writing skills to support academic success. They should also be able to think critically and creatively. Current approaches stress the importance of integrating the above language skills of listening, speaking, reading and writing.

Listening is necessary to develop speaking skills. Listening-comprehension, thinking and remembering all go together. However, the listening skill is the most neglected one, both in primary and second language teaching. In a classroom situation listening for content is assumed. Strategies involving listening to repeat, listening to understand and listening for communication should be emphasized. **Speaking** involves oral proficiency, expression, assimilating and producing discourse for interpersonal information and comprehension/production of cognitive/academic language. Oral practice can be guided practice, communicative practice and free conversation.

Reading involves decoding the text and construction of meaning. It is not just reading mechanics and it is acquiring knowledge. Can be accomplished more effectively through reading in a larger context, working collaboratively and by reading/writing for the purpose of communication. **Writing** is an opportunity for students to learn with the language and communicate effectively. Strategies for literacy instruction include pre-reading activities, Language Experience Approach and Directed Reading-Thinking Activity (DRTA).

A number of activities and games can be effectively planned for developing listening, speaking, reading and writing in a classroom. Listening- and reading-comprehension form an important aspect of language competence development, which in turn is a prerequisite for academic achievement. Teachers should actively seek innovative ways to achieve this based on the level of the students and their pace of learning.

Teacher's Role in Teaching English

In ELD classes, teachers must focus on both language and content. The teacher must modify their talk, attend to clarification, use appropriate questioning strategies and must know how to deal with the errors.

- There is a natural order in development of student's communicative competence in second language. Teacher must be aware of this and make use of this to build communicative competence. These consist of Memorization, Formulaic expressions (greetings), answering in unison, talking to self, elaboration, anticipating answers, monitoring, asking for assistance, request for clarification and role playing.
- Provide comprehensive input and output. This can be done by using visuals and context, implementing listening activities, using multi modal activities, asking questions in a variety of ways to suit the students' needs, link new information to the already learnt, exposing students to higher levels of comprehensible language.
- Using appropriate language modifications like precise pronunciation, using simple/shorter sentences, pausing frequently, repeating information, slower rate of speaking, elaborating and paraphrasing.
- Checking for clarification by pausing and asking if the students have understood, asking questions requiring simple responses, asking students to repeat the directions.
- Using questioning strategies like those requiring answering by actions (in the initial stages), incorporating two choices in the question, and gradually move to "wh" questions.
- Dealing with the errors in a reasonable way like accepting the errors initially, modelling the appropriate language and error correction with older students (in such a way that it should foster self-correction).
- Making use of material resources in the class: Classroom should contain picture charts/pictures, maps and globes, charts and posters, books, catalogues, magazines, puzzles, science equipment, manipulatives, computer software etc.

English Language Development among School Children in India

Though some Indian schools seem to have coped up well with reference to ELD and academic performance in a complex multilingual context, much more needs to be done to improve the quality of education in general. Inputs from the school system into the child's scientific thinking, felicitous use of language, competence to search for information and to work out solutions are crucial. Educators and parents in India have to seriously consider if schools are providing such inputs. Evaluation of ELD/ELT programmes followed in India and subsequent effect on academic performance should be carried out.

Much of the literature and evidence support that language learning in general proceeds in the order of listening, speaking, reading and writing. However, majority of schools in India starts teaching English language by emphasizing writing at a very early stage of language learning. Students would have mastered reading and writing with some relative competence, however, their listening skills would be poorly developed. Further, literacy based approaches with limited content-based ELD would not provide a good language competence essential for academic performance/learning. It is possible that teachers resort to using rote learning practices in order to cope with operational difficulties in larger classrooms commonly seen in Indian schools. Many of the activity- and experience-based language enrichment programmes get neglected. Many schools at best limit to teaching what is in the English Language textbooks prescribed for different grade/class levels and make minimal attempts to develop English language from the academic perspective at large. The systematic testing of language development/progress described earlier is rarely conducted in Indian schools and evaluation may be limited to regular written examination and some oral skills testing (even that may be limited to testing what the students acquired through rote learning or practice drills during the classes!).

On English Language Teaching, the report by the Committee for Improvement of Quality of Education to the Government of India states that wrong sentence structure, use of inappropriate vocabulary and spelling mistakes are very common due to lack of speaking skills and correct grammatical knowledge. Further the report highlights that the teachers ignore the linguistic aspects. The most important problem, which needs serious attention, is lack of language comprehension and exposure to reading materials among the students.

Mallikarjun has tried to identify the importance of multi-lingual situation in India and advocates a multilingual approach towards language learning in schools. He has criticized that the curriculum objectives for the three languages (as per the National Policy on Languages) taught in schools as being same. The educators should specify goals for each language to be taught in schools and methodologies to achieve them.

Teachers gathered to discuss the possibility, scope and methodology of setting up an ELTeCS in South India (English Language Teaching Contacts Scheme with British Council, U.K.) identified the key concerns for English language teaching. They were inadequate language and methodology competencies among teachers, lack of teacher-friendly and learner-friendly materials for use in classrooms and absence of innovative evaluation methods for teachers in primary/elementary schools. Such problems in addition to the mushrooming of English medium schools in urban and semi-urban India can have a negative impact on the quality of education.

With such diversity in languages and educational needs of the people, educators in India have to seriously look at the English Language Development in terms of language proficiency as well as academic performance. Though methods/ programmes found useful in the U.S. schools may not be directly applicable to us they do provide some useful insights into ELD among our school children. They highlight the importance of continuous improvisation of teaching methodologies/programmes, development of teacher's competence, systematic language evaluation as well as academic success. Concepts based on language acquisition in terms of development of Basic Interpersonal Communication Skills and Cognitive Academic Language Proficiency can be useful in designing English Language Development programmes. Now the following questions arise: Are some Indian schools overzealous of teaching English language neglect the proficiency in the primary language? Also, do we have a subgroup of children who at the end of 12 years of English medium education neither have proficiency in English nor perform well in academics? If yes, how can we overcome such problems? Can two-language/dual immersion programme (primary language and English) be effective in Indian schools? Systematic study in these areas may help educators develop suitable programmes to meet the challenges of ELD and academic success in multi-linguistic environments.

WORKS CITED

Jack C. Richards and Theodore S. Rodgers. *"Approaches and Methods in Language Teaching: A Description and Analysis."* Cambridge, U.K.: Cambridge University Press, 1986.

Lynne T. Diaz-Rico and Kathryn Z. Weed. "*The Cross-cultural Language and Academic Development Handbook—A Complete K-12 Reference Guide.*" Second Edition. Boston: Allyn and Bacon—A Pearson Education Company, 2002.

Mallikarjun B. A Multilingual Approach towards Language Teaching in Indian Schools. *Language in India*, Volume 2: 1 March 2002.

Maya Manon. The ELTeCS Launch in Cochin: English Language Teaching Contacts Scheme—British Council, U.K. India. www.ELTeCS-English-The British Council United Kingdom.htm, March 2002.

M.S. Thirumalai. "An Introduction to TESOL—Teaching English to Speakers of Other Languages." *Language in India*, Volume 2: 2 April 2002.

Lecture by Samuel O. Ortiz, Ph.D.

Sridhar Kumaraswami. "Teaching methods flawed" in *Hindusthan Times*, New Delhi: Hindusthan Times Com.htm, 18 October 2002.

Vineland School English Language Development Resource Books. California, U.S.A.: Vineland School District, 2002.

2

USING NEWS MEDIA IN ELT CLASSROOMS AT THE UNIVERSITY LEVEL

MEENAKSHI RAMAN

Language is the medium through which we transmit and interchange our ideas, feelings, courses of action and also various other types of information. As we all know, language is not a natural phenomenon but a creation of man's social needs. Hence each society depends as much on language as it is on air and water for its survival. The moment we think of communication in a society, we cannot help thinking instantly about language and media. Among the various types of communication contents brought forth through the media, news items occupy very significant position in reflecting the day-to-day, hour-to-hour happenings in the society. News media, both print and visual use language extensively and play a crucial role in communicating various types of information to people across diverse cultural settings. The fact that this media mirrors the society is itself adequate to use it invariably in the ELT classrooms which mainly aim at inculcating and developing communication skills in the learners thereby enabling them become more useful and responsible members of the society.

Dedicated teachers are always eager to return to the basic question of what to teach and how particularly in this age of information explosion (World Bank 1981, 07). At the university level an adequate and appropriate use of news media would enable the learners to familiarize them with the journalistic language, register and other stylistic devices that are at play when a piece of news is presented either in print or through a television channel. The tasks accompanying each text would give the learners confidence to read and view English language news items in print and on the television for themselves outside the classroom. Ultimately, this would achieve autonomous learning by enhancing their strategic competence.

Teaching is a continuous transformational process and teacher educators at the university level must adopt innovative strategies and provide leadership to revamp the education programmes they are dealing with. The paper attempts to discuss the issues involved in using news media both from the teacher's and the learner's perspective. It mainly focuses on the advantages and the large variety of thought provoking tasks that can be derived from viewing, reading and analysing the news items presented through print as well as visual media. The paper also discusses the methodology, which may be adopted in implementing these language activities in the ELT classrooms.

Advantages of using News Media in ELT Classrooms

Everyday, the students are invariably exposed to both written and oral information coming from press and television. Both modes of presenting news and feature stories provide creative and original ideas for making effective use of the wealth of readily accessible, authentic and up-to-date English. So why not this powerful tool is used in ELT classrooms? Using news media in ELT classrooms would help to develop a critical analysis and understanding of the various aspects of English language namely pronunciation, accent, vocabulary, idiomatic expression, sentence structure, cohesive devices etc. In addition, it would help in various language activities such as listening and reading comprehension and dictogloss. Editorials and gossip columns, serious and light-hearted newspapers can be used to teach formal and informal varieties of English; editorials and feature articles can provide passages for summary and comprehension; letters to the editor can demonstrate good features of letter writing; reports on court proceedings can illustrate questioning techniques; and various articles can provide direct and indirect speech for grammar samples of study. Both the oral and written contents of news media can also help to organize certain other skill building exercises such as conversation and role-play. The tasks accompanying each text would give the students confidence not only to read and view news in English language in print and on the television but also to understand and appreciate the nuances of phonetic, semantic, syntactic and stylistic features of the English language used in the news items and articles. Moreover, the students could be challenged with increasingly demanding and thought provoking tasks, which are practical and focused to helping them enhance their power of thinking and develop their critical skills (Meriono and Massi, 1998, 17). For example, students would be able to learn and develop the inverted pyramid practice, which is followed in preparing news items. This refers to the conventional practice in most news media, which uses the beginning of the report as a spot for emphasis. In most cases reporters put what they consider to be the most important aspects of the story at the beginning and the least important at the end (Chaffee and Petrick 1975, 36). Use of news media in ELT classrooms would hone the editorial skills of the students to a great extent. In all, this would ultimately develop their strategic competence and lead to autonomous learning. The most significant advantage of this practice is that one recording of a news programme or one single issue of a newspaper may contain material for teaching various types of writing: description, analysis and synthesis, comparison and contrast, and process description; and they provide models of good written form: paragraphing, topic sentence, introduction, conclusions, etc. (Pemagbi 1995, 53).

Methodology

When we decide to use the news medium, we need to bear in mind that they are a resource to be used in our classroom instruction. They are in no way intended to be the only activity used during the course. They need to be specifically designed to provide our students with stimulating, challenging topical and real material to support the course syllabus. To facilitate task-based learning (TBL) the teachers should see to it that a sequence of communicative tasks to be carried about in English. "*Communicative task is a piece of classroom work which involves learners in comprehending, manipulating, producing or interacting in the target language while their attention is principally focused on meaning rather than form*" (Carter and Nunan 2001, 173).

Language in a communicative task is seen as bringing about an outcome through exchange of meanings. Therefore the teacher who wishes to use the powerful News media in ELT classroom should plan and decide the methodology. The following points may be considered in designing this methodology:

- Frequency of using News Items
- Analysis of Material
- Selection of Print and TV News Items
- Planning the Sessions
- Classroom Activity
- Post Viewing/Reading/Listening

Frequency of using News Items

Depending upon the quantum of syllabus, availability of facilities and the suitability of time, the teacher should decide when it is the most convenient moment to expose the students to news items. The teacher should also decide how frequently this activity can be organized in the ELT classroom. In fact the news or TV clip should not be dated when shown to the students. In a more specific situation such as the case of students of Business Communication, Technical Report Writing etc. who come under the ESP learner category the criteria may be slightly different. This is because ESP has always seen itself as materials-driven and as a classroom-based activity concerned with Practical Outcomes. The key-defining feature of ESP is that its teaching and materials are founded on the results of needs analysis (Carter and Nunan 2001, 131). This needs analysis would turn out to be beneficial only when these ESP learners are exposed to up-dated, daily material which they have to process, that is understand, retrieve and reconstruct after viewing or reading the news item. This is precisely what they are expected to do in their professional lives. Therefore the frequency of exposure should depend on the students' needs, interests linguistic aspects to be practised and time availability.

Analysis of the Material

Before choosing the news items for use in ELT classrooms, the teachers should consider text structure, length, linguistic difficulty (including vocabulary) and content of both the press and television news. All of these are important to any task to be presented to the student, and each can be manipulated as a variable in itself. Apart from dealing with the linguistic aspect, attention should also be drawn to the discovery of the macro structure of the whole text, since this constitutes a crucial criterion for the selection of the material.

Thus teachers should set out to explore different texts so they can recognize the text patterns in each text. Then, this strategy should be explicitly taught and fostered as a skill in its own right. Passages should be analysed for differences which may predispose writers of certain subjects to use some strategies over others.

The learner should be able to recognize different patterns, such as an expository presentation with a problem-solution pattern, an argumentation or debate with a hypotheses-confirmation format, or a sequencing of events presented in a narrative text. Likewise, the analysis and retrieval of information based on the layout, pictures, and personal responses to news stories should be encouraged.

The lesson should also develop critical viewing by providing the learner with problem-solving and research skill through the use of news clips and newspaper cuttings and fast-paced graphics which depict formats and features. In the case of the broadcast news, the teacher should tape the programme when it airs and show all or part of it to the class. For example, a teacher may begin with a review of the day or week's top news stories. Discussion may focus on current issues and trends unfolding in the news. International news should be brought to the class so that students can explore selected events around the globe. All sorts of topics may be discussed including business and commerce, science and medical achievements, and special features such as art, drama, music and literature. As stated above this choice should be based on course requirements, objectives, and the learner's interests.

The learning of English can actually be facilitated and optimised by explicitly teaching the linguistic features, plus helping the learner become aware of the strategy required to extract meaning when confronted with oral or written media texts.

Hence the teacher need to put lot of effort in analysing the various news items with special reference to the level of students and the aspects of language to be taught or practised. This analysis is fundamental to the process of using news media in their ELT classrooms.

Selection of Appropriate Print and TV News Items

After careful analysis of various news items the teachers should proceed towards choosing appropriate reading or viewing news material for their classroom teaching. Both print and television news items can extend the language learning horizons concerned by showing language being used by a great variety of people for a number of different purposes in a wide range of contexts. For example different newspapers adopt different styles of presenting the news items; similarly different TV channels use different way of presenting the news items; even within the news items some channels use narratives (ETIC 1979: 26).

The following factors should be considered for the selection of suitable news items:

- Length
- Level of difficulty
- Subject matter (persuasive, descriptive, narrative)
- Mode
- Variety.

Length

Length is an important factor in text selection. The news item selected should neither be too long nor too short. If it is too long the students would become fatigued by the demands of the task; if it is too short there may not be enough material or time for the students to become involved in reading and viewing. Of course, less proficient learners may be asked to read or view shorter passages so that they do not feel the burden of reading or viewing news items and feel motivated to go for longer items. Generally a length of about ten or fifteen minutes seems to be appropriate under most conditions (approximately 1500 words).

Level of Difficulty

The next factor is the level of difficulty. The teachers should realize that the cognitive load imposed by reading and viewing the news item should not be so great that the learners are prevented from being able to process what they have seen or read. They also should see to it that the text does not fall so far below the learner's ability that it is only perceived at a superficial level and involves very little use of strategies. The level of difficulty necessarily includes the level of conceptual competence, analytical skills, language proficiency, familiarity with the topics etc. of the learners. Hence, the teachers need to consider all these factors while finding out the level of difficulty of the news items to be chosen.

Subject Matter

It's better to avoid the material with subject matter entirely unfamiliar to the learners. For example if the students are in their first year of undergraduate programme they may not be very familiar with corporate news items; they may be more interested in sports news items. But as we are aware, the possible subject matter variables in news items include topics related to human conditions such as family relationships, education, health and environmental issues, aspects of everyday life, political issues, international relationships, sports affairs, etc. They may provide interesting material as long as they are easily comprehended by the learners. Hence the teachers should choose those news items which may not only interest the learners but also benefit them in understanding the cultural, social, political, economical and commercial aspects of their nation and other nations.

Mode

Depending upon the convenience and the available facilities, the teachers can select oral (TV) or written mode (newspapers or internet) of news items for their use in ELT classes. Besides considering the convenience and available facilities, the teachers should keep in mind the necessity in terms of the skills to be developed in their students. For example, to hone the phonetic or listening skills of the students, they should use the oral mode whereas to sharpen the reading or critical skills of the students they may use written mode. Again it would be appropriate to use both the modes for carrying out reconstruction activities through Dicto-composition exercises. In fact it would be emphatic if the teachers try to arrange for presenting the same piece of news in both the modes—oral and written—from different angles as far as possible. This would enable the learners to come conversant with the news item by first reading about it and then watching it on television or *vice versa*.

Variety

To foster a critical debate among students, the teachers may obtain news items from several newspapers or their websites so that the learners might be able to compare and contrast different treatments of the same news item. With the selection of a variety of newspapers or news channels, the learners may be asked to identify different points of view and comment on the subjectivity of the news item. Further this variety would enable the learners to understand the function of persuasion in the news which is supposed to be very vital for presenting news items. By going for a variety of newspapers or TV channels, the learners can retrieve the most important aspects of the news story, take the roles of the journalists and reconstruct the news items in their own language and style. A sample exercise for comparative analysis is given at the end of this article (Jones Leo 1998, 182-83).

PLANNING THE SESSIONS

Previewing

The learners should be provided an initial focus on the context in which the news event has taken place. By means of certain warm-up activities such as role playing, discussing the meanings of certain unfamiliar or difficult words in the text etc. the learners may be motivated and guided for the task of reading or viewing the news item. If the oral mode is to be used, the learners may be asked to go through the corresponding written mode of the text in advance. It is better to use the recorded news items of TV as frequently as possible since this would interest learners more than newspaper items because of the use of lot of visuals.

CLASSROOM ACTIVITY

Viewing/Reading/Listening

News items and feature stories are good means to develop the skill of listening and other related skills. The visual support such as people speaking, gesture body language, eye contact etc. they provide help to a great extent in comprehending the text better. Similarly news items and features stories used from print media serve as good means to develop the skills of reading and other related skills. The learner is actively involved in solving problems through hands—on tasks that involve locating and extracting specific information, matching, sequencing, selecting appropriate answers; agreeing/disagreeing with certain statements, taking notes, summarizing, and so on. These activities are aimed at developing not only language but also text organization.

The teachers should always keep in mind that the learners are viewing or reading the news items for a purpose. In fact the learners are interacting with and reacting to the text rather than passively absorbing the written and oral information transmitted to them. After completing such tasks the learners should practice and extend the language read or heard in the sequence and to analyse the types of interaction by closely observing the linguistic input of the selected material.

Reconstructing

Since the learners bring much background acknowledge to the reading, listening or viewing task, the main objective of the teachers should be to help the learner reconstruct one possible version of the news item under discussion. Dicto-composition (dictation and composition), also known as dictogloss, is one of the important language learning activities. Basically it is a reconstruction activity which improves several skills: the ability to listen, to retain and recall, to spell and punctuate properly, to construct appropriate sentences in a given context and to use linguistic devices that bind phrases and sentences into a text.

The teachers should make the learners try to use the linguistic and strategic power that they have as L1 users and transfer these abilities to the tasks at hand. Strategies of guessing, predicting and inferring are fostered because they are of paramount importance in text processing and reconstructing activities. To facilitate the learners elicit the most meaningful units of information, the teachers can implement the traditional five Ws (Who/Whom, What, When, Where and Why/How) as the starting point. Once the learners answer these questions (clippings may be shown again or read out in between), the learners should be engaged in more challenging activities oriented towards the reconstruction of the story. More demanding tasks can be provided to help the learners unravel aspects related to the tone, subjectivity and tendentiousness of the text under discussion at a later stage.

Analysing

Once the learners are at ease with the meaning, they can identify the rhetorical aspects such as the general pattern of text organization as well as the use of cohesive signals, different syntactic patterns, particular lexical items, and idiomatic expressions, etc. Similarly, the learners' attention should be drawn to the stylistic devices and the tone of the story. By focusing on these formal aspects of the language the learners would develop their receptive abilities and comprehension of the indicators of additional meanings. Acquiring proficiency in analysing and understanding the formal aspects of the language would enable the learners become more effective in speaking and writing the language used. A sample worksheet for analysing news is given at the end of this article.

Post-viewing/Reading/Listening

Keeping the ultimate aim of this approach that is to achieve autonomous learning by developing the strategic competence of the learners, additional follow-up tasks can be provided. These will offer opportunities for the further consolidation of language functions, forms and vocabulary as well as enriching background knowledge and cultural. Special projects should be fostered to enrich and expand the learners' command of the language and knowledge of specific tasks. In an increasingly competitive and globalised market, the teachers of English need to ensure that the learners' benefit from their English classes by exposing them to authentic texts and practical approaches through enjoyable learning activities.

Using news media in ELT classrooms has not yet become popular in Indian ELT scenario. But, by knowing what strategies the language learners actually use when reading or listening/ viewing the teacher only improve their comprehension of these skills as communicative acts but also their understanding of how they might be taught. Further research is needed on how reading/viewing strategies may vary depending on the background of the reader and the reader reading/viewing task itself.

Planning viewing activities based on BBC and CNN news in particular may be intimating at first but once the teachers begin to pilot some materials and gauge the students' interests and involvement, the possibilities begin to open up. Similarly newspaper articles and items from a variety of newspapers both national and international would help a long way in understanding the nuances of English language in terms of form and function.

Exercise (comprehension and comparative analysis)

Find the answers to these questions in the newspaper article given below:

1. How many papers reported Professor Heinz Wolff's death?
2. How many papers reported Dr. Heinz Wolff's death?
3. Why did *The Sun* confuse the two Heinz Wolffs?
4. Why was Joan Wolff particularly worried about The Sun report?
5. What did the two Heinz Wolffs have in common?
6. Why do you think every sentence is a new paragraph in *The Sun* report? How is the style of *The Guardian* report different?

Great Egg Race Prof dies at 61

Zany scientist Dr Heinz Wolff, who shot to fame in the BBC's loony inventions series The Great Egg Race, has died in hospital.

The balding 61 years-old professor founded a world-beating research unit at London's Brunel University.

But with his fly-away hairstyle, half-moon specs and bow tie, he become best known for his part in wacky computer advents in which he was crushed under a ten-ton weight.

In 1939 his family fled from Berlin to start a new life in Britain.

Genius Dr Wolff, who spent 30 years with the Medical Research Council, once refused a place at Oxford and deliberately failed his Cambridge University entrance exams.

(from *The Sun*)

SUN TRIBUTE CRIED THE WRONG WOLFF

Ed Vulliamy

Professor Heinz Wolff, the distinguished director of the Brunel Institute for Bio-engineering, whose tragic death was reported in *The Sun* last Monday, spoke cheerfully enough to *The Guardian* yesterday, using not a ouija board of spirit medium but a telephone from a Dutch seaside town called Noordwijk.

"Great Egg Race Prof Dies at 61," announced *The Sun*, referring to Professor Wolff's role in what the paper called the "loony inventions series" on BBC TV and sparked off a bizarre chain of events throughout which Professor Wolff remained alive and well.

Within days of *The Sun's* story, two obituaries appeared in *The Times* and the Independent, detailing the career of Dr Heinz Wolff, a leading psychodynamic psychiatrist, who had died at 73.

Dr Wolff had, sadly, died—but *The Sun* had got the wrong Heinz Wolff.

Professor Heinz Wolff was in Holland yesterday to make a presentation to a research laboratory. "I have started to receive cards in the post saying "I'm glad you are still alive," he said, "The main thing has been the tremendous number of phone calls I've still doing it."

When his death was announced, organisers of a meeting he was due to attend decided to cancel, out of respect, and telephoned his home to offer condolences. His wife, Joan, said yesterday: "The switchboard at Brunel was jammed with people ringing up on Monday morning. But our first thoughts were for the family, and the terrible worry that people would hear second hand—I mean, most of the our friends don't read *The Sun*."

Both Professor Heinz Wolff and Dr Heinz Wolff were born in Berlin and settled in London. At one time, when Professor Wolff lived in Hampstead Garden Suburb and Dr Wolff lived in Hampstead, their telephone numbers differed by one digit.

Professor Wolff is a graduate of University College, London: Dr Wolff trained, and later became a department head, at University College Hospital. "We have been confused before," said Professor Wolff, "but never in such a horrifying way."

Several famous names have read of their own deaths in the newspapers, the most celebrated being Mark Twain, who complained that "reports of my death are grossly exaggerated." George Bernard Shaw read his own obituary and Ernest Hemingway was killed in print twice before he died. *The Guardian* also paid last respects to the writer Ngaio Marsh before she was quite ready to accept them.

Sample Worksheet for Analysing News

This worksheet may suit any news item/article used in the classroom.

- Write the name of the TV programme.
- What are the various events that are covered in this news report?
- What background material (visual texts, graphics, statistics, charts, etc.) is used to support the linguistic information (reports, interviews)?
- Is the background material sufficient for the understanding of the events?
- Write down key words that will help you reconstruct the story presented in the news item.
- How would you describe the tone of the documentary? Does it change throughout the story? If so, why do you think so?

- Provide another headline for your own written version of the piece of news.

WORKS CITED

Carter, Ronald and David Nunan (eds.). *Teaching English to Speakers of Other Languages.* UK: Cambridge University Press, 2001.

Chaffee, Seven H. and Michael J. Petrick. *Using the Mass Media.* USA: McGraw-Hill Book Company, 1975.

ETIC Publications, *105—The Use of Media in English Language Teaching.* London: The British Council, 1979.

Jones, Leo. *Cambridge Advanced English.* New Delhi: Cambridge University Press, 1998.

Merino, Adriana and Maria Palmira Massi. Using the News in the Classroom: A Discourse Approach. *English Teaching Forum,* Vol. 36, No. 3, July-September, 1998.

Pemagbi, Joe. "Using Newspapers and Radio in English Language Teaching." *English Teaching Forum,* Volume 33, Number 3, July 1995.

World Bank Staff Working Paper No. 491. (1981) *The Educational Use of Mass Media.* USA: The World Bank.

3

Teaching English Intonation to EFL/ESL Students

MEHMET CELIK

This article proposes a workable, teachable, generalisable as well as communicatively efficient framework for the teaching of the intonation of English to non-native speakers of English. It is proposed that a framework of English intonation should include four major intonational features: intonation units, stress, tones, and pitch range. Consequently, the phenomena of intonation in English should have a piece of utterance, intonation unit, as its basis to study all kinds of voice movements and features. Every intonation unit has a type of tonic stress: (unmarked) utterance-final tonic stress, or emphatic, or contrastive, or new information stress, the last of which is more frequently used in utterances given to wh-questions. Further, intonation units have typically one of these tones; fall, low-rise, high-rise, and fall-rise. Tones are assigned to intonation units in relation to the type of voice movement on the tonic syllable. Finally, all intonation units have to be spoken in one of the three pitch levels (keys): high, mid and low.

Introduction

At a time when the language learning task is geared to instant interpersonal communication with efficiency and precision, the intonation phenomena could not have gone unnoticed in the preparation of English teaching syllabuses in the threshold of a new millennium. What to include and what not to in the teaching of intonation to learners of English as a second/foreign language (ESL/EFL) has caused uncertainty and lack of confidence, and consequently ignoring of the intonation in syllabuses to a great extent, which is, as Underhill (1994: 75) rightly notes, because "[...] we are not in control of a practical, workable and trustworthy system through which we can make intonation comprehensible."

A major feature of communication, suprasegmental (prosodic) features of speech have usually been avoided in the design of syllabuses for teaching English, partly due to the unduly little importance attached to the teaching of them, and partly due to the unavailability of a concise, salient, practical, and workable framework (Underhill, 1994: 47; Kenworthy, 1987). There are some attempts, of course, to come up with a scheme that is practical. However, they usually concentrate on certain areas of intonation rather than embracing the whole phenomenon of intonation (Coulthard, 1977; Underhill, 1994; Levis, 1999). Levis (1999), for instance, falls short of providing a coherent scheme by which foreign language teachers can utilize in their syllabuses for improving oral skills; it studies, in passing, intonational features such as significant pitch, pitch levels, intonation patterns, and placement of nuclear stress.

For Cruttenden (1986: 35), intonation has three important features: (1) division of a (dividing) a stream of speech into intonation units; (2) selection of a syllable (of a word), which is assigned the 'tonic' status; and (3) selection of a tone for the intonation unit. To this list, another feature can be added: pitch range, or key (Brazil *et al.*, 1980). In the experience of the present author in teaching oral skills to prospective teachers of English as a second/foreign language, a conception incorporating these four major features of intonation in the teaching syllabus has efficiently worked and proved very useful. This system, it is believed, may prove to be useful for other practitioners in the field of ESL/EFL.

This article explains the four major features in the teaching of English suprasegmentals: intonation units, stress, tone, and pitch range by reviewing relevant and current research. As such, this article provides a framework of English intonation for the teaching of English as a second/foreign language.

What the framework proposes is primarily based on what is most salient in the more recent scholarly studies of intonation phenomena, and secondarily, on what can be teachable given the author's own experience in the teaching of the phenomena. Later, the need to teach intonational features in meaningful contexts with realistic language rather than fabricated language as well as the need to consider intonation, not as a luxury but a necessity for an efficient interchange in English is pointed out.

Intonation Units

An 'intonation unit' is a piece of utterance, a continuous stream of sounds, bounded by a fairly perceptible pause. Pausing in some sense is a way of packaging the information such that the lexical items put together in an intonation unit form certain psychological and lexic-grammatical realities. Typical examples would be the inclusion of subordinate clauses and prepositional phrases in intonation units.

It is proposed here that any feature of intonation should be analyzed and discussed against a background of this phenomenon: tonic stress placement, choke of tones and keys are applicable to almost all intonation units. Closely related with the notion of pausing is that a change of meaning may be brought about; certain pauses in a stream of speech can have significant meaning variations in the message to be conveyed. Consider the example below, in which slashes correspond to pauses (Roach, 1983: 146) (see Halliday, 1967; Leech & Svartvik, 1975 for more): the meaning is given in brackets.

- Those who sold quickly/ made a profit
  (A profit is made by those who sold quickly.)
- Those who sold/ quickly made a profit
  (A profit was quickly made by those who sold.)

More examples can be used in order to illustrate the significance of pausing, and further, it can be pointed out that right pausing may become a necessity to understand and to be understood well.

Stress

This section addresses the notion of stress in words as perceived in connected speech. In addition, the existence and discovery of tonic stress is discussed, and the major types of stresses are explicated. Four major types of stress are identified:

- Unmarked tonic stress
- Emphatic stress
- Contrastive stress
- New information stress

An important prosodic feature, 'stress' applies to individual syllables, and involves, most commonly, loudness, length, and higher pitch (Roach, 1983: 73). Each of these features may contribute in differing degrees at different times. Stress is an essential feature of word identity in English (Kenworthy, 1987: 18). It is evident that not all syllables of a polysyllabic English word receive the same level of stress; in connected speech, usually two levels of stress appear to be perceptible, to non-native speakers in particular, regardless of the number of syllables: stressed and unstressed (Ladefoged, 1973; Kenworthy, 1987). What is known as the primary stress is regarded as the stressed syllable while the rest, secondary, tertiary, and weak, are rendered as unstressed syllables.

At the clausal level, normally, words that carry higher information content in the utterance are given higher stress than those carrying lower input (information) and those that are predictable in the context. It is generally the case that one word is stressed more than any other since it possesses the highest information content for the discourse utterance, that is, it informs the hearer most. The group of words described above are largely from what is called 'content' words as opposed to 'function' words. Content words are nouns, verbs, adjectives, and adverbs while function words are articles, prepositions, conjunctions, and modal auxiliaries. Furthermore, it is content words that are polysyllabic, not function words. This classification conforms to grammatical considerations. The classification we present here from a suprasegmental viewpoint, that is on the basis of being stressed or not, is slightly different from that of grammar. Consider the following:

Content/Stressed Words	*Function/Unstressed Words*
verbs	modal auxiliaries
nouns	articles
adjectives	conjunctions
adverbs	prepositions
question words	*pronouns*
prepositional adverbs	
negatives	

In other words, the items on the left hand column are stressable in unmarked utterances whereas the ones on the right column are not.

Tonic Stress

An intonation unit almost always has one peak of stress, which is called 'tonic stress,' or 'nucleus.' Because stress applies to syllables, the syllable that receives the tonic stress is called 'tonic syllable.' The term tonic stress is usually preferred to refer to this kind of stress in referring, proclaiming, and reporting utterances. Tonic stress is almost always found in a content word in utterance final position. Consider the following, in which the tonic syllable is underlined:

- I'm going.
- I'm going to London.
- I'm going to London for a holiday.

A question does arise as to what happens to the previously tonic assigned syllables. They still get stressed, however, not as much as the tonic syllable, producing a three level stress for utterances. Then, the following is arrived at, where the tonic syllable is further capitalized:

- I'm going to London for HOliday.

Emphatic Stress

One reason to move the tonic stress from its utterance to final position is to assign an emphasis to a content word, which is usually a modal auxiliary, an intensifier, an adverb, etc. Compare the following examples. The first two examples are adapted from Roach (1983: 144).

(i) It was very BOring. (unmarked)
(ii) It was VEry boring. (emphatic)

(i) You mustn't talk so LOUDly. (unmarked)
(ii) You MUSTN'T talk so loudly. (emphatic)

Some intensifying adverbs and modifiers (or their derivatives) that are emphatic by nature are (Leech & Svartvik, 1975: 135):

> indeed, utterly, absolute, terrific, tremendous, awfully, terribly, great, grand, really, definitely, truly, literally, extremely, surely, completely, barely, entirely, very (adverb), very (adjective), quite, too, enough, pretty, far, especially, alone, only, own, -self.

Contrastive Stress

In contrastive contexts, the stress pattern is quite different from the emphatic and non-emphatic stresses in that any lexical item in an utterance can receive the tonic stress provided that the contrastively stressed item can be contrastable in that universe of speech. No distinction exists between content and function words regarding this. The contrasted item receives the tonic stress provided that it is contrastive with some lexical element (notion.) in the stimulus utterance. Syllables that are normally stressed in the utterance almost always get the same treatment they do in non-emphatic contexts. Consider the following examples:

(a) Do you like this one or THAT one?
(b) I like THIS one.

Many other larger contrastive contexts (dialogues) can be found or worked out, or even selected from literary works for a study of contrastive stress. Consider the following:

- She played the piano yesterday. (It was her who....)
- She played the piano yesterday. [She only played (not harmed)....]
- She played the piano yesterday. (It was the piano that...)
- She played the piano yesterday. (It was yesterday....)

New Information Stress

In a response given to a wh-question, the information supplied, naturally enough, is stressed. That is, it is pronounced with more breath force, since it is more prominent against a background given information in the question. The concept of new information is much clearer to students of English in responses to wh-questions than in declarative statements. Therefore, it is best to start with teaching the stressing of the new information supplied to questions with a question word:

(a) What's your NAME?
(b) My name's GEORGE.

(a) Where are you FROM?
(b) I'm from WALES.

(a) Where do you LIVE?
(b) I live in BONN.

(a) When does the school term END?
(b) It ends in MAY.

(a) What do you DO?
(b) I'm a STUdent.

The questions given above could also be answered in short form except for the last one, in which case the answers are:

- George
- Wales
- in Bonn
- in May

In other words, 'given' information is omitted, not repeated. In the exchange:

(a) What's your name?

(b) (My name's) George.

The 'new' information in this response is 'George.' The part referring to his name is given in the question, so it may be omitted.

Regarding the significance of new information declarative statements, Ladefoged (1982: 100) states:

> 'In general, new information is more likely to receive a tonic accent than material that has already been mentioned. The topic of a sentence is less likely to receive the tonic accent than the comment that is made on the topic.'

Furthermore, Bolinger (1968: 603) notes that speakers '[...] depend on stress to highlight the most important and informative *idea* in the sentence' (the italics is original). I think that Bolinger's 'the most important and informative idea' coincides with the concept of 'new information.' So the stressed lexical item is that which carries the information enveloping communicative intent and purpose. The information in the stressed item is the core of the message within the utterance. Therefore, it is the most important element in the utterance. Consider the following example taken from Dickerson (1989: 20, cited in Levis, 1999: 45):

(a) It sounds like there was some excitement last night.

(b) Didn't you hear? There was a tor<u>NA</u>do in the area.

Here in this example, the most prominent information appears to be stored in 'tornado' rather than the last content word in the utterance, as expected according to the guidelines given under 'Emphatic Stress.'

Tone

A unit of speech bounded by pauses has movement, of music and rhythm, associated with the pitch of voice (Roach, 1983: 113). This certain pattern of voice movement is called 'tone.' A tone is a *certain* pattern, not an arbitrary one, because it is meaningful in discourse. By means of tones, speakers signal whether to refer, proclaim, agree, disagree, question or hesitate, or indicate completion and continuation of turn-taking, in speech.

Pointing to extensive variations in the taxonomy of English tones, Cruttenden (1986: 58) rightly notes that "This is an area where almost every analyst varies in his judgment of what constitutes a 'major difference of meaning' and hence in the number of nuclear tones which are set up." He adds: "[...] intonational meanings are often so intangible and nebulous [...] (that) it is difficult to see how a wholly convincing case for any one set of nuclear tones [...]" (parenthetical statement is mine). Crystal (1969) and Ladefoged (1982) identify four basic tones (fall, rise-fall, rise, and fail-rise) while O'Connor and Arnold (1973) distinguish only two (rise and fall). Brazil *et al.* (1980) and Roach (1983) endorse five tones (fall, rise, rise-fall, fall-rise, and level) whereas Cruttenden (1986) recognizes seven tones (high-fall, low-fall, high-rise, low-rise, fall-rise, rise-fall, and mid-level).

It appeared in the author's teaching experience that only four types of tones can be efficiently taught to non-native speakers of English:

- fall
- low-rise
- high-rise
- fall-rise

What makes a tone a rising or falling or any other type of tone is the direction of the pitch movement on the last stressed (tonic) syllable (Brown, 1977: 45). If the tonic syllable is in non-final position, the glide continues over the rest of the syllables. A fall in pitch on the tonic syllable renders the tone as 'fall.' A 'rise' tone is one in which the tonic syllable is the start of an upward glide of pitch. This glide is of two kinds: if the upward movement is higher, then it is 'high rise'; if it is lower, then it is 'low rise.' 'Fall-rise' has first a pitch fall and then a rise.

Fall **(A Falling Tone)**

A falling tone is by far the most common used tone of all. It signals a sense of finality, completion, belief in the content of the utterance, and so on. A speaker, by choosing a falling tone, also indicates to the addressee that that is all he has to say, and offers a chance (turn-taking) to the addressee to comment on, agree or disagree with, or add to his utterance. However, it is up to the addressee to do either of these. This tone does in no way solicit a response from the addressee. Nonetheless, it would be polite for the addressee to at least acknowledge in some manner or form that he is part of the discourse. Now, let us see the areas in which a falling tone is used. The following is a proclamation in which a teacher is informing a student of the consequences of his unacceptable behaviour.

- I'll re<u>port</u> you to the <u>HEAD</u>master

A falling tone may be used in referring expressions as well.

- I've <u>spo</u>ken with the <u>CLEA</u>ner.

Questions that begin with wh-questions are generally pronounced with a falling tone:

- Where is the PENcil?

Imperative statements have a falling tone.

(i) Go and see a DOCtor.

(ii) Take a SEAT.

Requests or orders have a falling tone too.

(i) Please sit DOWN.

(ii) Call him IN.

Exclamations:

- Watch OUT!

Yes/No questions and tag questions seeking or expecting confirmation can be uttered with a falling tone. And the response to it may be lengthened. Consider the following example:

(a) You like it, DON'T you?

(b) YES.

In a Yes/No question structure, if the speaker uses a falling tone, we assume that he already knows the answer, or at least he is sure that he knows, and the purpose of asking the question, as far as the speaker is concerned, is to put the answer on record. In the following exchange, the speaker is sure to get a 'Yes' answer from the addressee:

(a) Have you MET him?

(b) YES.

Low-Rise **(A Rising Tone)**

This tone is used in genuine 'Yes/No' questions where the speaker is sure that he does not know the answer, and that the addressee knows the answer. Such Yes/No questions are uttered with a rising tone. For instance, consider the following question uttered with a rising tone, the answer of which could be either of the three options:

(A) Isn't he NICE?

(B) (i) Yes.

(ii) No.

(iii) I don't know.

Compare the above example with the following example, which is uttered with a falling tone, and which can only have one appropriate answer in the context:

(a) Isn't he NICE?

(b) YES.

Other examples which are uttered with a rising tone are:

- Do you want some COFfee?
- Do you take CREAM in your coffee?

High-Rise **(A Rising Tone)**

If the tonic stress is uttered with extra pitch height, as in the following intonation units, we may think that the speaker is asking for a repetition or clarification, or indicating disbelief.

(a) I'm taking up TAxidermy this autumn.
(b) Taking up WHAT? (clarification)

(a) She passed her DRIving test.
(b) She PASSED? (disbelief)

Fall-Rise (followed by Fall)

While the three tones explicated so far can be used in independent, single intonation unit, the fourth tone, fall-rise, appears to be generally used in what may be called 'dependent' intonation units such as those involving sentential adverbs, subordinate clauses, compound sentences, and so on. Fall-rise signals dependency, continuity, and non-finality (Cruttenden, 1986: 102). It generally occurs in sentence non-final intonation units. Consider the following in which the former of the intonation units are uttered with a fall-rise tone (the slash indicates a pause):

- Private enterPRISE / is always EFficient.
- A quick tour of the CIty / would be NICE.
- PreSUmably / he thinks he CAN.
- Usually / he comes on SUNday.

One of the most frequent complex clause types in English is one that has dependent (adverbial or subordinate) clause followed by an independent (main) clause. When such a clause has two intonation units, the first, non-final, normally has a fall-rise while the second, final, has falling tone. Therefore, the tone observed in non-final intonation units can be said to have a 'dependency' tone, which is fall-rise (The explication of tone patterns as well as some of the examples in this section are largely based on Cruttenden, 1986). Consider the following:

- When I passed my REAding test / I was VEry happy.
- If you SEE him / give my MESsage.

When the order of complex clause is reversed, we may still observe the pattern fall-rise and fall respectively, as in

- I WON'T deliver the goods / unless I receive the PAYment.
- The moon revolves around the EARTH / as we ALL know.
- Private enterprise is always EFficient / whereas public ownership means INefficient.

All in all, final intonation units have a falling tone while non-final ones have fall-rise. Consider further complex clauses:

- He joined the ARmy / and spent all his time in ALdershot.
- My sister who is a NURSE / has ONE child.

This completes the four major tones selected for the framework. As is the case in this section, some of these tones can be used in combination when a syntactic unit (sentence) has more than one intonation unit. This section has reviewed the (fall-rise + fall) and (fall + fall-rise) patterns. In the following two sections, two patterns, namely (fall-rise + low rise) and (fall + fall), are examined respectively.

Fall-rise + Low Rise

Typically this tone pattern involves a dependent clause followed by a Yes/No question.

- If I HELPED you / would you try aGAIN?
- Despite its DRAWbacks / do you favour it or NOT?

Fall + Fall

A fall tone can be followed by another fall tone when the speaker expects or demands agreement as in tag questions.

- It's a bit TOO good to be true / ISN'T it?

Reinforcing adverbials can also have a fall when place utterance finally as an expression of after-thought.

- Ann said she'd help as much as she COULD / NATUrally.

If the two actions are part of a sequence of related events, it has (fall + fall) tone pattern, as in the following in which the information in the first intonation unit and the one in the second one do not have dependency:

- She's 28 years OLD / and lives in GiPPSland.

Pitch and Pitch Range (Key)

Pitch is one of the acoustic correlates of stress (Underhill 1994: 57). From a physiological point of view, '[...] pitch is primarily dependent on the rate of vibration of vocal cords [...]' (Cruttenden, 1986: 3). When the vocal cords are stretched, the pitch of voice increases. Pitch variations in speech are realized by the alteration of the tension of vocal cords (Ladefoged, 1982: 226). The rate of vibration in vocal cords is increased by more air pressure from the lungs. In an overwhelming majority of syllables that are stressed, a higher pitch is observed. Therefore, loudness to a certain extent contributes to the make-up of pitch. That is, higher pitch is heard louder than lower pitch. Further, syllable length tends to contribute to the perception of the utterance-final tonic stress more than pitch because of the natural decline of speech force as it comes to conclusion, contrary to acoustic facts (Levis, 1999: 42).

The term 'key' can be described as utterance pitch; specific and/or meaningful sequences of pitches in an intonation unit. Keys that are linguistically meaningful and significant are worth being included in a syllabus. For a key to be significant, (1) it should be under speaker's control; (2) it should be perceptible to ordinary speakers; and (3) it should represent a contrast (Roach, 1983: 113). Usually, three keys are identified: high, mid and low (Coulthard, 1977; Brazil *et al.*, 1980).

For each intonation unit, speaker must choose one of the three keys as required for the conversation. Most of the speech for a speaker takes place at the mid (unmarked) key, employed in normal and unemotional speech. In contrast, high and low keys are marked: high key is used for emotionally charged intonation units while use of low key indicates an existence of equivalence (as in appositive expressions), and relatively less significant contribution to the speech. The relationship between pitch and key is a comparative one in that syllabic pitch is always higher than the utterance pitch; in some sense, syllabic pitch is one step ahead of the utterance pitch.

High Key

Exclamation

Exclamation is usually the cover term used to refer to actions described by verbs such as cry, scream, shout, wail, shriek, roar, yell, whoop, bellow, bark, thunder, howl, echo, and so on. Speakers do these to express their strong feelings such as excitement, surprise, anger, irritation, rage, fury, wrath, fume, agitation, cheer, merriment, gaiety, fun, etc. Speakers generally exploit high pitch when they exclaim.

The extract "'Have you guessed?' he whispered at last. 'Oh God!' burst in a terrible wail from her breast.'" can be schematized as

high She: oh GOD
mid
low He: / have you GUESSED? /

Contrastivity

Another function of high pitch is to indicate contrastivity. Brazil *et al.* (1980: 26) note the following: "It is proposed as a general truth that the choice of high key presents the matter of the tone unit as if in the context of an existentially-valid opposition." Consider the following adapted example, in which the word uttered with a high key has contrastive stress (Brazil *et al.*, 1980: 26):

high BOGnor /
mid / we're going to MARgate this year / not
low

In addition to the high key for *Bognor,* either referring (fall-rise) or proclaiming (fall) tone should be selected. Use of high key with referring tone indicates that the contrast was established prior to this utterance whereas a proclaiming tone reports what the two options are as part of the news. The following example, adapted from Pennington (1996:132), also illustrates the utilization of high key for contrast:

high YALE /
mid / I'm going to HARvard / not
low

Echo/Repeat

The act of echoing/repeating is almost always done with high pitch. It may involve a genuine attempt to recover unrecognized, unheard information, or to indicate disbelief, disappointment and so on. The tone to be utilized in such intonation units is high-rise. Consider the following exchange where a case of disbelief is in question:

(a) 'Four thousand,' said Barney sadly.
(b) 'Four thousand?' But it's just a shack!
high B: four THOUsand
mid / but it's just a SHACK /
low A: / four THOUsand /

In the following examples, a repetition and/or clarification and disbelief is sought, respectively:

(a) I'm taking up taxidermy.
(b) Taking up what?
high B: taking up WHAT /
mid A: / I'm taking up TAxidermy /
low

Low Key

Co-reference, Appositives

Lower pitch is used to indicate co-referential, additional or supplementary information. Consider the following example, in which the word *dummy* in low key is co-referential with *you* in mid key (Pennington, 1996: 152):

high
mid / I TOLD you already /
low DUMmy /

Non-defining Relative Clauses

The type of information uttered in low pitch may be non-defining relative clauses, parenthetical statements expressions of dis/agreement, reduced clauses etc. Consider the following:

high
mid / my DOCtor / / is very WELL-known /
low who's a neurologist

Statements of Opinion

There are times when short statements of opinion, involving clarification, certainty/uncertainty, are attached to propositional statements. Look at the examples below:

high
mid / the GOvernment / / will agree with our deMANDS
low I THINK

Conclusion

This study has argued for the inclusion of intonational features of English in the syllabuses designed for the teaching of English as a second/foreign language, and provided a practical framework of English intonation, which is based on the present author's experiences. Intonation, the non-grammatical, non-lexical component of communication, is an inseparable component of utterances. Speech without intonational features is no more than a machine output. Intonation is a paralinguistic device in vocal communication. It reveals many facets of the communication process taking into consideration all factors present in the discourse context. Therefore, it is an indispensable part of speech. Tones are important discourse strategies to communicate effectively; simply, it is not what you say, it is how you say it. Therefore, a proficiency in intonation is a requirement for non-native learners of English for a better communicative discourse with native or non-native speakers of English.

WORKS CITED

Bolinger, D. *Aspects of Language.* New York: Harcourt Brace Jovanovich, 1968.

Brazil, D., M. Coulthart and C. Johns. *Discourse Intonation and Language Teaching.* Harlow (Essex): Longman, 1980.

Brown, G. *Listening to Spoken English.* Harlow (Essex): Longman, 1977.

Coulthard, M. *An Introduction to Discourse Analysis.* Harlow (Essex): Longman, 1977.

Cruttenden, A. *Intonation.* Cambridge: Cambridge University Press, 1986.

Crystal, D. *Prosodic Systems and Intonation in English.* Cambridge: Cambridge University Press, 1969.

Dickerson, W.B. *Stress in the Speech Stream: The Rhythm of Spoken English.* Urbana: University of Illinois Press, 1989.

Halliday, M.A.K. *Intonation and Grammar in British English.* The Hague: Mouton, 1967.

Kenworthy, J. *Teaching English Pronunciation.* London: Longman, 1987.

Ladefoged, P. *A Course in Phonetics.* New York: Harcourt Jovanovich, 1982 (1975).

Levis, M.K. "Intonation in Theory and Practice, Revisited." *TESOL Quarterly,* 3: 37-63, 1999.

O'Connor, J.D. & G.K. Arnold. *Intonation of Colloquial English.* London: Longman, 1973.

Pennington, M.C. *Phonology in English Language Teaching.* London: Longman, 1996.

Roach, P. *English Phonetics and Phonology: A Practical Coursebook.* Cambridge: Cambridge University Press, 1983.

Underhill, A. *Sound Foundations: Living Phonology.* Oxford: Heinemann, 1994.

4

Test Taking Strategies in Reading Comprehension

MALAVIKA SHARMA

The aim of this article is to highlight the importance of the mental processes employed by students when reading. In the normal course of teaching and testing we are concerned with the product of reading, that is, the answers students give to comprehension questions, not the underlying process which leads them to provide these answers. Information about the product only tells us of the level of their proficiency, but knowledge of the process would enable us to know why they get certain questions right and not others. The reasons could be either linguistic, that is, they interpret a passage in a particular way because of the limitations of their understanding of certain words or constructions or they could alternatively be cognitive, that is, a failure to perform certain mental operations, such as analytical or interpretative thinking. The mental processing of 'better' contrasted against those who fare less well, in order to determine what characterizes the good reader. The strategies employed by the proficient student could then be taught in class, in order to make the teaching of reading a principled procedure. Merely providing students with practice in the activity appears to be less likely to achieve the same result as fast.

Reading theorists have regarded reading for some time as an active rather than a passive process. The reader's understanding of a text is conditioned by what he already knows, and the availability of that knowledge during the reading process (Carroll 1971, Bransford 1979, *et al.*). It is also seen that individual readers have different purposes and motivations for reading, which lead to different ways of processing information in the text, and variation in what they derive from it. Therefore, different readers are likely to interpret texts in varied ways. As Widdowson (1979) says, "texts do not have one meaning, waiting to be extracted by the reader, but rather that they have meaning potential, which is only realized in the interaction between reader and writer."

Reading is not merely an educational requirement. It is required in all aspects of life. The importance of accessing new information and modern trends in thought is necessarily felt, for example, in white-collar jobs. However, even students whose medium of instruction has been English, throughout their educational careers, are unable to read efficiently in English. They have not been trained in developing their cognitive abilities and applying their minds to the tasks that are set, which demand precision and relevance. The problem, therefore, is not only linguistic. It is also a question of thinking when reading.

Perhaps when teaching reading, the teacher does not generally direct the students' attention to the purpose for which they are reading, and the different possible ways of extracting meaning from text. Lack of efficient training along with unsuitable test formats (which in their turn condition teaching in the classroom) has in fact been the major causes of student failure to comprehend texts. The comprehension texts at school and college have passages followed by questions that are not actually geared to testing the linguistic or the cognitive ability of the students. The concern appears to be not testing comprehension in a principled way, but fulfilling a routine requirement. Yet these students are expected to read and understand their course books in all their subjects and demonstrate knowledge of these at the examination. The compulsory English course at an English-medium University has to address these issues, which determine students success in their academic careers.

Therefore, it is essential even in the teaching of reading that the teacher trains students in developing their ability to think, to relate new experiences to what they already know, and to process and organize information. Good comprehension tests are required in order to make students reflect on what they are reading. As Lunzer and Gardner (1979) say, 'it is not enough for the teacher to say think.' In order to promote reflection, precise questions must be set. A bad test is one that can be answered without prior and thorough reading of the text; simply by 'looking up' the right phrases or sentence to answer each question. Such as test offers little stimulus for thought.

Courses, thus, need to be designed to meet the real life needs of the learner, that is, his current requirement in the practical world. Such an approach is usually termed "learner-centred." Graded objectives can help. So as to ensure a surrender value to each level of attainment, as well as an emphasis on the use of realistic sample of language, or "authentic" texts. Relevance to learner's needs would lead to better learning.

A slightly different, but, also valuable approach to learning could be to train learners to select the learning modes suited to them, to use one another as learning resources, to negotiate the content of their learning with the teacher, and generally to take responsibility for the management of their own learning. The teacher is then seen as only one of the resources available to the learner. The role of the teacher would be to make the learners aware of other possible resources, and help them in deciding which to use and in what manner. The ultimate goal in this case is to give rise to the autonomous learner and the individualization of learning.

It is felt that these kinds of changes in teaching methodology will help encourage the learner to complete his given tasks with confidence. It will also enable him to work with tasks he personally finds challenging. By keeping a record of the progress of the students, the teacher can find out why the student answered a particular question the way he did. The way each individual arrives at an answer to a question may vary a great deal. Evaluation of learning is, therefore, important as feedback for teaching.

It is possible to evaluate both the 'product' of learning and also the 'process.' The 'product' approach looks at the results or the 'product,' that is, the correctness of the answer. The 'process' approach helps the teacher in understanding the different ways in which the learner approached his task, by using different processes, strategies or skills. Alderson (1985, 1986) demonstrates that getting the right answer to a test question may not even reflect an understanding of the text. It is possible, he says, to get a question right for the wrong reasons, especially multiple-choice items. Conversely, it is possible to get comprehension questions wrong and yet understand the text. It is the 'process' which gives rise to the product or their answer. Therefore, talking to students about how they have arrived at particular answers, what makes them think they are right, what exactly they have understood will be of use to the teacher and test framer.

Research in the teaching of reading shows that the emphasis in teaching reading has shifted from teaching it as a passive skill to demanding active participation from the student readers. The current view goes further than this and asserts that it is an interactive process, whereby the reader attempts to understand what the writer intended to mean. As Frank Smith (1971) says, "Readers must bring meaning to print rather than expect to receive meaning from it."

Early work in second language reading, specifically in reading English as a second language, assumed a 'bottom-up' view of second language reading. This meant that second language reading was primarily viewed as a process of reconstructing the author's intended meaning by starting with the printed letters and words, that is, moving from the smallest textual units or the 'bottom' to larger and larger units at the top, that is, from phrases to clauses to entire texts. Therefore, problems of second language reading were viewed as being essentially problems of decoding, that is, making sense first of letters, then words, then grammatical structures, and finally deriving connected meaning from these.

The 'bottom-up' approach to second language reading is similar to the linguistic approach. The focus of the linguistic approach is on language. Linguists are not so much concerned with how or why people read the way they do. They are mainly concerned with the structure and nature of the linguistic knowledge that underlies what is read.

The linguistic approach is mainly concerned with the

product of reading, that is, what the reader has 'got out' of the text. What a student has understood of a text is not the same as how he arrives at such an understanding. The product of reading may vary in terms of the various meanings assigned to the text by the reader, but this does not imply the use of different skills. The approach does not attempt to describe the mental processes of the reader as he was reading the text.

The product approach to teaching reading comprehension aims at assessing whether comprehension has occurred. The typical form of such "product-oriented" courses is that students are given a text to read and then asked questions to check whether they have understood.

Even though current linguistically-oriented courses train students to find the correct answers to questions on an unseen text, they generally use a mechanical system of asking questions, for example, the answers to the first question generally lies in the first sentence of the passage, or the words in the question direct the students to the answer in the text because it is in the same words. Even if this strategy is not specifically taught, the student imbibes it in the course of answering questions in the text.

This does not mean that the product approach is a wrong approach to teaching reading comprehension. Any approach will obviously aim at the product, that is, the outcome or the answer. What really matters is, however, what underlies the product, that is, the process by which the teacher aims at effective reading comprehension, needs to be altered. While focusing on the outcome, attention should be aimed at teaching students the various strategies, which are essential in the process of reading. The focus should be on the techniques, which will help the student deal independently with any text in his subject area, by teaching him different ways of approaching a text through what Blum & Levenston (1978) call a "systematic series of steps." Bialystok (1991) says that 'reading strategies,' such as the use of background knowledge, skimming, scanning, predicting guessing the meaning of different words, and so on, help learners accomplish their reading tasks. The product approach is useful in the sense that teachers can determine what reading strategy has been used through the answer provided by the student. Cavalcanti (1991), examining the reading process of students, found that students vary their strategies according to the nature of the problem encountered.

This approach to reading comprehension has been described as the 'process approach' where the main idea is to teach the students the strategies necessary to arrive at the required result. The idea behind this approach is that students will be able to handle difficult reading tasks, once they are familiar with the nature of the strategies they need to use. Blum and Levenston (1978) say that the repeated use of the strategies "can lead to internal change in the organization of the second language." Bialystok (1979) refers to 'strategies' as an "additional element" whereby the reader is "trying to change his normal routine in order to arrive at the expected form of response." This suggests that every language has its own system of organization of information and while there may be general strategies for reading, there are also language-specific strategies.

The value of concentrating on reading strategies in teaching is that if the processes can be isolated, they may be found to contain elements that can be generalized over different texts. Learners can then learn specific strategies in order to improve their reading ability. The basic rationale behind attempts to describe the process of reading is that this will enable us to distinguish successful from unsuccessful readers. It also opens up the possibility of using the strategies of successful readers to teach the less successful, or at least making them aware of the existence of other processing strategies.

In order to determine the strategies typically used by students in reading, a group of Junior College students from Bombay University were made to perform reading comprehension tasks on a given passage. The questions demanded, in addition to knowledge of the language, the ability to perform operations involving the cognitive skills of Identification, Interpretation and Analysis. The reading tasks were somewhat different from those that students were used to encountering. The passages were based on the kind of reading tests they would be likely to encounter in their area of specialization, namely the Fine Arts. The tasks all involved thinking. They could not be performed on the basis of general knowledge or a mechanical matching of the words in the question with those in the passage. After the test, all of them were interviewed individually, to find out the reasons why they had given the answers they had (regardless of whether the answers were right or wrong). All students were interviewed within two days of the test, so that the task was fresh in their minds.

On the basis of these interviews, a series of strategies used by the students who had fared well on the test were listed, as well as those strategies used by those who had done badly. These became the starting point of a course in reading that was conducted for these students. The attempt here was to determine whether reading strategies could be developed through training. Consequently, an experiment was designed, using two matched groups of Junior College students. The Experimental Group received the experimental treatment, namely specific training in appropriate strategies of reading, while the Control Group merely had practice in performing comprehension tasks, without specific training in how to perform these. A series of six sessions (including the first session mentioned above) was held with each of these groups, with the Experimental Group being interviewed individually after each comprehension task. The Control Group was interviewed only after the first and last tasks in order to ascertain the degree of progress made, without benefit of specific training. The progress of the Experimental Group (with training) was contrasted with that of the Control Group (without specific training in the strategies to use) from Entry Stage to Exit Stage, to determine whether specific training in reading strategies led to better performance on comprehension tasks. The developmental progress of the Experimental Group was also studied, to ascertain how long it took for certain strategies to develop.

The findings indicate that the performance of the Experimental Group was significantly (in statistical terms) better than that of the Control Group. More specifically, the Experimental Group was significantly better than the Control Group on tasks involving analytical thinking, but on other tasks involving identification of clearly stated information, or interpretation of statements, there was no appreciable difference in the performance of the two groups. This indicates that the most difficult skill of analysis requires specific training.

The qualitative analysis of students' verbalization of the techniques employed by them in answering questions also showed a considerable improvement in the Experimental Group's strategies, providing support for the hypothesis.

A comparison of t-values in the sub-skills, and rate of progress at Entry and Exit Stages of the Experimental and Control Groups is given in the following Table 1.

TABLE 1

Comparison of t-values in the sub-skills, and rate of progress at Entry and Exit Stages of the Experimental and Control Groups

Experimental Group	*Entry-Exit Stages*			*Control Group*		
Sub-skills	t-values of diff. in means	The sig. level	Rate of progress	t-values of diff. in means	The sig. level	Rate of progress
IDENTIFIC	2.06	p>.05	18.57%	3.69	p>.001	48.40%
INTERPRET	12.3	P>.001	43.93%	5.47	p>.001	30.52%
ANALYSIS	5.69	p>.001	61.42%	0		0
Total of all sub-skills	9.2	p>.001	44.40%	9.16	p>.001	43.30%

Table 1 compares the t-values of the difference in mean scores and the rate of progress of the Experimental and the Control Groups from the Entry to the Exit stages.

In IDENTIFICATION, the t-value of the difference in the scores of the Control Group (p>.01) is seen to be at a higher level of significance than that of the Experimental Group (p>.05) from Entry to Exit point. The rate of progress in IDENTIFICATION is also higher for the Control Group than the Experimental Group. It must be borne in mind that the scores of the Control Group on IDENTIFICATION are lower at Entry point, yet they are able to reach the same level as the Experimental Group without having undergone the training sessions. In other words, students are able to handle questions related to IDENTIFICATION with excessive practice.

In INTERPRETATION and ANALYSIS, however, the rate of progress for the Experimental Group is greater than that of the Control Group. The t-value of the difference in the mean scores also indicates that the Experimental Group performs better. We can thus, conclude that students need training in the relevant reading strategies in order to undertake questions related to INTERPRETATION and ANALYSIS. Having undergone the training they are able to perform better than students without such training.

The qualitative response of both the Experimental and the Control Groups also brings out the difference in their attempt to answer reading comprehension questions. Table 2 shows the differences in the use of the strategies of the Experimental and the Control Groups at the Exit Stage.

TABLE 2

Comparison of the Strategies of the Experimental and the Control Groups at the Exit Stage

Differences	
Experimental Group	*Control Group*
1. Skimming the text in order to get the overall idea.	1. Reading the text several times to get the overall idea.
2. Guessing at the meaning of unfamiliar words or phrases from the overall meaning.	2. Ignoring unfamiliar words, not attempting to guess at their meaning.
3. Isolating and selecting the specific information required from the text.	3. No attempt in selecting information.
4. Analysing and classifying information in the text.	4. No attempt at analyzing and classifying infor-mation.
5. Using their background knowledge of the topic, or their knowledge of the world to guess at meaning.	5. Using background knowledge in order to elucidate the text.

The comparison of the strategies used by the Experimental and the Control Groups at the Exit Stage indicates the relevance of the training sessions given to the Experimental Group. It was expected that the Experimental Group students would show considerable progress from Entry to Exit Stage in the strategies they claim to be using. The findings have confirmed this. The students of the Experimental Group take less time to answer questions, and they do not answer at random. Moreover, they do not get bogged down when they come across an unfamiliar word in the passage. They try to guess its meaning from the given context. Even though sometimes their guesses are incorrect, the fact that they are using their cognitive abilities indicates the success of the teaching programme. In addition, skimming to get at the gist of the passage, scanning for specific information, answering questions in a logical order, analyzing and classifying information given in the text and so on, are the other cognitive abilities used by the students. Control Group students, on the other hand, as seen above, are unable to do this, and seem to use most of the same strategies they had used at Entry Stage. This development is cognitive as well as linguistic abilities makes the Experimental Group students better readers at the Exit Stage than the Control Group students.

As an extension of the study the Experimental Group was studied after the period of a year to ascertain the long-term benefits of training in reading strategies, that is, whether they continued to use the reading strategies they had been taught. This required a comprehension test and individual interviews. It was found that they made good use of the strategies like skimming and scanning the text for information, activating the use of background knowledge, and attempting intelligent guesses at the meaning of unfamiliar words. This provided further justification for developing courses, which aimed at training in the use of reading strategies.

Another experiment (Experiment II) was conducted at the degree college level. Students of the F.Y.B.A. in three different colleges were tested in the second term, when they had undergone one term's work in the course 'Communication Skills in English,' where they would already have received training in developing reading skills. The colleges were selected on the basis of their results at University exams to represent different categories of students. The breakdown is given below:

College 1: Above-Average Group (30 students)

College 2: (a) Above-Average Group (30 students)
(b) Average Group (60 students)

College 3: Below-Average Group (60 students)

All the students were given a comprehension test and then individually interviewed to ascertain the strategies used by them in answering. From their responses it was found that the Above-Average Group students used the following strategies:

1. Skimming to get at the gist of the passage.
2. Scanning for specific information in the passage.
3. Guessing at the meaning of difficult words on the basis of the relevant sentence, the content of the passage, or from their previous encounter with these words.
4. Predicting from the title what the passage would contain.
5. Using background knowledge.
6. Classifying, analyzing and evaluating information and ideas.
7. Inferring the writer's opinion regarding information/ ideas in the passage.

On the other hand the Average-Group students used the following strategies:

1. Reading the text several times to get the overall idea.
2. Reading the test items and attempting to understand what is demanded from them, even though they were unable to find the answers.
3. Reading the text again after reading the test items.
4. Trying to guess at the meaning of unfamiliar words or phrases, though much time was not spent on this.

The Weaker-Group students used the following strategies:

1. Matching words and phrases used in the question with those in the text.

2. Avoiding reading the text, and instead, proceeding directly with answering the test items.
3. Answering questions based on the assumption that the first few sentences would contain the overall idea of the text, and the concluding sentences would contain the writer's opinion.
4. Answering questions in general terms, not in terms of the specific information required.

From the above analysis we can say that the Weaker-Group students in spite of studying the "Communication Skills in English" course, did not seem to have been trained in the area of reading strategies and therefore found it very difficult to attempt the given tasks. On the other hand, the Average-Group knew how to attempt the given task, though more practice was required in order for them to be efficient. In contrast the Above-Average Group students are aware of the relevance and significance of the use of reading strategies and show a high level of confidence in their use of these.

We can therefore conclude that good readers use the following strategies in reading comprehension tests:

1. Skimming in order to get the overall idea of the passage.
2. Scanning for specific information.
3. Predicting from the given title the content of the passage.
4. Using their background knowledge.
5. Guessing the meanings of unfamiliar words from the context.
6. Classifying, analyzing and evaluating.
7. Reading the passage for key ideas or words.
8. Using textual aids to anticipate information.
9. Paraphrasing the text.
10. Inferring the writer's opinion regarding information/ ideas in the passage.

Our knowledge of the strategies used by good readers will enable us to train poor readers to overcome their reading difficulties. The steps needed for the fulfilment of this purpose is as follows:

1. The structure of larger units such as the paragraph or the whole unit is more important than individual sentences. It is no good studying a text as though it was a series of independent units. This leads students to becoming dependent on understanding every single sentence in a text, even when this is not necessary to fulfil their reading purpose.

2. Students should be trained to attempt global understanding of a text before approaching details. When constructing reading comprehension tasks, it is preferable to start with the overall meaning of the text, its function and aim, rather than working on specific areas, or linguistic features like vocabulary. It is possible, for instance, to develop the students' powers of inference through systematic practice, or introduce questions, which encourage students to anticipate the content of a text from its title and illustration, or the end of a story from the preceding paragraphs. Students should be trained to guess, predict, check and ask themselves questions to understand unknown elements, whether these are ideas or single words.

3. Care should be taken to introduce exercises in which there is no single straightforward answer. This would help students develop their powers of creativity, interpretation and evaluation. Exercises should be framed in order to lead to greater discussion and reflection on the text.

4. Tasks should be flexible and varied. Students must be taught to tackle varied reading tasks and perform a variety of different cognitive operations. The nature of the texts should also vary. Exercises could contain open-ended questions, multiple-choice items, tasks requiring the completion of tables, and so on, in order to train readers to be flexible in their approach to handling information in a text.

5. The aim of the exercises must also be clearly defined. Exercises should be purpose-oriented, and devised in such a way as to illicit and develop specific skills. This can help to give rise to independent and efficient readers.

6. Reading is an interactive activity whereby the reader not only gets meaning from the text but also brings meaning to it, and readers have to be trained to make use of their knowledge of the world in approaching a text.

WORKS CITED

Alderson, J.C. and Urquhart, A. (eds.). *Reading in a Foreign Language.* London: Longman, 1986.

Alderson, J.C. and Lukmani, Yasmeen. "Cognition and Reading: Cognitive Levels as embodied in Test Questions." *Reading in a Foreign Language,* Vol. 5, no. 2, 1989.

Alderson, J.C. "Testing Reading Comprehension Skills" (Part One). *Reading in a Foreign Language,* Vol. 6, no. 2, 1990.

Alderson, J.C. "Reading in a Foreign Language: A Reading Problem or a Language Problem?" In *Reading in a Foreign Language.* London: Longman, 1986.

Baker, Linda. "How Do We Know When We Don't Understand?" *Standards for Evaluating Text Comprehension.* New York: Academic Press, 1985.

Bialystok, Ellen. "A theoretical model of second language learning." *Language Learning,* Vol. 28, no. 1, 1978.

Bialystok, Ellen. *Communication Strategies: A Psychological Analysis of Second Language Use.* Applied Language Studies, Oxford: Basil Blackwell, Inc., 1990.

Carell, Patricia L., Devine, Joanne and Eskey, David E. *Interactive Approaches to Second Language Reading.* Cambridge: Cambridge University Press, 1988.

Grellet, Francoise. *Developing Reading Skills.* Cambridge: Cambridge University Press, 1981.

Harri-Augstein Sheila, Smith, Michael and Thomas Laurrie. *Reading to Learn.* London: Longman, 1982.

Nunan, David. *Designing Tasks for the Communicative Classroom.* Cambridge: Cambridge University Press, 1989: 32-35.

Pugh, A.K. *Silent Reading: An Introduction to its Study and Teaching.* London: Heinemann Educational Books, 1978.

Rivers, Wilga M. *Teaching Foreign Language Skills.* Chicago: The University of Chicago Press, 1968.

Tadros, Agnela. *Prediction in Text.* Birmingham: English Language Research, University of Birmingham, 1985.

5

ESP and Course Design for ELT

KRISHNA MOHAN and MEERA BANERJI

The paper examines the concept of ESP in the context of ELT in India and proposes a fresh taxonomy of the latter. It attempts to show that some confusion about ESP has been caused by interpreting this acronym as denoting a variety of English rather than referring to a type of ELT. It suggests that the principles and concerns of ESP should shape the ELT course design at the university level in India.

Though the study of English in India began as a historical accident, even today it continues to be a language of intellection and communication for meeting the specialized needs of education, business, commerce, law, politics, science and technology. In the absence of any Indian language enjoying the status of a common link language in the country, the social environment strongly supports the use of English. The constitutional provision about English as an associate official language of the Central Government is recognition of this role of English in the country and represents the collective will of the nation. In continuing to accord a place of importance to English, we have simply accepted a reality and ensured a smooth and workable linguistic intercourse among the various states of India.

Whereas there has been, in general, a satisfactory change in our attitude towards the place of English in society, all is not well with its teaching. Even today ELT continues to be in disarray, ineffective, irrelevant and perhaps, irresponsible. In a developing country such as ours where the need of the hour is rapid social and economic growth and where there are too many heavy demands on existing meagre resources, utmost economy in every sphere of activity is essential. No less important is the time factor. Unfortunately so far as ELT is concerned, there is hardly any conclusive evidence to show that we have been guided, to the extent desirable, by these important considerations. Despite efforts during the last four decades or so ELT at the university level is not yet marked by a spirit of dedicated professionalism. A modern professional is alert and wide-awake to significant developments and aware of the outflow of investigations in his field. He is in constant search for what can optimize the results. No such direction is discernable so far as ELT is concerned. For example, the current emphasis on language as a social phenomenon does not seem to have exercised any noticeable impact on the shaping of our ELT programmes. Partly as a result of sociolinguistic studies, the imparting of communicative competence (CC) as the principal objective of L2 teaching programmes is getting wide recognition. But we have yet to make a vigorous and comprehensive attempt to examine the relevance of the results from the emergence of this concept and to consider their application to the Indian situation. Similarly, the earlier emphasis of ELT on how to teach (methodology) has given way to what to teach (contents specification and syllabus design). Another direction in which one can observe new efforts is the development of courses to teach special English to meet the needs of students of certain disciplines, notably science and technology. This has led to the birth of the concept of English for Special Purposes (ESP). In fact, the notions of CC and ESP interlock and so their birth has been simultaneous. These developments have tended to change the methods and procedures of syllabus construction and techniques of teaching by introducing an element of scientific rigour in ELT operation. But so far as India is concerned, the impact has been minimal.

We may define ESP courses as those where the syllabus and materials are determined in all essentials by the prior analysis of the communication needs of the learner, rather than by non-learner centred criteria such as the teacher's or institution's predetermined preference for General English (GE) or for treating English as part of general education.

The words 'special' and 'purpose' in ESP are contentious and hence before we proceed further, let us resolve this issue. Barnett (1977: 11) and Munby (1978: 2-3) distinguish these two notions clearly. The word 'special' is in common use with reference to the specialized registers that are associated with such restricted varieties as 'legal English,' 'technical English,' etc. These varieties of English are statistically quantifiable and definable in terms of formal linguistic properties, lexical items, collocations and sentence structures. Further, the statement that a purpose is 'special' seems to imply that it is not ordinary but this is not necessarily the case with what an ESP course aims at. Another intended meaning of the phrase 'special purpose' is that it is not general. But then this intention is better conveyed by 'specific' as it directs attention not to specialised varieties of English of the kind mentioned above but to distinctly formulated purposes. The 'purpose' may well encompass the learning of specialised and restricted varieties but the focus is directed on the learner and the purposes for which he requires the target language and the ESP programmes are designed, keeping this consideration in mind. An ESP course for scientists in this sense, for example, would not be limited to the language of scientific texts; instead, it would include all the identified skills and components relevant to the language tasks he performs or is likely to perform in playing the role of a scientist. For designing an ESP course of this type the identification of such skills and abilities would be done carefully by following the techniques of scientific investigation. Candlin (1978: ix) has rightly pointed out that "ESP should remain loyal to collected rather than invented data" and we may add that it should not entirely rely on experience as well. Thus by its very nature ESP demands a rigorous approach to course design, using insights and findings from sociolinguistics, discourse analysis and the communicative approach to language learning. Studies in these areas have shown the way to identify, collect and analyse the relevant data for the purpose of designing an ESP course. For doing this, the procedure suggested is identifying homogenous groups of language users and characterizing their uses of language in particular circumstances together with a representative selection of linguistic usages habitually employed. This will provide base-line data which can then be distilled to construct a course.

The question raised about P in ESP is whether it means 'purpose' or 'purposes.' According to Noss and Rodgers (1976) the two forms of ESP can be (i) English for a Special Purpose and (ii) English for Special Purposes. The former "assumes a restricted corpus selected from the totality of the English language with a particular group of learners. The basis for selecting such a corpus must be its assumed frequency of use in a particular academic, vocational, or other specialized field." (Noss and Rodgers 1976: 53). Some of the examples given of this kind of English are Business English, English for Hostel Staff, etc. The second term ESP (Plural) is used to refer to the aggregate of such restricted corpora as are designated by the term ESP (singular). This 'aggregate,' it is argued, would approach the totality of what we call English. Further, each 'restricted corpus' will have much in common with some other such corpus. And collectively these may form a network around some kind of 'common core' which would be less than the totality of English. At present there is no agreed definition of this presumed common core but it is assumed that it is not likely to be any different from what is termed as elementary or General English. This distinction between ESP (singular) and ESP (plural) does not appear to be significant, as we shall presently see, in the face of our earlier discussion of the notion of ESP. There is nothing new in saying that ESP (plural) is an aggregate of different types of ESP (singular). All along ESP has referred either to one course or many, depending upon what one is discussing. The important thing to note is that it is a type of ELT course which lays stress on the attainment of the terminal objectives based on the purpose of learning language.

In fact, there is no need to draw a distinction between ESP (singular) and ESP (plural) in order to arrive at the conclusion that there is a common core, which is less than the 'totality of English.' On the one hand, even such a narrow-ranged ESP course of English for hotel staff cannot wholly ignore the importance of grammaticality of utterances likely to be made in highly specific situations as would have to be envisaged in designing a course of this type. On the other hand, no course, ESP or otherwise, can claim to teach the totality of English. However, in their discussion of ESP (plural) Noss and Rodgers seem to imply that it should be possible to discover common areas among groups of language restricted areas of human activity and on this basis to indicate the nature of the contents of an ESP course. This idea is relevant for our purposes and we shall return to it later.

Having thus looked briefly at the nature of ESOP we can conclude that S in ESP should be construed to mean 'specific' rather than 'special' and P for 'purposes.' Mackay and Mountford (1978) have appropriately titled their book and Moody and Moore (1977) their Report as *English for Specified Purposes,* though these contain material for which one could also use the phrase '*English for Special Purposes.*' Since these two notions overlap, it would be advisable to indicate one's preference in any serious discussion of the subject. In India in all L2 situations English is learnt for certain specific reasons and we use it to meet certain well-defined demands. This is an additional reason for our preference to 'specific.' One could have used 'particular' instead of 'special' or 'specific' to solve the problem of S in ESP. But that would have meant the changing of a widely used and understood acronym, ESP. The readily accepted acronyms are like newly minted coins and without sufficient reason one should not attempt to withdraw them from circulation.

Having said this we now proceed to examine very briefly the notions conveyed by these acronyms and also to refer to some of the confusion that is caused by them. We shall also examine whether there is sufficient reason to modify them. On the basis of the brief discussion that follows it is difficult to say with certainty whether some of the currently used acronyms need to be thrown out of circulation. But one outflow of what we are going to say is that it helps us in attempting to construct a fresh taxonomy of ESP and to discuss the notions that shaped them.

The world of English teaching is crowded with acronyms and they seem to be multiplying with the ever-increasing concern of scholars for refinement of concepts and precision of communication. We shall try to limit ourselves to the minimum essential for the purposes of the present discussion.

With the proliferation of acronyms to describe various types of English threatening to grow into an over-rich diet of alphabet soup, it is best at the outset to try to limit ourselves to as few as possible that will serve our purpose and to indicate clearly what we will mean by them. Let us then begin with the beginning.

The emergence of the concept of ELT can be traced to the need for imparting proficiency in the use of English for practical purposes (a functional tool of communication) as distinct from the need for teaching English literature as part of general education.

A greater need was felt to do so when the newly independent countries like India which were formerly under the British rule decided in favour of retaining English as means of national communication out of sheer practical necessity (political cohesion, educational growth, science and technology development, etc.). English, in fact, assumed a range of functions no other language exercised before and to see that the innumerable kinds and degrees of ability to use the language are attainable by those who need them became a tremendous educational problem. It is partly as a result of this emphasis on imparting practical ability to use English, that the name ESP was given to meet the diverse needs and fulfil the specific purposes for which English was retained by the erstwhile British dominated countries. In India GE in various garbs with the intended emphasis on imparting linguistic proficiency began to be taught but this acronym did not become current. In fact, it merged with the internationally used acronym, ELT. The concept denoted by ESP can on the face of it be appropriately stated to be that it is a variety of English, a kind of English used for certain specific purposes. But ELT of which it is an 'offspring' refers to an operation and a process. And it seems inappropriate to suggest that a teaching process can 'breed' a teaching variety. What the coiners of this phrase had in mind was 'teaching English for specific purposes' and hence a more appropriate acronym to indicate their idea would be TESP. It may not be entirely wrong to suggest that part of the confusion about whether ESP refers to discipline-based or registral varieties of English or to teaching language for attainment of certain specific objectives was caused by this acronym. The term TESP may not have created this confusion. This literature available on the subject, in fact, already uses ESP in this sense but does not term it as such.

Similarly, in the context of our situation we wonder why the phrase "Teaching English for General Purposes" (TEGP) was not introduced. GE is vague in its connotation and no wonder anything goes under the umbrella of GE. Each university in India has interpreted it according to its own perception of the needs of its students and educational policies of the government. What we are suggesting is that GE has been wrongly regarded in terms of samples taken from a variety of different sources, just as ESP has been in terms of samples taken from subject-specific resources. Both GE and ESP are the first offsprings of ELT and hence refer to the operation called teaching English, the only difference being that in the former the purposes are not so specifically indicated as in the case of the latter. We are inclined to agree with Barnett (1977: 11) when he says that "ESP is surely as old as specific reasons for learning a language and anyone who learns it sufficiently well is likely to use it for specific purposes [...]. ESP therefore has its roots in acknowledged ELT principles of the past—in the basic recognition that learners' needs differ and in the value of formulating clear objectives." This statement seems to suggest that perhaps too much is being made of the difference between these two concepts.

Our further classification of ESP relates to what kind of purposes one has in mind in devising a course of this type. So far as higher education in India is concerned, we teach English for two purposes; one, to enable the student to have an easy access to knowledge by giving him the benefit of another medium and two, to prepare him to operate successfully in the professional world after he graduates. So our concern is with both 'Teaching English for Academic Purposes' (TEAP) and 'Teaching English for Professional Purposes' (TEPP). To be considered useful, any course, by whatever name we may call it, must take care of both these types of needs. This leads us to ask the question whether scientific English should be taught to students of science, business and commercial English to students of business and commerce, and so on and so forth. To answer this question, we need to give a new name to the teaching situations just mentioned. It would be more appropriate to rechristen EST as TEST (Teaching English for Science and Technology) and on the same analogy coin acronyms such as TEBC (Teaching English for Business and Commerce) etc. EST does not indicate the teaching activity we have in mind. Whether ST English is a type of discourse or a variety of English defined in terms of its formal properties is outside the scope of the present discussion. But a brief reference to Widdowson's (1975) view on the subject would not be out of place here. It would justify our suggestion to modify EST to TEST and the same arguments should hold good for the modification of other such acronyms. EST shows how language is used to express some reasoning processes, defining, classifying generalizing, making hypotheses and drawing conclusions. Thus merely learning some linguistic forms occurring frequently (universal tense, passive forms, for example) and a specialist vocabulary would not help. Giving examples of the language system does not show what kind of communication it is. The focus in teaching should be on the techniques of activating the dormant competence of the learner and extending it by relating his linguistic knowledge to meaningful realizations of the language system. There is a seemingly direct and easy route which tempts us when we are given the responsibility to teach students whose professional goals are well-defined. This route is to choose engineering texts, for example, for teaching English to engineering students but this route may not teach or effectively prepare a student for more general communicative strategies over a wider range of language use as required by the professional situation in which he will have to operate. Thus the presentation of authentic language on the ground that the learners will have to use such language is an undue compliance with needs specification. It may work in certain situations but for universal acceptance it has to be established by reference to pedagogic criteria. It would be wrong to adjust our pedagogy to the latest linguistic fashion; the over-riding concern should be to work out what would meet the essential needs of the learner.

Thus one significant result of the intellectual turmoil caused by ESP in the world of ELT is the realization that the main concern of language teachers should be with how the language system is put to use for communication purposes. This concern has naturally led to an effort to understand clearly the role the learner is expected to play and consequential need to define the learning objectives in more concrete terms, indicating precisely the kind of terminal behaviour expected of him. And these are the concerns that should govern our ELT courses. It has been rightly pointed out that ESP approach is not a harmonized body doctrine. Rather, it serves to gather into one body of knowledge a variety of insights and intuitions about the teaching of English. These should regulate our effort if we wish our English courses to deliver the good. We may sum up as follows the ideas thrown up by ESP:

1. The purposes for which English is used should be clearly identified.
2. The communication needs of the learner should be discovered through scientific investigation.
3. The stress in teaching should be put on language as a communication system and not as a grammatical system.
4. The preoccupation with the rules of 'usage' should give place to the concern with the rules of 'use.'
5. The teaching should be learner-centred and the objectives of teaching should be specified in terms of the terminal behaviour of the learner.

English in India is mainly learnt as tool of acquiring communicative ability relevant for real-life situations. Hence as ESP course which is designed, using the above mentioned insights, would necessarily cater to the needs of the various professions into which our university graduates enter. We may call this kind of teaching operation as TEPP as distinct from EOP. We propose the replacement of 'O' by 'P' deliberately because the word 'profession' more appropriately expresses the kind of work done by students who graduate from our universities. The addition of T is for the same reasons as we advanced for modifying ESP to TESP.

We may now summarise our classification of ELT as follows:

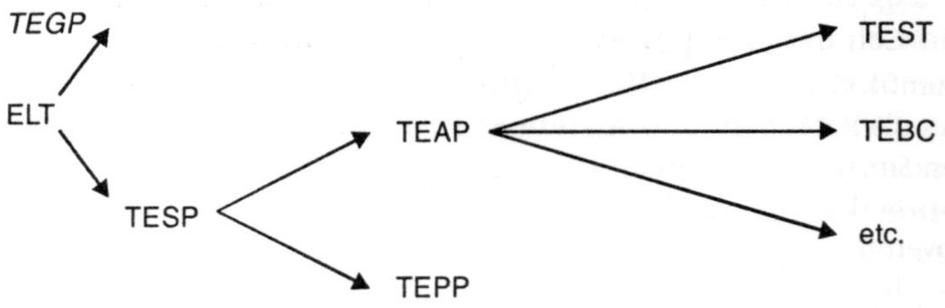

It appears that no useful purpose would be served by further classification of TEPP in the context of teaching English at the university level in India. The type of courses which are generally mentioned for exemplification in the literature on TEPP are: Courses for diplomats, bank officers, meteorologists, air hostesses, air traffic controllers, telephone operators, etc. The kind of English these professional groups need has a narrow range and serves a very limited purpose. It is not the responsibility of universities to prepare students for meeting the specific communicative needs of such specialized jobs. University education must be broad-based and impart fundamental communicative skills so that the student, whatever profession he joins, is able to activate his competence to meet the specific requirements of individual professional situations. In fact, what should be done is to enable the student to achieve some real fluency in a broad area and this can be extended later as the need arises. If this is done, there may not be any need to ground the learner in discipline-based courses; for once the basic communicative competence is acquired, it can be used by the learner also while he is a student. The communicative ability consists in the art of negotiating meaning and whosoever is involved in intellectual work cannot but learn, among other things, to use language for the kinds of activities which, for example, the advocates of TEST think, are relevant only for scientists and engineers. We are aware that this thought blurs the distinction made between TEAP and TEPP, perhaps TEGP and TESP as well. Further investigation may reveal that the kind of English teaching our university students require can be termed only as TEPP and that TEGP, though drawing on the principles of TESP, should remain the concern of the school system alone.

BIBLIOGRAPHY

Barnett, J.A. 'Keynote Address: ESP in ELT' in *English for Specific Purposes*, a Report on the International Seminar, 17-22 April, 1977. Paipa, Bagota Colwnbia, 1977.

Brumfit, C.J. Reprint. *Problems and Principles in English Teaching*. Oxford: Pergamon Press Ltd., 1981.

Candlin, C.N. 'Preface' in *English for Specific Purposes* Ed. By Ronald Mackay and Alan Mountford. London: Longman Group Limited, 1978.

Government of India. *Report of the Study Group of Teaching of English*. New Delhi: Ministry of Education and Youth Services, 1971.

Kachru, Braj B. 'English in India: A Pan-Indian and International Link' in *English Around the World*, New York: May 1971, 1971.

——. 'Models of English for the Third World: white Man's Linguistic Burden or Language Pragmatics? In *TESOL Quarterly*, Vol. 10, No. l, June 1976, 1976.

Leaver, Betty Lou and Boris Shekhtman (Eds.). *Developing Professional-level Proficiency*. Cambridge: Cambridge University Press, 2003.

Mackay, Ronald and Alan Mountford (ed.). *English for Specific Purposes*. London: Longman Group Limited, 1978.

Macmillan, Mathew. 'A Survey of Recent Trends in the Development of English Courses for Students of Science and Technology' in *Curriculum Development and Syllabus Design for English Teaching* edited by G.H. Wilson. Singapore: SEAMEO Regional English Language Centre, 1976.

Mehrotra, R.R. *Indian English* (Text Series) Ed. by M. Gorlack. Heidelberg: Groos Verlaf, 1982.

Mohan, Krishna. 'ESP, EST or EPP: What Do Our Students Need?' in *English Teaching Forum*, Vol. XIX Number 3, July 1981, 1981.

Moody, H.L.B. and J.D. Moore (eds.). *English for Specific Purposes*, a Report on the International Seminar Paipa, Bagota, Colwnbia, 1977.

Munby, John. *Communicative Syllabus Design*. Cambridge: Cambridge University Press, 1978.

Noss, Richard B. and Theodore S. Rodgers. 'Does English for Special Purposes Imply a New Kind of Language Syllabus?' in *Curriculum Development and Syllabus Design for English Teaching* edited by G.H. Wilson. Singapore SEAMEO Regional English Language Centre, 1976.

Richard, Jack C. and Willy A. Renandya. *Methodology in Language Teaching*. Cambridge: Cambridge University Press, 2003.

Soundararaj, Francis. *Teaching Spoken English and Communication Skills*. Madras: T.R. Publications, 1995.

Widdowson, H.G. EST in Theory and Practice. *English for Academic Study*. An LTIC Occasional in Paper. London: The British Council, 1975.

6

KILLING TWO BIRDS WITH ONE STONE: A DYNAMIC APPROACH TO ELT

MIMI SINGH SANDHU

Teaching English as a second language can be made much more interesting than it often appears to be. My focus here is on the college students who enter their first year with a good knowledge of grammar, but even when they leave college after five years, they are not as fluent in the language as they are expected to be. Invariably, they need to be motivated to come out of their shell and communicate in English. A moral support is not enough. Nor is the knowledge of parsing or precis writing. They need to use English in their daily life not merely as a library language (as most of them learn to use), but as a lingua franca. They need to feel the language.

My understanding of the college students in my two decades of teaching experience is based on the fact that despite a good knowledge of grammar, many students, who study English as a second language, are unable to communicate with ease in English. There needs to be, therefore, a more dynamic approach to the teaching of English as a second language at the college level. The teaching of interactive grammar is a very familiar concept in modern teaching. What is required, today, is a viable approach to develop fluency in speech. This requires a basic knowledge of the phonology of English and also a basic idea of the intonation. It is not important for the student to learn the intricacies of phonology and intonational patterns. But the teacher, undoubtedly, must be trained to use a discrete approach in relation to the level of the learner.

Exercises in accent, rhythm and intonation can be used to reinforce the students' knowledge of grammar and develop fluency in spoken English. The effort can be very easy in the early stages of teaching when only that level of proficiency is targeted which makes the language incapable of being misunderstood. What needs to be pointed out is the importance of word accent in sentences and in homonyms like: *con`duct* and *`conduct; pro`ject* and *`project.*

At a higher level, certain grammatical norms need to be preserved. Take for instance, the rule, which says, "The verb immediately following do/does/did is always in its base form." (Verma and Nagarajan, 1999: 16). A very common mistake made by the undergraduate students is that despite the knowledge of the rule, they use the past form of the verb (instead of the base form) when they need to refer to the past. They construct sentences like: **They didn't came.* The following phonetic drill in the particular rhythmic pattern, (as illustrated in CIEFL: Exercises in Spoken English Part-1, 1977: 20) serves as a good remedy:

> *He didn't come.* (ti tum ti tum)
> *She didn't come.* (ti tum ti tum)
> *You didn't come.* (ti tum ti tum)
> *I didn't come.* (ti tum ti tum)
> *So nobody came.* (ti tum ti ti tum)

The last sentence uttered in a different rhythmic pattern: *ti 'tum ti ti`tum* (CIEFL: Exercises in Spoken English Part-1, 1977: 21) helps in establishing the grammatical difference between the past and the base form of the verb in accordance with the above-mentioned rule.

Grammatical corrections made subconsciously is sometimes more effective than the conscious attempt. The spontaneity of the utterance is often marred when the learner makes a deliberate effort. The teacher can, therefore, bring about this change in the garb of intonation exercises. The interogative sentences like **What you are doing?* etc. can be dealt with by using the correct word order in an intonation drill. It does become as convenient as killing two birds with one stone.

At a still higher level, the students can be trained to manipulate language through intonation. This manipulation of language is actually a double-edged sword: the purpose is to communicate, but the intention is to negotiate or win a diplomatic battle. The writer who supplies the most convenient tools (weapons!) for this negotiative process (battle) is David Brazil.

It was during my M.Phil. Dissertation work, under the guidance of Professor Kamlesh Sadanand (of the Central Institute of English and Foreign Languages, Hyderabad), while I was going through David Brazil's *Discourse Intonation* that I thought of teaching language through intonation. Brazil's "engagement with the semantics of intonation [...] proposes that intonation is more satisfactorily accounted for at the level of discourse than at the level of grammar" (Brazil, 1977: 2-3).

In the Foreword to *Communicative Value of Intonation in English* (Brazil, 1997), Martin Hewings and Richard Cauldwell speak of the manageability of *Discourse Intonation* for both "teachers and researchers." Brazil's description "recognizes significant intonation choices as being made within a very small number of systems—four in all: *Prominence, tone, key* and *termination.*" I am indebted to my supervisor, Professor Sadanand for a couple of modifications in Brazil's classification of tones. She helped me to perceive a distinct difference between level tones which prompt the speaker to withhold or withdraw from interactive situation and those level tones, which as Crystal describes, are "functionally rise-like" (Cystal, 1969: 217). She also asked me to refrain from using Brazil's symbol 'zero' (0) for level tone because zero gives the impression of no sound at all. Thus, Brazil's systems contain a total of thirteen (*PLUS ONE*) choices, summarized in the following table:

System	**Choices**	**Number**
Prominence	prominent/non-prominent	2
Tone	rise-fall, fall, level, *low-rise*, rise, fall	5+1
Key	high, mid, low	3
Termination	high, mid, low	3

In terms of the economy of variables, Brazil stands apart because the approaches of other phoneticians "result in far greater complexity and a potentially openended list of meanings" (Brazil, 1997, *Foreword*, vii). Since the focus is on discourse analysis and discourse is, obviously, based on "real, situated speech," the thrust is towards communication skill. If a taped conversation is analyzed in accordance with Brazil's model, the revelations can be startling. His explanation of the pitch-sequence (Brazil, 1979: 18), a unit higher than the tone-unit, gives a wider scope of communication.

The tones are not tied to lexically derived notions like "expectancy" and "surprise," but make "direct reference to the interactive process," which is "implicit in every spoken utterance" (Brazil, 1977: 3). For the classification of tone, Brazil takes the cue from Daniel Jones who spoke of two tunes in English: One whose final pitch movement is rising and the other whose final pitch movement is falling. According to Brazil, there exists a contrast between two main tones: the 'falling' and the 'falling-rising.' The fall-rise tone "marks the matter of the tone-group as shared, already negotiated, common ground occupied by the participants at a particular moment in an ongoing relationship. Choice of falling tone, by contrast, marks the matter new:" (Brazil, 1977: 8).

Brazil's approach to intonation considers "relative pitch" as its "defining-factor" (Brazil, 1979: 4). "The physical correlates of key are a set of phonetic features no single one of which is essentially present." A speaker makes a "potentially meaningful choice to pitch each successive tone group at, above, or below the level which for him can be regarded as the norm."

The Pitch Concord is Brazil's most remarkable contribution to the world of Intonational Analysis. It is the relationship between "the final tone unit of one move and the initial key choice of the next move" (Brazil, Coulthart and John 1981: 75). It deals with "an area of phonology" which describes pitch-sequence as a "stretch of discourse within which each speaker's actual behaviour can be judged against the expectation of utterance-to-utterance locking." Brazil's "method" is to note what the effects of this locking "are when they do and, when they do not, occur" (Brazil, 1977: 120).

The learner needs only to be familiar with the fourteen (13+1) choices illustrated above. Exploiting the tone and the key combination is a matter of individual discretion, which is facilitated by the human nervous system. Then the student will not only "be able to speak English with an intonation that will strike the native speaker as correct," but "his own power of imitation will enable him to supply the refinements" (Kingdon, 1958: xvi-xvii), and use the language to kill as many birds as possible.

WORKS CITED

Brazil, David. *Discourse Intonation*, 1977.

——. *Discourse Intonation* Vol. II. Birmingham Instant Print Limited, 1979.

Brazil, D., Coulthart, M. and Johns, C. *Discourse Intonation and Language Teaching*. Longman, 1981.

Brazil, D. *Communicative Value of Intonation in English.* Cambridge, 1997.

Central Institute of English and Foreign Languages. *Exercises in Spoken English Part-I.* C.I.E.F.L., 1977.

Kingdon, R. *The Groundwork of English Intonation.* Longman, 1958.

Verma, S.K. and Nagarajan, H. *An Interactive Grammar of Modern English.* Frank Bros. & Co. (Publishers) Ltd., 1999.

7

THE CONCEPTUAL VALIDITY OF LEARNER CENTRED APPROACH IN DISTANCE EDUCATION FOR ELT

PUSHP LATA

Introduction

It is often maintained that teachers do not slavishly follow a pre-specified plan, and that learners do not always learn what teachers teach. Other observation is that teachers seem to do all the work and exhaust themselves in the process. Also teachers often feel they work harder than their students. This is true of language teaching too. The most prominent reason for this seems to be that the traditional curriculum consists of what the course designers and writers think that learners ought to learn. Moreover, language teaching and learning has so far been kept outside the educational mainstream. Language learning has been seen as a linguistic, rather than an educational matter, as there has been a tendency to overlook research and development as well as planning processes related to general educational principles for second language acquisition research (David Nunan 1989: 15). A hiatus that exists between theory and practice in curriculum planning is visible particularly in case of adults learning a second language. Lawton (1973) delves deep into this issue and considers this gap between 'what should be' and 'what is,' quite momentus. He comments as following:

> This gap exists at a number of levels; for examples, the difference between what teachers suggest should happen and what can be observed in the classroom, the gap between educational theory as taught in colleges and

> universities and the 'common-sense' practical approach of teachers in schools. Students leaving college and entering universities are sometimes advised by practising teachers to 'forget all the theory and get on with the real teaching.' (Lawton 1973: 7)

Thus the major burden actually lies on teachers and to reduce teachers' 'overload' would mean involving the learner in doing work more profitably for himself. This concept resembles to Curran's 'investment,' a deep involvement relating to the whole person. It stems from the idea that students' participation should be encouraged not merely in the classroom activities but also in decision-making regarding the selection of teaching methods and materials. Therefore, primarily the main focus will remain on management of Language learning.

In distance education too the learners on account of the absence of immediate support from teachers and lecturers are often imposed with a curriculum which often lacks the least consideration of what the learners want and why they want it. It is amazing to find that for ages the theoreticians and educationists have been voicing for "needs analysis of the learners" before providing them with a final set of learning materials, yet it has not materialised so far especially at the tertiary level. Besides, distance learners' limitations and learning conditions have been quite often condoned while designing curriculum of English Language for them.

If a curriculum for the regular set-up students is not a need-based or learner-centred one, there is a teacher in the classroom, who can take care of the things and the facts lacking in the curriculum, as Stern suggests for these teachers:

> Language teachers can be said to regard themselves as practical people and not as theorists. Some might even say they are opposed to 'theory' expressing their opposition in such remarks as 'it is all very well in theory, but it would not work in practice.'

This statement can be questioned for its validity, as every teacher cannot articulate things on his own. But at the same time it compels the distance curricula planners to think that on account of the absence of immediate learning support and supervision, the distance learners who are adults must be provided with a set of materials which interest them and help them teach themselves. It should be made learner-centred in its nature, since we intend to prepare them for sharing the responsibility for learning. In brief, after we acknowledge the fact that learners can acquire the management ability they lack, we need to devise the ways of conducting learner-training.

Hence, the researchers have started redressing and broadening the concept of adult second language learning and curriculum planning (*e.g.* Stern 1983, Yalden 1983, Richards 1984, Nunan 1983a, Dubin and Olshtain 1986, Brumfit 1984). All of them support the concept of learner-centredness to be applied while planning curricula.

The Theoretical Framework of Learner-centred Curriculum

The ways learners go about learning a second language have been investigated from varied angles. In the recent trend much interest has been evinced in learner-centred approaches. In fact the development of learner-centred approaches to language teaching has stemmed from the researches and experiments in the area of adult learning. In the learner-centred approach as stated by David Nunan (1989: 19), information by and from learners need to be used in planning, implementing and evaluating language programmes. Hence, if we aim at evaluating the any English Language curricula and Teaching materials from a learner-centred perspective, it becomes essential for us to talk briefly about the theory and practice of adult learning first.

Brudage and Mackeracher, the well-known theorists of adult learning, have stated some of the principles of adult learning as follows:

> Adults who value their own experience as a resource for further learning or whose experience is valued by others are better learners.
>
> Adults learn best when they are involved in developing learning objectives for themselves which are congruent with their current and idealized self-concept.
>
> Adults have already developed organized ways of focusing on, talking in and processing information. These are referred to as cognitive styles. The learner reacts to all

experiences as he perceives it, not as the teacher presents it.

Adults enter into learning activities with an organized set of descriptions and feelings about themselves which influence the learning process.

Adults are more concerned with whether they are changing in the direction of their own idealised self-concept or whether they are meeting standards and objectives set for them by others.

Adults do not learn when over-stimulated or when experiencing extreme stress or anxiety. Those adults who can process information through multiple channels and who have learnt 'how to learn' are the most productive learners.

Adults learn best when the content is personally relevant to past experience or present concerns and the learning process is relevant to life experience. Adults learn best when novel information is presented through a variety of sensory modes and experiences, with sufficient repetitions and variations on themes to allow distinctions in patterns to emerge. (Brudage and Mackeracher 1980: 21-31)

The above statements certify the view that adult learners are not merely passive recipients of knowledge. Instead they are willing to participate actively while learning. They, therefore, should be given enough opportunity to make their own decisions whether it is objectives or contents or methods of learning. Brindley (1984, 1986) in the survey emphasizes upon making every learning activity learner-centred. He strongly advocates the development of language curricula towards learner-centredness rather than subject-centredness or teacher-centredness. In a traditional curriculum, there are course writers and teachers who are entirely responsible for the curriculum but recent research has revealed that if the learners contribute to the curriculum process, curriculum will be more interesting, effective and feasible for the learners.

Breen, in his book *Language Learning Tasks* concentrates on learner-centred language teaching. He establishes a link between the concept of learner-centredness and learning activities and also proves how advantageous this relationship is. Wilkins (1988), too, supports the view of allowing learners' choices in deciding 'what to do' and 'how to do.' While discussing the reasons for adopting a learner-centred approach, it can be reinforced by research into second language acquisition as well as the work done in the area of learning styles. The National Policy of Education 1986 has also emphasized that each individual's growth presents a different range of problems and requirements, at every stage from "womb to the tomb," implying that an individual's individuality and his needs, interests, aptitudes and abilities should be taken into account by the educational system (NPE 1986: 2). This policy, thus, has advocated "a learner-centred and activity-based process of learning" (*NPE* 1986: 11).

This concept, certainly implies a major change in the roles assigned to teachers and learners in a closed-classroom set-up. This approach has attributed the teacher of the closed classroom a role of a facilitator of the learning process and an organizer of the learning situation, wherein he has to "simulate curiosity and independent thinking, promote planning and execution of projects and acquisition of knowledge through observation of phenomena, creative thinking and activities" (*NPE* 1987: 6). But in distance education, since the teacher is not there on the scene, instructions given in the text-book can perform this type of changed role. In distance/open education it requires a change in the role of instructional programming as well as that of the learners themselves.

Briefly, the learner-centred approach implies that the 'learner' should be the main focus of the educational programme. If we aim at learners attaining their autonomy, we need to sharpen our focus on the learner as Learner. In learner training it is firmly believed that the learners' awareness about their own learning behaviour can be increased. Language Learning thus would focus on inculcating the various learning strategies: Meta cognitive strategies such as planning, monitoring or evaluating learner activities; Cognitive strategies like manipulation and organization of new information; and Social affective strategies that are mediated by social interaction. The language curriculum, according to this approach, should be based upon the needs, interests, aptitudes, and abilities for enabling the learners to acquire the necessary skills, knowledge, attitudes and values. This requires a shift of attention from 'teaching' to 'learning.' Distance learners are especially prepared to develop the skills of learning to learn and have active interaction on their own while going through their study material.

Now the question which emerges after this discussion is whether a curriculum can be entirely learner-centred.

It would of course, be unrealistic to assume so. No curriculum can ever be entirely either learner-centred or subject-centred. However, if possible, the curriculum designer can make it learner-centred, whatever its content selection or methodology of evaluation be.

Self-instruction and Learner Training

The term 'self-instructional' refers to situations in which a learner, with others or alone, works without the direct help of a teacher. Therefore, self-instructional materials need to be prepared for Distance Learning students. There are two types of self-instruction:

1. Learner-centred
2. Materials-centred

Leslie Dickinson (1987: 5) makes a distinction between the two by saying that the former is characterized by modes which place responsibility on the learner, while the latter builds the teacher's role into the teaching materials. Self-instruction is mainly concerned with responsibility in learning. Several advocates of this concept (Self-directed Learning: Carver 1984, Learner Autonomy; Reley 1976, Self-Tutoring: Ager *et al.* 1988) lay emphasis on the desirability of weaning learners away from their heavy dependence on the institution or teacher and at the same time making them independent learners. For this they should exploit their general environment at the maximum and control their own learning. Learners are increasingly involved in the 'decision-making process' about learning. But an essential ingredient in learner's undertaking full responsibility is his own timely judgment as to whether he has been right and successful in his learning activity so far. 'Self-assessment' thus plays a vital part in self-instruction.

'Self-assessment' is feasible as it focuses on the learning process, rather than the results or the products.

Now let us see how far the 'Self-instructional materials' are justified to be given to students in Distance Education set-up; for this we need to discuss briefly the various characteristic features that make the Distance Education different from regular classroom teaching.

Justification for Self-instruction especially in DE

There are several reasons which may be considered responsible for introducing the concept of 'self-instruction' especially in case of DE.

Learners live at a considerable distance from the institution. Their job may not allow these distance learners even to attend the contact-programmes which are occasionally held for them at the study centre. Or they may not be free from their social liabilities to attend those classes. Sometimes learners are disabled and cannot attend classes. Some of the learners have a very little time to devote to their study. Moreover, they might want to fill in their gap of knowledge by doing a small portion of their syllabus. Quite often being adults, learners

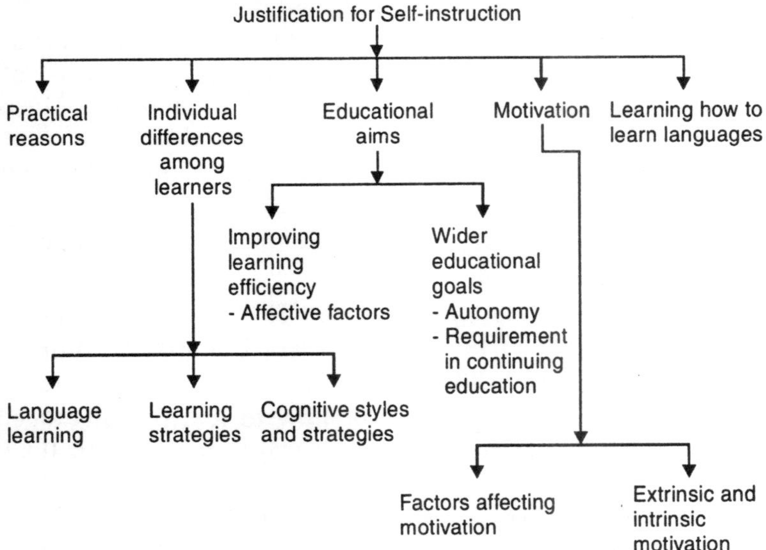

Figure: How learner-centred self-instructional mode works against teacher oriented teaching.

develop a sort of aloofness, so they wish to study on their own.

The above is not an exhaustive list of reasons, responsible for the need of self-instruction in DE. Leslie Dickinson (1986: 19) has explored this issue and has come up with a map showing 'justification for self-instruction.'

Distance Learner and Learner Training

However, it cannot be denied that making the learner autonomous largely depends on the learner himself. Therefore, learner training is increasingly being advocated. Learner training is a way of preparing learners to get the best out of the opportunity of autonomous learning. Dickinson rightly remarks:

> We teach advanced students some of those techniques we, as teachers, use so that they can take a much more important part in directing their own learning. (Dickinson 1974)

Holec (1981) also recognised the fact that learners who are aiming for some measure of autonomy require preparation of various sorts in learner training. The most recent movement in this field is mentioned by Howkins (1984 revised in 1987), in his book 'Awareness of Language of Language.' He aims at heightening the learners' awareness about the nature of language, about the nature of communication and the nature of language learning. Various proponents also argue that effective strategies of learning constitute the major difference between a good and bad language learner.

Dickinson (1988: 47) summarises the things in which a learner must be trained:

1. Clarification/verification. The learner asks for examples of how to use a word or expression etc. [...]. (Rubin 1981)
2. Making judgment about how to learn a language, and about what language learning is. (Wenden 1983 a, b)
3. Using gestures when cannot think of how to say something. (Ramirez 1986)

4. Self management: Understanding the conditions that help one learn, and arrange for the presence of those conditions. (O'Malley *et al.* 1985)
5. Memorising words through grouping them according to the similarity of their endings. (Cohen and Aphek 1981)
6. Learning how to organize self and peer assessment of written composition. (Dickinson 1987)
7. Learning that language has several different functions, *e.g.*, for description, for expression. (Crookball 1984)

In brief three necessary components of self-instruction that can be easily identified as are follows:

- Training in processes, strategies and activities which can be used for language learning;
- Instruction designed to highten awareness of the nature of the target language, and instructions in a description of metalanguage; and
- Instruction in aspects of the theory of language learning and language acquisition.

How to Implement Learner Training?

The distance learners need much learner training of this sort. But how can it be implemented? In a closed classroom set-up the teacher can play a major role and help his learners to become autonomous learners, *e.g.*, 'trouble shooting' as proposed by Dickinson and Carver (1981, 1982a). In a class session students are encouraged to specify just what they find difficult in their learning. However, in a distance education set-up it is not all that easy for the obvious reason that learners are not under immediate supervision of their tutors. Nonetheless, the best possible way for its implementation is to integrate such a programme into the language teaching materials. This means that the materials must be designed as self-instructional in nature and must include the time provision for self-assessment. Through such type of materials, learners can be trained sometimes consciously and sometimes unconsciously.

One sample module I have designed that is given below. In this module the learners are being guided in a subtle way on how to make notes from a given text. Though the text is rather simple and short but it will perfectly serve as an example for designing teaching materials and preparing exercises on self-instructional lines. It should be noted that due to space constraint a short example has been given here:

MODULE: READING PASSAGE

Read the following passage carefully and answer the questions given in exercise 1.

SATELLITES

You certainly know that the moon revolves round the earth and is, therefore, the earth's satellite. But do you know that some of the other planets have their moons?

Of the nine planets in the solar system Mercury, Venus and Pluto have no satellites. The other six have thirty-one satellites among them. Jupiter is the largest planet and it has the most satellites; it has four large and eight small ones. Saturn has nine; Uranus has five; Mars and Neptune have two each. The earth is the only planet that has a single satellite—the moon.

The largest satellite is one of Jupiter's twelve, and it is called Ganymede. The diameter of Ganymede is 5,500 Km. while that of the moon 3,475 Km. The smallest satellite is the other one of Mars, which is called Deimos. Deimos measures only 13.5 Km. from one side to the other.

The distance of the satellites from their parent planets varies enormously. Phobus, the inner satellite of Jupiter is over 23 million kilometres from its planet. The moon is 376,284 Km. from the earth.

In addition to these natural satellites, there are now several artificial satellites which revolve round the earth and some of the other planets. These man-made satellites have been put into orbit chiefly by America and Russia. The first artificial satellite Sputnik-I was put into orbit by Russia in 1957. It probably continued to orbit for ninety-two days.

Exercise 1

Fill in the blanks:

Note. Do not write the whole sentences. While taking down notes you should write the information as briefly and as precisely as you can.

1. NATURAL SATELLITES

(a) Definition: A satellite, a body which.......................

(b) Number	Planets	No. of satellites
(i)	Jupiter	12 total, 4 large 8 small
(ii)	________	____________________
(iii)	________	____________________
(iv)	________	____________________
(v)	________	____________________
(vi)	________	____________________
(vii)	________	____________________
(viii)	________	____________________
(ix)	________	____________________

(c) Size (i) Largest............. 5550 Km. in diam.

(ii) ....

(iii) The earth's ....

2. ARTIFICIAL SATELLITES

(i) Definition: ______________________________

(ii) The first satellite: Name: ______________________

Country: ______________________

Year : ______________________

Period: ______________________

Student Observation. In the above exercise you have tried to furnish the information you have obtained from the passage on the other hand, you can visualize how beautifully you can prepare notes from a given text. Don't you think it will require less time while you would feel like revising your unit for the examination. Now let us see how far you have learnt the <u>art of Note taking.</u>

Exercise 2

Make notes from the following passage:

The word medieval means 'the middle age.' It is used in

history, therefore, to refer to that period which has lies between the ancient and the modern periods and is quite literally the middle period. How do we know when the ancient period ends and the medieval period begins? We have taken the 8th century A.D. as the beginning and the 18th century A.D. as the end of the medieval period. Why? Because as you will see when you read this book, there were many changes taking place in Indian society in about the eighth century A.D. and during this time these changes influenced many aspects of Indian society. They influenced the political and economic aspects, social laws, religion, language, art—in short, almost everything. So we recognize that a new stage in Indian history had come about. We may say that this change took place around the eighth century.

We have to be just a little vague about the data because just as a person does not change suddenly in one year, similarly societies also take time to change. Nor does everybody become influenced by new ideas at the same time. Some of these changes in Indian history began earlier than the eighth century and in some parts of India their influence was felt a little later. But taking a general view of things, we can say that the new phase took root in the eighth century. In the same way with the break-up of the Mughal empire and the coming of the British, the 18th century also saw many changes. So we refer to the century as the closing of the medieval period. (*Medieval India*, Romila Thapar, NCERT, 1967)

In the above module students were expected to understand the information given in the text and by doing the first exercise indirectly they will also learn how to take down notes.

Conclusion

In brief, the educationists and theorists have always felt the need of introducing innovations within the existing constraints. They focus on receiving the attention of the heterogeneous group of learners and making the curriculum more relevant to the needs and interests of the learners in general and distance learners in particular because of the discernible difference in the learning environment. We need to administer the self-directed learning among the students so that they could become proficient in the use of English

Language. And this can be done by designing self-instructional materials which must in turn grade the learning process from elementary skills to pre-intermediate and intermediate levels to develop an awareness about their own learning process.

WORKS CITED

Brindley. *Needs Analysis and Objective Setting in the Adult migrant Education Programme.* Sydney: New Adult Migrant Education Service, 1984.

Brudage and Mackeracher. *Adult Learning Principles and Their Application to Program Learning.* Ontario: Ontario Institute for Studies in Education, 1980.

Brumfit, C.J. *Communicative Methodology in Language Teaching.* Cambridge: Cambridge University Press, 1984.

Dickinson, Leslie. *Self-instruction in Language Learning.* Cambridge: Cambridge University Press, 1987.

Dubin and Olshtain. *Course Design.* Cambridge: Cambridge University Press, 1986.

Lawton, D. *Social Change, Educational Theory and Curriculum Planning.* London: Hodder and Stoughton, 1973.

National Policy on Education. Government of India, 1986. Cited as *NPE.*

Nunan, D. *Language Teaching Course Design: Trends and Issues.* Adelaide: National Curriculum Resources Centre, 1985.

Stern, H.H. *Fundamental Concepts of Language Teaching.* Oxford: Oxford University Press, 1983.

Valden, J. *The Communicative Syllabus: Evolution, Design and Implementation.* Oxford: Pergamon, 1983.

8

Lexicology and Translations in the Language of Advertising

SANGEETA SHARMA

Advertising is changing with a wink. It has become a daunting task for the copywriter to create the messages which etch in the memory of the viewer for longer period. Even when advertising is ephemeral and transient the message conveyed remains indelible. The tools available to the copywriter are enormous and he exploits all his repertoire of language to create an impact on the reader. He has got a creative license to use the language as he wants. Of course we know that literary style and advertising style are entirely different. In literary style, writer's soul purpose is to derive aesthetic pleasure by displaying unique way of looking at the world the writer presents chiaroscuro of life in a manner that is very unique to him, therefore his style regardless the content, who the author is. In advertising writing the copywriter is anonymous, therefore he is not bothered about his ego for he has to reach the hoi polloi. Copywriter is like an actor who adapts himself according to the product and message strategy. He is constantly working on variegated products from Dettol Soap to Merceder Benz. His final aim is to create a message, which roil the enthusiasm in the reader and cajole him to buy the product. That is why he zeroes in on his effort by twisting and squeezing the language to have a mind-boggling impact. It is observed that by using *idiomatic language* he is able to achieve his objective in larger sense. Ad copy is written the way people talk after accepting the fact that different people talk in different ways in different situations. It is also called contemporary language therefore key phrases from vernacular are used to establish contemporary cue. It imbibes the concepts of *code mixing* and *code switching* as in Mummy Ka Magic Chalega for whirlpool refrigerator is an example for code mixing. Use of vernacular language across the country as in Zandu Balm is apt example of code switching. 'Neighbour's envy, owner's pride' is a contemporary phrase which had titillated the andier or for considerable tihae. Catching attention, stirring the imagination and aiding memory are perhaps the primary functions of advertising language. Unusually stylish short and crisp words remain effaced, as they are easy to remember and repeat. It has been found that language of advertising is enriched by using words with pun, words which are euphonious. In any advertisement, the most important part is brand name. We come across products, whose names fascinated us, excite us and ever conjure up images of the objects they refer to. We often wonder how the product got its nomenclature. But when we analyse we find there is a intriguing story behind the denomination of each of these products. The brand names can be classified into the six categories:

(i) Brand names after the person
Gillette, Binny, Godrej, Dunlop, Lipton, Pears, Raymonds, Hawkins, Johnson & Johnson, Colgate, ANZ Grindlay, Listuue, Kelvinator, Woodword's Gripe water.

(ii) Names borrowed from other languages
Lux, Anacin, Silvikish, Anne French, Cuticura, Dabur, Amul products, Lipton Taaza, Dollops.

(iii) Names derived to reflect the characteristics of the product
Finolex, Palmolive, Zodiac, Polar, Prudent, Promise, Woodword's Gripe water, Band aid, Max Factor, Aramusto, Margo, Sundrop, Camel, Sunrise, Oral-B.

(iv) Names coined
Sumeet SP-16, ECIL, MRF, HMT, (Acromyou) Vaseline, Lakme, Kissan, Brooke Bond, Red Label Tea.

(v) Names after a place or town
Sunblight, Bournvita, Hindware.

(vi) Names formed by modifying spellings
Brylcream, Kurl-on, Kwality.

Advertising language, where creativity is of the utmost significance, gives the copywriter a licence to deviate from the traditional rules and conventions just as a poet takes liberties with the language in order to enrich his expression. The copywriter widens and deepens the potentialities of language in several ways. His task is to find fresh, interesting and thought provoking ways of conveying meaningful information realistically. An advertisement should not only communicate effectively about the product but also incite curiosity, create understanding, build conviction and develop the urge to investigate. Advertising language is, at times, standard and unobtrusive but more often it attracts attention by being colourful and imaginative which in turn involves deviation from language usage. The study will focus on lexical deviation that is the limen of lexicology.

Lexical Deviations

Copywriters take unlimited advantage of lexical deviations for their creative copy as this constitutes one of the richest sources of new expressions for them. Major three types of such deviations observed in advertising are:

- Functional conversion
- Neologisms and nonce-formation
- Anomalous lexical collocation

Functional conversion

It is also known as zero affixation. In this one part of speech operates as another part of speech, providing fresh vitality and variety. A few examples of functional conversion as observed in few advertisements are as follows:

- Less oil is more health (n-adj)
- Trousering from Mafatlal (n-v)
- Have you gold spotted today (n-v)

Adjectives process of preponderance position in the lexicon of advertising. So a copywriter formulates new epithets by his imagination. These are the multiple hyphenated adjectival groups place before headwords. For example:

- Easy – to carry (Duckback travel goods)
- Built-in (Fallifan)

Neologisms

The copywriters share with poets the prerogative to coin new words, most of which remain nonce words, made for specific occasion ostracized by standard language. Neologisms expands the ambit of expression of a copywriter. The words are formed by compounding, affixation, composition or derivation. Examples for each category are cited.

Compounding—Skin care (Lakme), Tea Times (Marie), Liril freshness (Liril), Germfree (Dettol).

Affixation - Pre-lubricated (Yamaha)
Micro-components (ECTV)

Adjectival derivatives – Munchy (Biscuits)
Zingi (Gold spot)
Lemoni (Limca)

Anomalous lexical collocation

When a copywriter is in search of a scintillating new adjective or a noun, anomalous lexical collocation comes to his aid. This deviation consists of an unrestricted choice of nouns where only a noun from limited list of nouns is normally used. The deviation which occurs is in contrast to the expected occurrence. A few examples are as follows:

- Love at thirst site (Limca)
- Jo Peeta Wohi Sikandar (Cinkara)

So we reprise by saying that Lexicon of advertising is very creative and novelty is sustained by adopting different ways of coinage of new words.

The arena of advertising is boundless, the fringes unnoticed. The emergence of a largely borderless world has created a new reality for the existing companies. Today, world trade is driven by global competition among global companies for global consumers. With the development of faster communication, transportation and financial transaction, time and distance are no longer barriers to global marketing.

Products and services developed in a country quickly pave their way in the other country. Indians are so enthusiastic to accept goods, a varied range from China. Consumers around the world wear Nike shoes and Calvin Klein Jeans, eat at McDonald's outlet, shave with Gillette razors, use Gateway and Dell computers, drink Coca-Cola and Pepsi and Starbucks coffee, chat on cellular phones made by Nokia and Motorola and drive cars made by global automakers such as Ford, Honda and Nissan.

Just as with domestic marketing, companies engaging in international marketing must carefully analyze the major environmental factors of each market in which they compete, including economic, demographic, cultural and legal variables.

International advertisers often have problems with language. An old Italian adage translators are traitors still germane. The advertiser must know not only the native language of the country but also its nuances, idioms and subtleties. International marketers must be aware of connotations of words and symbols used in their messages and understand how advertising copy and slogans are translated, which is usually very arduous. Of course, translation is always slightly different from the original, but unwary translators can fall in any of the two traps: (1) translating word for word and believing this linguistic accuracy is a good translation; (2) summarizing the content of a message and believing that epitomizing is good translation. Because good translation involves processing ideas rather than merely processing words, neither approach achieves the equivalence of meaning necessary for effective communication. Word to word of semantic translation not only impedes communication but also results in embarrassing blunders that can damage a company's or brand's credibility or image and cost to customers. Mistranslations and faulty word choices often have created problems for firm engaging in International marketing. Study of some of the gaffe resulted because of mistranslation are stated below:

1. Pepsi's slogan: "Come Alive with Pepsi"

   German: Come out of the grave

   Chinese: Pepsi brings your ancestors back from the dead
2. A United States Airlines competing in Brazil advertised "Rendezvous Lounges" in its planes.

   In Brazilian dialect it means "a place to make love."

3. Budweiser's long time slogan was—King of Beers. But in Spanish, it became "Queen of Beers" because the noun cerveza (beer) has a feminine ending.
4. When Coca-Cola slogan was adopted in China, copywriters tried to put together Chinese alphabets to make it sound like Coca-Cola. The first attempt Ke-keu-ke-la meant *bite wax tadpole* and the second attempt produced Ko-kou-ko-le which meant *happiness in the mouth.*
5. The spanish translation for Perdue chickens slogan read—"It takes a sexually excited man to make a chick affectionate" which was actually meant to be "it takes a strong man to make a tender chicken."
6. The word four in Japanese (Shih) sounds like that for death. Hence IBM's series 44 computers had different number classification in Japan.
7. Kellogg had to rename its product "Brah Buds" in Sweden because it meant "Buned Farmer."
8. The Coors slogan "Turn it loose" became "Suffer from diarhoea" in Spanish.
9. Clariol introduced—m\Mist stick-curling iron into German only to find out that 'mist' is a slang for manure. Not too many people had used for the 'manure stick.'
10. The American slogan for Salem cigarettes was "Salem—feeling free." In the Japanese market, they advertised as "when smoking Salem, you will feel so refreshed that your mind seem to be free and empty.
11. Gerber started selling baby food in Africa with the same packaging as in US, with a cherubic baby on the label. In Africa, companies usually put the pictures on the label of what's inside, since most people can't read English.
12. Colgate toothpaste introduced a toothpaste in France called cue, and later found that it was the name of a notorious porne magazine here.
13. An American T-shirt maker in Miami printed shirts for the Spanish market which promoted the pope's

visit. Instead of "I saw the pope" (el papa), the shirts read "I saw the potato" (la papa).

14. In Italy, Schweppes tonic water translated the name into Schweppes Toilet water.
15. Parker Pen wanted to market a ballpoint pen in Mexico as "It won't lack in your pocket and embarrass you." Instead it thought embarazar (impragnate) meant to embarrass and so it read "It won't leak in your pocket and make you pregnant."
16. Chevrolet introduced a new vehicle in Spain in 1960 called Nova. But is Spanish, 'Nova' meant 'It doesn't go anywhere!'
17. Kentucky fried chicken slogan—"Finger Lickin' good" became "Eat your fingers off" in Chinese.
18. Signalling by making a circle with the thumb and forefinger has different meaning in various cultures:

    OK or the best—in most European and American countries.

    Money in Japanese.

    Rudeness in Brazilian.

    Vulgar connotation in Latin American countries.
19. Pepsodent toothpaste is unsuccessful in South East Asia because it promises white teeth to a culture where black and yellow teeth are symbols of prestige.
20. American ad campaign using various shades of green was a disaster in Malaysia, where the colour symbolizes death and disease.

One may want to translate safety precautions for non-English speaking employees in his company or may want to translate advertising slogans to market the products globally. Either way there is a need for some way of proofing those translations.

The best option is back-translation—a two step process in which a translator encodes the message into another language, and then new translator retranslates (back translates) your message into the original language. This back translation is compared with the original message to discover any errors or discrepancies. No two languages represent same social reality as they are unique. The dextrous translator knows not only the grammar and lexicon but also the language, and good Advertiser knows that you have to test the translation before trusting it.

Advertisers should follow some basic rules in using translations:

- Translators should live in the country for whom they are translating to know of their culture, and habit, and social attitude.
- Translator must also be a creative copywriter. Word to word translation is not enough but more suitable would be translating the concept—literal translation.
- Translator should get familiar with product and its features. He should have a some concept clarity of marketing.
- Translator must be very cautious of pun, idiomatic expressions and rhetoric language. It is a Herculean task for him to translate the language of advertising.

BIBLIOGRAPHY

Arens William F. *Contemporary Advertising*. 6th edition. Chicago: Irwin, 1996.

Belch, George E. and Michael A. Belch. *Advertising and Promotion—An Integrated Marketing Communication Perspective*. 5th edition. New Delhi: Tata McGraw Hill Publishing Company Limited, 2001.

Bovee, Courtland L. and John V. Thill. *Business Communication Today*. 4th edition. USA: McGraw Hill, 1995.

Czinkota, Michael R. and Ilkka A. Ronkainer. *Global Business*. 3rd edition. Texas, USA: The Dryden Press, 2000.

Weir, Walter. *On Writing of Advertising*. New York: McGraw Hill, Inc., 1960.

Wright, John S. and Daniel S. Warner. *Advertising*. 2nd edition. USA: McGraw Hill Book Company, 1996.

9

Communicative Language Teaching in a Multimedia Language Lab

SHIH-JEN HUANG and HSIAO-FANG LIU

Introduction

Due to the impact and influence of information technology on society and education, computer-assisted language learning is becoming the trend in foreign language teaching. Interactive computer network allows students to test the result of learning without the risk of being punished for any mistake. Learning does not have to be a pressure. Computer-assisted language learning can reduce the anxiety of students and turns out to be a positive side of learning (Gates, 1997).

The study is the extension of Huang (1997). As a result, the aim of this study tends to explore how students adjust themselves in learning English with the aid of multimedia computers and the interaction between students and multimedia computers. The literature of past research in the Communicative Language Teaching Approach and computer-assisted language learning usually look into the topics in their own domain. The research combining the two fields is not common so far, which makes this study important.

This study would like to address three questions. First, what are the similarities and differences of language teaching and learning between a traditional classroom and a multimedia language lab under the communicative framework? Second, are there any changes in the roles of teachers and students when they are in a different teaching environment from traditional classroom? Third, what are the implications of the

Communicative Language Teaching Approach (CLT approach hereafter) in a multimedia computer language lab in teaching?

Review of Literature

Many researchers have helped develop the theory and practice the Communicative Language Teaching Approach (Brown, 1987; Brumfit & Johnson, 1979; Hymes, 1972; Nattinger, 1984; Nunan, 1987 & 1989; Richards & Rodgers, 1986; Rossner, 1988; Savingnon, 1983; White, 1989; Yalden, 1983). The underlying theory of the CLT approach is the communicative competence (Hymes, 1972). Students do not simply learn the linguistic structures and grammar rules. They have to learn how to use the language properly. Littlewood (1981) described the CLT approach that one of the most characteristic features of communicative language teaching is that it pay systematic attention to functional as well as structural aspects of language. In reaction to the grammar-translation and audio-lingual methods, the CLT approach emphasizes the communicative activities that involve the real use of language in daily life situation.

To combine the CLT approach with a framework of computer-assisted language learning, computer simulation seems to be the best strategy to fit both. Huang (1997) categorized computer simulations into two types: instruction-oriented and fun-oriented. Their categorization depends on their primary purpose, the nature of computer-human interaction, and the amount of control (see table below).

	Primary purpose	*Computer-human interaction*	*User control*
Instruction-oriented	Teaching & learning	Unbalanced	Limited
Fun-oriented	Motivational & entertaining	Balanced	Multiple

The primary purpose is remarkably significant as it will determine the nature of the computer simulations. The instruction-oriented computer simulation aims at teaching or helping people learn. Consequently, the primary purpose of this type of computer simulation will be giving instructions and placing the responsibility of learning on the users for most of the time and constantly monitoring them to see whether they have successfully achieved the goal. Moreover, the nature of computer-human interaction is not balanced. Users receive instructions passively, then respond, and wait further instructions. The computer becomes dominant in the interaction. Subsequently, the user's choice during the interaction is rather limited. Users do not have much choice since all available choices are predetermined. The outcome of the user's move becomes predictable. The user's limited control over the computer is partly due to the fact that users in an instruction-oriented simulation are expected to accomplish a pre-set goal in learning. The simulation guides users in a certain direction. Therefore, the user's choices are restricted by simulation's primary purpose.

Take the famous Living Books series (Broderbund) for example. Users can click on a paragraph and the text will be read out loud. When users click on any objects in the background, the object will move accompanied by sound effects. Users can continue clicking as often as they like, but the one-click-one-move interaction remains the same.

On the contrary, the primary purpose of fun-oriented simulations is to be both motivational and entertaining. Instruction in a particular subject is not the primary concern in fun-oriented simulations. This type of computer simulation tends to motivate users to get interested in the simulation itself. Entertainment is the goal. As a result, both user and computer share equal opportunities to receive instructions from and respond to each other. Furthermore, the user has multiple choice for taking control. Fewer restrictions are imposed. The user's move could lead to another multiplicity of choices and the prompting of an unexpected response from the computer.

However, the two categories of computer simulations are not mutually exclusive of each other. Rather, they would be better regarded as the two ends of a continuum. All computer simulation activities fall somewhere in between. In other words, it is very possible that a computer simulation possesses both instruction-oriented and fun-oriented features.

Methodology

Subjects

The present study was conducted in the spring semester of 1998. Subjects were 45 second-year students in the five-year programme of the Department of Foreign Languages at Fooyin Institute of Technology, Taiwan. The study took place in the setting of the students' "Oral Practice" course. The aim of the course in the second semester was to further expand students' English oral skills to a more composition-like style. The teacher and students met for one 2 hour session every week.

All of the students graduated from junior high school. They had completed 4 years of English study (3 years in junior high school, one year at Fooyin). Also, students were familiar with the basic operation of computers such as saving and retrieving files because they took a required computer introductory course at the first year and meanwhile were taking a required word processing course.

Setting

The instructor did not instruct and guide the English conversation practice in a classroom merely equipped with only desks, chairs, and a large blackboard. Instead, the course was carried out in a multimedia computer language lab (multimedia lab hereafter). There are fifty-six Pentium class desktops in the lab. They are all networked. Two computers are set for instructor use only.

The multimedia lab shares some features with the traditional audio-lingual language lab. The teacher can broadcast the teaching materials by playing audio tapes, video-tapes, or CDs. Students practice with each other in pairs by themselves. The instructor assigns a pair of students as the model group.

The multimedia lab has some features that traditional language lab cannot compete. First, a traditional language lab does not have the function of video on demand. Students can choose an English teaching programme they are interested in and learn on their pace of learning. The English learning programme will just serve the student's desired goal of learning.

In one sense, students easily get the individual attention from the computer. Second, the function of a multimedia lab is multiple. It cannot only assume the role of a traditional language lab, but also offer teachers more powerful teaching tools with the aid of modern computer technology.

Design

The design of this study basically follows Huang (1997). The subjects were paired in groups. Students were assigned a topic for every meeting in the class. First, students began to play a computer simulation software, SimTown, and designed a simulated town on the computer. Next, they had to work on the assignment based on the assigned topic and the created city.

To be more specific, each session consisted of five stages. First, the teacher oriented students to the basic operation of computers again. Then, the teacher needed to present the simulation software. Second, after students learned how to play SimTown, they must build their own simulation town. Students were required to build the town in collaboration with the partner. They played the role of mayor of the simulated town. At this stage, students merely enjoyed the fun of playing. What they did not know was that they were establishing their own computer simulation environment for language learning. They were allowed to build the city in whichever way they desired. Third, after students finished building their city, the city itself then became the simulation world as students' learning materials. Students were required to practise an assigned topic. Fourth, students presented their simulated town to the class based on the assigned topic. The presentation was oral and in English. The student presentations could be given either individually or in groups. This presentation stage includes two parts: presentation and interaction. In addition to the presentation itself, the other class members might ask questions. It usually took place in a multimedia lab because each group simulation town would be broadcast to every student monitor screen.

Before leaving this section, it stands to reason that a short introduction of the computer simulation software employed in this study is necessary. SimTown is a computer simulation programme created by Maxis/Electronic Arts. It is designed for children at the age of 3 to 10. As a result, it happens to be very suitable for EFL students at the intermediate level for the following reasons. First, the layout and graphic design are very appealing to students. They will not easily feel bored and keep being interested in the software. Second, the vocabulary in the software is easy to understand. Since the software is about a town, it provides several name list of trees, houses, buildings and the like. Students will increase their vocabulary by playing the software. Third, unlike SimCity, SimTown's counterpart for adults, every creature in this software has its name and personal information such as favourite food and sports. The player can even create his own character and track the character location in the town. It adds more realism to the software.

The challenge of this simulation is that the player must build a town from scratch and then manage it. The town will become a ghost town if it is poorly managed. The computer simulation computes every decision the player makes. The computer simulation will respond to every move the player makes.

Data Collection

The data was obtained through teacher classroom observation and a group interview of five randomly selected students. The purpose of the interview session tended to further understand the student's attitudes toward the CLT approach and the multimedia lab. The students, including three male students and two female students, were randomly selected. The interview was conducted in Chinese at the end of the 1998 spring semester. The interview session lasted about twenty minutes in a question and answer manner and the contents of the interview were noted down. Before the group interview, the five students were briefed about the nature of the interview.

Discussion

What are the similarities and differences of language teaching and learning between a traditional classroom and a multimedia language lab under the communicative framework?

The study presents two types of communication in the multimedia lab from the perspective of the CLT teaching. First, the CLT teaching in the multimedia lab presents a large impact on the student-teacher communication. The student-teacher communication seemed to be blocked to some extent by the layout of the multimedia lab. Physically, the multimedia lab is larger than the traditional classroom. The physical distance enlarged the psychological distance. It has the tendency that the two-way communication between the teacher and the students turned to be the one-way teacher to student communication.

Second, the student-computer communication is relatively new to students. For most of the students, it was the first time for them to take so much time "talking" to a computer. Here we need to clarify the concept of communication with a computer. As mentioned above, SimTown is an interactive software. By interaction, we mean that the computer software will respond to students' move and every decision will lead to different ends. The computer software and students do not communicate with each other by "words." Instead, students need to learn another communication system. The computers communicate by means of graphic presentation, sound effect, and animated characters. Students have to learn how to communicate with the computer so that they know what move they should make next.

Next, the layouts of the traditional classroom and the multimedia lab look similar. The seats and computers are all arranged in a matrix. One important difference is that the teacher can easily reach students by walking in the aisle between two columns of seats and initiate the communication. Students can also easily rearrange the seats for the communicative activities in the classroom. It does not happen that way in a multimedia lab. All computers are fixed on the floor in the same matrix as the seat arrangement in a traditional classroom. All of sudden the teacher has the difficulty reaching students. A multimedia lab is far larger than a traditional classroom. Thus, the teacher needs to talk to students through the broadcasting system. The "intimacy" between the student and the teacher is gone. All students can see a teacher hiding behind the control console.

Also, the communicative activities are different. In a traditional classroom, the teacher provides the topic-specific situation for students to make use of language as much as they can. Since the traditional classroom is far from any similarities to the real life situation, the teacher has to tell students to use their imagination and place themselves in that situation. Nevertheless, the multimedia lab offers the opportunity for students to visualize the situation. The computer software creates a virtual world that is very similar to the real world. It is a world that you can see.

Are there any changes in the roles of teachers and students when they are in a different teaching environment from traditional classroom?

The role of teachers and students apparently change. The teacher assumes the role of coach or director. He or she orchestrates the flow of communication for the whole class. However, the teacher must realize that to some extent a teacher has been shared with the computer. In this study, the computer software is not designed for teaching. Therefore, the intervention of computer in a teacher's teaching is not very obvious yet. In case that a learning-oriented computer software is used in a multimedia lab, teachers have to be aware that students no longer depend on the only source of knowledge. The computer software will 'teach' students the knowledge that teachers are supposed to teach. As a result, a teacher must transform his role from a coach or a director under the communicative framework to a coordinator. The teacher coordinates the flow of communication between the teacher and the student as well as between the student and the computer.

On the other hand, students should elevate their learning motivation and independence on learning. Students' higher motivation is reflected by the interest of participation. When the communicative task requires the student and his partner to complete the town building task on the computer, the negotiation is initiated. Although they might not necessarily speak English when they negotiate about the town building, some students felt the need to communicate in English. Also, they felt that they could set the pace of learning. They did not have to finish the town building in one hour. Rather, they would discuss with the partner and built the town according to their pace of learning.

What are the implications of the Communicative Language Teaching Approach in a multimedia computer language lab in teaching?

First, the choice of appropriate computer software that fits into the setting of a multimedia lab is one of the keys to success. As discussed above, the setting of a multimedia lab is different from a traditional classroom. Computer software is not used at all in a traditional classroom. Textbooks and audio-tapes are the main teaching sources. They are still very helpful teaching tools in a multimedia lab. However, the medium of teaching ought to go along with the computers. The other dimension that should be taken into consideration is that the teaching tool is also different in a multimedia lab. Chalks and blackboard are obsolete. The computer is the most appropriate teaching tool in a multimedia lab. Accordingly, using computer software in a multimedia lab should be fun and interactive.

Second, orientation is import. The problems come from two aspects. One is the computer software itself. One extra job that students have to do is to learn how to manipulate the computer software. For the first few weeks, students have to become familiar with the manipulation of the computer software so that they can begin to make use of the software. Teachers should be aware of the possible frustration resulting from the unfamiliarity of computer software. The student's difficulty in the manipulation of the software usually undermine the student's interest in the class. The computer software is completely new to students. Consequently, negative interactions between students and the computer proved to be very frustrating for most students. Alexis & Trollop warns (1985) that

> less threat and anxiety were as an advantage of simulations, but the opposite can also be true, because simulations call for intensive interaction among participants, and the results of decisions and suggestions

> a student may make are immediately apparent to participants. Simulations can be more threatening and more anxiety provoking than traditional lecture methods. (185)

They must experiment playing with it. However, the teacher assistance will help them smooth out the difficulty and they will be very glad to engage in all communicative activities based on the computer software.

The other is the technical problems in the management of the multimedia lab. For most of teachers, it demonstrates a major challenge. In a multimedia lab, the management demands not only the fundamental knowledge of computer, but also the advanced knowledge of computer, which is almost impossible for the majority of English teachers. In other words, you need to be familiar with the computer software you are using in the class, answer students' technical questions, and diagnose the temporary shut-down of computer. In comparison with the work in a traditional classroom, managing a conversation class under the communicative framework in a multimedia lab is relatively demanding.

Limitations and Implication

In conclusion, on the basis of the previous discussion, this study does not present enough evidence to show that the communicative language teaching method is more effective than it is in the traditional classroom. However, this study would like to suggest some directions for teachers' reference.

First, teachers should prepare themselves for the use of modern computer technology. Foreign language training will not always take place in a traditional classroom. With the help of a setting such as a multimedia lab, foreign language training will be more efficient. Teachers should have the clear idea of how a traditional classroom is different from a multimedia lab. To serve that purpose well, this study summarizes the previous discussion as below:

	Traditional Classroom	Multimedia Lab
Layout	Matrix	Matrix
Teaching tools	Chalk, blackboard, audio tapes	Local computer network, video on demand
Teaching materials	Textbook	Interactive computer software
Communicative activities	Imaginative role-play	Realistic computer-simulated environment
Student-teacher	Direct communication and more "intimacy"	Indirect communication and less "intimacy"
Student-computer	Not available	Interactive

Moreover, regarding the procedures of carrying out the project, orientation is the key factor in determining success with the project. Teachers must clearly state the goals and linguistic skills students are expected to attain by playing the computer simulation. Students had to keep in mind their purpose for playing the simulation. Otherwise, they would tend to indulge themselves in simply playing. Also, since SimTown is an English-version software, it is essential that teachers get students familiarized with necessary vocabulary to play the computer simulation before the group project. Moreover, SimTown is an interactive software. That is, messages regarding the city during its stages of development could pop out in English at anytime. The computer simulation has its own "advisors" who are always willing to offer their valuable suggestions to help students run a better city. Students would also encounter difficulties building their city if they could not understand the on-line interactive messages.

Although this study shows that the CLT approach is not as successful as we had expected in a setting of the multimedia lab, this study suggests that with the fast development of computer technology, foreign language teaching in a setting other than the traditional classroom is still a promising trend.

WORKS CITED

Alexis, S.M. & Trollop, S.R. *Computer-based instruction: methods and development.* New Jersey: Prentice Hall, 1985.

Brown, H.D. *Principles of Language Learning and Teaching.* MA: Addison-Wesley Publishing Company, 1987.

Brumfit, C. and Johnson, K. (ed.). *The Communicative Approach to Language Teaching*. New York: OUP, 1979.

Gates, B. *The Road Ahead*, 1997.

Huang, S.J. The Preliminary Study of the Indirect Use of Computer Simulation in EFL Teaching. Paper presented at the First International Conference of CALL, Naval Academy, Taiwan, 1997.

Hymes, D. "On Communicative Competence." In J.B. Pride and J. Holmes (eds.) *Sociolinguistics*, 269-93. Harmondsworth: Penguin, 1972.

Levy, Michael. *Compuier-assisted Language Learning*. Oxford: Clarendon Paperbacks, 1997.

Littlewood, W. *Communicative Language Teaching*. New York: Cambridge University Press, 1981.

Nattinger, J.R. "Communicative Language Teaching: A New Metaphor." *TESOL Quarterly*, 18 (3), 391-407, 1984.

Nunan, D. *Designing Tasks for the Communicative Classroom*. New York: Cambridge University Press, 1989.

Nunan, D. Communicative Language Teaching: Making it work. *ELT Journal*, 41(2), 136-45, 1987.

Richards, J.C. & Rodgers, T.S. *Approaches and Methods in Language Teaching: A Descriptions and Analysis*. New York: Cambridge University Press, 1986.

Rossner, Richard. Materials for Communicative Language Teaching and Learning. *Annual Review of Applied Linguistics*, 8, 140-63, 1988.

Savingnon, S.J. *Communicative Competence: Theory and Classroom Practice*. Reading, Mass.: Addison-Wesley Publishing Company, 1983.

White, C.J. Negotiating Communicative Language Learning in a Traditional Setting. *ELT Journal*, 43(3), 213-20, 1989.

Yalden, J. *The Communicative Syllabus: Evolution, Design and Implementation*. Oxford: Pergamon Press, 1983.

10

Chutnifying the Text: A View on the Split of Synchrony and Literary Globalisation

ALESSANDRO MONTI

> *Caõnî*: Sauce, indigenous sauce; a kind of acid sauce or marmalade.
>
> (*Hindi Dictionary*)
>
> *Caõnî Banânâ*: To transform into pulp, to beat up thoroughly.
>
> (*Hindi Dictionary*)
>
> *Caõnî*: Chutneys can be made from different ingredients but popular chutneys include mango chutney, tamarind chutney and coriander. Coconut chutney is generally served with south Indian food.
>
> (*Hindu and Urdu Phrasebook*)
>
> *Chutney*: A type of pickle, originally from India, made with fruit, vinegar, spices, sugar.
>
> (*British Dictionary*)
>
> *Chutney*: A sweet and spicy relish made from fruit, spices, sugar and vinegar.
>
> (*American World English Dictionary*)

Chutney is a word "across," a sort of now settled semantic migrant that has been scattered into the interstices of another's language. It indicates retroactively a colonial encounter and a deliberate mixture concerning difference, either in taste or in flavour. It constitutes an extended metaphor of contact and change, of colonial expansion and of cultural backdrop. A concise text in itself, chutney stretches the "national allegory" of affiliated identity up to the continuous slippage of values introduced by high hybridisation. Its procedures of transcolonial assimilation into the Western (or British, at least) dietary system reveal gluttony and simultaneously restore to visibility the archaic and voracious "gaster" figure that disrupts the linear genealogies that indicate development and span different acts of enunciation. My transoceanic metaphor concerning food represents a contested territory of postcolonial writing, beyond and notwithstanding the dubious or vicarious pleasures of change and assimilation. This step provides a loaded battleground for performative repetitions of meaning and organised affective diet. In a nutshell, my metaphor is caught, rather than being illustrated by it, in the diglossic transition from the phonetically hostile *caõnî* to the more familiar and palatable term chutney. Such an act of lexical migrancy releases parodic strategies of narrational rhetoric, whose catachrestic nature illustrates displacement and deformation.

The emergence of a literary language grounded on disjunctive sequences of lexical diaspora lays bare what is "untranslatable" in this aesthetic of exchange. The gap goes beyond the mere severance of continuity and *does* transcend the blessed proliferation of cross-cultural texts. We should be able to identify an element of resistance in such operations that re-inscribe identities or meanings. The lexeme chutney is obscured by a borderline feeling of anxiety and retroactive belonging, one that dramatises hybridity as an unfinished zone of regret and self-effacement. This hybrid discourse of disavowal appears in the non-dialogic script of the Anglo-Indian voice. We should mention the now forgotten Chutney Lyrics (R.C. Caldwell, 1871), sketches of mild-flavoured colonial apories of differentiated presence that half-work the notion of linguistic and cultural "chutnification," through a dispossessing feeling of migrancy from the native West to the East.

Thus, the term chutney suggests a double passage of sour assimilation in the fragmented system of signs, one that produces heterogeneous forms of diasporic human identities and simultaneously rehearses suburban fantasies of tamed exoticism: from composite "masala" to cockney pickle, I would say. This early instance of colonial globalisation raises however the issue of difference, seen as the agency that defers the inscribed meaning to a retroactive fantasy of modified genealogical belonging. Bhabha argues the debate in terms of "gathering": a chiasmatic rescue of the past and the refusal of whatever apologetic nostalgia (Bhabha 139). As such, "chutnification" transfers a scattered meaning across the middle passage of metaphor, so as to start a distanced view through an impression of imagined contiguity. This colonial incorporation of the archaic gathers authority by means of a decisive slippage of ingredients and selective procedures: assimilation represents a disseminative strategy of previous struggle and final globalised counter-liminality.

The harsh conflict with the archaic of which Bhabha speaks is signified by Rushdie in *Midnight's Children*, when in the first pages of his novel he illustrates his selective procedures of discursive strategy by introducing a mixed, or "chutnified," metaphor of similarity between the narrative text, food (or the dietary norms concerning it) and the human body:

> Family history, of course, has its proper dietary laws. One is supposed to swallow and digest only the permitted parts of it, the halal portions of the past, drained of their redness, their blood. Unfortunately, this makes the stories less juicy; so I am about to become the first and only member of the family to flout the laws of halal. Letting no blood escape from the body of the tale, I arrive at the unspeakable part; and, undaunted, press on. (Rushdie 62)

The term "halal" (one that is fraught with stiff overtones of self-righteous purity and assertions of un-negotiable discrimination) foregrounds a kind of critically loaded globalisation, one that excludes any possibility of free movement across the interstices of communal belonging and only recognises affiliated identities. Rusdhie cuts across such exclusive "areas of darkness" and by doing so he disrupts the archives nourished by sectarian belonging and sequences of uninterrupted cultural lineage. His textual policy of "chutnification" surmounts discrimination and inscribes *de facto* his script into the sphere of the forbidden ("haram"). Whereas colonial hybridisation assimilates and modifies according to taste, the category of "halal" globalises by means of taboos and exclusions. Instead of proposing a unified point of view it introduces division, so as to pull the discourse away from the present, and consequently takes archaic modes of homogenisation. Rusdhie replaces heterogeneity for this kind of homogeneity. His gargantuan rediscovery of the body and its equalisation with a full-blooded text ("letting no blood escape from the body of the tale") restores analogical constructs that are grounded on globalising images of food.

To find a similar vision of reactive resistance we have to move back to the body of Bharat Devi in *Anandamath* by Bankimchandra, in which we view the stages of anticolonial resistance through the different aspects taken on by the goddess. These two instances "authorise" the religious or national archive through select representations of the body seen as a reconstituted unique—a cultural continuum whose morphological features correspond to the decent and anti-grotesque body of which Bakhtin speaks: a closed whole, with no blemishes or fissures, a stopped hole that allows neither passage nor reproduction (350). This body is interpreted by Rushdie in specific terms of grotesque representation: "the past has drifted into me [...] history pours out of my fissured body" (37). Of course, the paradigmatic sequence "into"-"out" evokes the grotesque and unique image of the "eaten-eating" world that Bakhtin finds in Rabelais (242). In particular, the very act of death ("pours out of my fissured body," in Rusdhie) coincides with the act of birth, such as analysed by Bakhtin apropos of the episode that narrates how Gargantua came to the world. This reorganisation of the body seen as a sign (or rather, as a system of signs) introduces us to the notion of the "leaking" archive, that is the response that Rushdie gives to the imagined un-fissured body of the anti-grotesque tradition. Here two different and antinomic models of globalisation (respectively the archaic and the grotesque) are at hand. The former postulates indivisibility and claims globalisation to itself, as an exclusive pattern that allows only "halal" rules, whereas the latter acts within an interstitial space, within an in-between zone of contact, whose archaeological roots must be found in the "bicorporeal" image outlined by Bakhtin and whose slightly chaotic growth occurs in Bhabha. We should refer, for instance, to his "imagined" version of the migrant, one who lives (or thrives or survives, following circumstances) in a borderline condition between metaphorical states of death and rebirth, loss ("pouring out") and change or even gain.

To me, the discursive strategies of postcolonial discourse adopted by Bhabha endorse the demarginalised figure of the migrant in terms of excess and too oblique presence. However, I would not argue at all, in the wake of Gayatri Spivak and Bhabha himself, about a catachrestic agency that opens up an interruptive time-lag in the "progressive" myth of modernity.[1] I would rather speak of the "exorbitance" introduced by the migrant in the western scenario. The notion of *exorbitance* deploys possibilities of grotesque representation, that is, it recognises the functional role assumed by the separate and autonomous parts into the definition of individuality. Then, the fact of "splitting apart" constitutes a metaphor of fullness, a multiplicity (or a multiplication) of the cracks (or in more mundane language, of the body fissures) that explode in *Midnight's Children*:

> Please Believe that I am falling apart.
>
> I am not speaking metaphorically, nor is this the opening gambit of some melodramatic, riddling, grubby appeal for pity. I mean quite simply that I have begun to crack all over like an old jug—that my poor body, singular, unlovely, buffeted by too much history, subjected to drainage above and drainage below, mutilated by doors, brained by spittoons, has started coming apart at the seams. In short, I am literally disintegrating, slowly for the moment, although there are signs of acceleration. I ask you only to accept (as I have accepted) that I shall eventually crumble in (approximately) six hundred and thirty million particles of anonymous, and necessarily oblivious dust. This is why I have resolved to confide in paper, before I forget. (We are a nation of forgetters) (36)

The Rabelaisian quality of this mock "extended" catalogue transposes the culturally bloated identity of the migrant, such as seen by Bhabha, from the "underworld" of dissonance and miscellaneous gathering, one that turns ascription into hybridity, to the imagined dual intersecting body figured by Bakhtin. In particular, Rushdie locates the body of Saleem in a zone of encounter between the collapse of death and the revival of memory. In Rabelais the act of ravenous gluttony that precedes the birth of Gargantua integrates the heavy physiological surface of the episode with a simultaneously generative movement. Likewise, the battered and splintered body of Saleem substitutes an implied metaphor of continuity (represented by the possibilities of keeping a total memory of the past) for the forbidding notion of the archive. A further element of correlation with the analysis developed by Bakhtin is given by the analogy between the falling apart of the imagined body of the narrator and the falling apart of the social body. Of course, this unbalancing split could be viewed as a parody of some myths of origin, such as the ones embodied by the Hindu Purusa story. However, the processes of splitting and successive chutnification in *Midnight's Children* suggest a genealogical deconstruction of identity, rather than foregrounding stereotyped images of social order and unruffled accommodation of integrated cultures.

According to Bhabha, the subaltern or metonymic are neither empty nor fully, neither part nor wholly. This exercise of authority is then grounded on conflict and evokes a kind of supplementary disavowal in the enunciation of national identity. The "double inscription" of which Bhabha speaks operates on lines that are analogous to the metamorphoses implied by the globalising act of chutnification, whose teleology of partial homogeneity is surmounted by the adaptive reconstruction of the archaic (in my instance, the native "*caõnî*," that is tamed into the more palatable "chutney"). I would like to extrapolate two more hints from the discourse of belonging (or re-possession), one that I would reproduce by assimilating the terms of translated enunciation and transferential subversion articulated by Bhabha. Namely, the metonymical quality that we should be able to recognize in the globalising text of the migrant writer and the acknowledgment of growth (expressed by the emergence of the organic) as an inter-cutting (or "hybrid") process. Consequently, we should focus our attention on the close connection between the foetus of the future narrator in his mother's womb and the correlative expansion of the intensified discourse into a text, a book, even an encyclopaedia:

> By the time the rains came at the end of June, the foetus was fully formed inside her womb. Knees and nose were present; and as many heads as would grow were already in position. What had been (at the beginning) no bigger than a full stop had expanded into a comma, a word, a sentence, a paragraph, a chapter; now it was bursting into more complex developments, becoming, one might say, a book—perhaps an encyclopaedia—even a whole language. (111)

The organic metaphor that equates the human body and its growth to the book and its normative power ("the encyclopaedia") is structurally rendered into the apparently "low" language of food, an idiom that Bakhtin hyphenates in the composed definition "material-physical" (that is, pertaining to the body). This transgressive strategy instructs analogies of discursive synecdoche, so as to posit a borderline identity of the migrant, one that defuses the sliding inscription of his belonging into the liminality of the assimilated stranger and finally re-inscribes a transnational statement of the globalised (or open) archive. Thus, the correlated motifs of birth and growth (whose starting points are constituted by the formation of the foetus) involve both the human body and the postcolonial text. They may be developed so as to shape a superorganic image of reproduction beyond decay and waste. "To preserve" (in other words, "to chutnify") becomes a further key metaphor of organic (and textual as well) imagery, one that finally encapsulates disseminative sequences of identity, which remind me of the principle of "superindividual" life (or multi-semantic body, to me) argued by Bakhtin (247).

Rushdie abolishes whatever difference between the truth of the narrator and the rhetoric construction of the text, between the period of pregnancy, the "low" act of delivery and the generative act of writing. However, we cannot just interpret this movement towards homogeneity in terms of "situational consciousness," the "national allegory" of which Fredric Jameson speaks, perhaps a too comprehensive notion that sublimates how "the telling of the individual story and the individual experience cannot but ultimately involve the whole laborious telling of the community itself" (69). We should disconnect this analogical discourse of national memory that has been retold and of private affiliation that has been made general. Such loaded moments of cohesion are questioned *in toto* by Rushdie, who begins *Midnight's Children* by articulating disjunctive sequences of synchronic ambivalence, between the crumbling body of the narrator and the growth in progress of the fictional text. This imagined condition of emptiness and simultaneously of coming fullness (or re-birth) might be referred to estranging strategies of calculated synecdoche, one in which the holistic unity of the narrative is indicated by the impending dispersal or fragmentation of the body. Of course, this procedure reminds me of the well-known "low" feasting that in Rabelais anticipates the birth of Gargantua, to the effect that the physiological dissolution of the maternal bowels coincides with the "coming out" of the hero. This state of falling apart requires counter-images of preservation against the flowing away of the vital fluids that give life to the body (the cracks and fissures of the bloated and bursting off Saleem).

The multisemantic process of fragmentation, involving as it does procedures both of filling and emptying, is forelighted by Rushdie at the beginning of the novel: "while I sit like an empty pickle jar in the pool of Angle-posed light" (14). We should be able to detect in the whole passage a strategy of narration that regulates the continuous slippage from family story to categories of national affiliation (or dis-affiliation), from the apparently smooth surface of amnestic communality to the cleavage introduced by the "Anglo-poised light." Chutnification stands here as a sign of compromised nationality: it preserves the otherwise interrupted flow of memory but displays simultaneously a bitter sense of displacement. It makes also possible intersections of meaning, ones whose hybridised nature is well exemplified by the difference in taste and spelling between the "deshi" food and the English-transferred chutney. Thus the term lays bare globalisation with a difference: as a literary marker of style and language it deploys a Janus-like quality, one of dissonance and agonistic co-presence rather than of interfaced continuity of values. To misquote Bhabha, Rushdie adopts chutnification to express temporality rather than historicity. He has no apologies to show (Bhabha 140).

The case is different with another chutnified (rather than chutnifying) text, *The God of Small Things* by Arundhati Roy. In this novel the metaphor of preservation dramatises the narrative of individual experiences as the rhetorical device that illustrates history. The huge vats in which fruit and vegetables are boiled and reduced to formless pulp represent a sweetened version of the national archive. The ultimate and too clever symbol of this synthesis is well represented by the finally "hot" encounter between the subaltern and the lady. Arundhati Roy replaces the easy pathos of the love story for the splintering image of the grotesque body. She restores tears and copulation, whereas Rushdie had introduced laugh and sexual impotence. The effective move from Salman Rushdie to Arundhati Roy strikes a note of bourgeois feasting and reductive manipulation of the organic metaphor of textual growth. She churns words into sophisticated and useless puns, whose transgressive range had already been questioned, and shrugged away, by a wiser Bharati Mukherjee in her novel *The Tiger's Daughter*:

> That first winter in Poughkeepsie she had been given Sartre and Camus, Rilke and Mann, and the Joyce beyond Dubliners, and her closed little heart had been flooded. She had even begun writing stories about Calcutta based on the style and subtleties of Joyce and she had stopped only when they had become too easy, too obvious. (45)

Whereas Bharati Mukherjee adopts a stance of disaffiliation from the memories of the "archaic" margin that she has left at home, Arundhati Roy saturates the same interstitial space of vacancy. Both writers refuse the regret expressed by the chutnification of the literary text and separate the act of resistance from a condition of existential "maroonage." Instead of bursting away as Rushdie does, they re-imagine the details of loss and nostalgia in the lives of the migrants, so as to avoid underdevelopment and defeat: both of them scatter apologies and disseminate fantasies that foreground the select disavowal of their origin.

They interpret the language of "modernity" in personalised

terms of displacing intersections between their own (imagined) biographies and the national symbols of "locality." Their critical gaze moves through subjectivity as the unique form of "lived historical memory," well against the disruptive exercise of narrative authority embodied by Salman Rushdie. If we want to detect crucial forms of ubiquitous presence, and analyse unquestionable movements of "doubleness" in writing, we should consider again the initial generative metaphor of birth in *Midnight's Children.* The analogical foetus of the future narrator grows before our astonished eyes, a powerful object of discursive signification that turns the petty chronicle of family life into an iterated sign of decentred belonging: from physiological accumulation to the recursive pedagogy of the performed text.

However, this passage deploys a further projection of "affective" memories that negotiate identity by means of a contested transition of territories. The ambiguous hint to the many heads possessed by the foetus ("and as many heads would grow were already in position") constitutes an image that should remind us of the multiple limbs that sprout from the bodies of the Hindu gods and goddesses. Such a collapse of the rules of finitude that we usually associate with the rational configuration of the human body indicates cultural and ironic misgenation. It does invert the rigidity of the "halal" imposition in favour of the plastic re-thinking of the "full" body. This process of regained exorbitance from the rules that circumscribe identity and claim select belonging may be viewed as a modern adaptation of the grotesque globalisation of the human body made by Rabelais. It also shifts the agencies of signification from the dietary rules of "halal" to the plastic sites figured by the culture and the myths of the Hindus. This ability in transferring or translating the grounds of knowledge, beyond the punishing practice of negation, posits the issue of literary globalisation in terms of supplementary iteration of meanings: the virtually many-headed Saleem.

Once again Rushdie, the magic tightrope walker, moves across the boundaries and the closures of the postcolonial writer. He eludes the vexed question of the origin, such as represented by the stereotyped aura of revenge that the western and the westernising script usually associate with the proliferating reproduction of the "archaic" traits in the culture of the East. To illustrate my point, and testify how Rushdie goes beyond the estranging movement that confirms the binary vision of the "authoritative" migrant, it is worth considering the cases of *Jasmine* and *Wife*. In both of them Bharati Mukherjee metamorphoses her persecuted heroines into the savage persona of Kali, so as to make possible and underline the metonymic intervention of difference in the "deferred" maintenance of a performative and exhibited identity. In particular, the writer accommodates the anxiety of her counter-response and produces an imagined construct of racial fantasy, expressed by the gothic figure of the American would-be rapist "Half-Face" (a character drawn directly from the pages of *Dick Tracy*).

Bharati Mukherjee masquerades the "grotesque" vision of the represented body in the discursive images of alien presence and menace, so as to shift our gaze from the East to the West. Her reaction is however grounded on a sign of atavistic memory and regressive power of competitive reaction:

> It was the murkiness of the mirror and a sudden sense of mission that stopped me. What if my mission was not yet over? I didn't feel the passionate embrace of Lord Yama that could turn a kerosene flame into a lover's caress. I could not let my personal dishonor disrupt my mission. There would be plenty of time to die; I had not yet burned my husband's suit. I had not stood under the palm tree of the college campus.
>
> I extended my tongue, and sliced it. Hot blood dripped immediately in the sink [...] I wanted that moment when he saw me above him as he had last seen me, naked, but now with my mouth open, pouring blood, my red tongue out. (*Jasmine* 117-18)

A similar tactic is rehearsed in the slightly controversial *Wife*, in which the killing of the husband reminds us of the ritual sacrifice of a goat to the goddess Kali:

> She sneaked up on him and chose a spot, her favourite spot just under the hairline, where the mole was getting larger and browner, and she drew an imaginary line of kisses because she did not want him to think she was

> the impulsive, foolish sort who acted like a maniac just because the husband was suffering from insomnia. She touched the mole very lightly and let her fingers draw a circle around the delectable spot, then she brought her right hand up and with the knife stabbed the magical circle once, twice, seven times, each time a little harder, until the milk in the bowl of cereal was a pretty pink and the flakes were mushy and would have embarrassed any advertiser, and then she saw the head fall off. (212-13)

The fetished reaction and reactive appearance of Kali, to redeem an undervalued feminine identity, represents a fulfilled and retroactive imposition of difference. The return of the darkened Devi is poised against a hegemonic sign of gendered authority, one that imposes rape or subtle discrimination. Kali embodies here a movement against ambivalence and separation, so as to lend authority to the individualised conflicts that restore comforting rules of rigid self-identification and prejudicial authority. Bharati Mukherjee recuperates, through strategies of "archaic" resistance, a de-hybridised source of power and primal identification.

With Arundhati Roy the eastern body (whose representative identity is conveyed to us by the copulating pair at the end of the book, the union of Shiva with Kali, as an overenthusiastic western commentator wrote), can be only viewed through an act of vulgar voyeurism. Bharati Mukherjee returns overtly to the folk Hindu type, given that her avenging women are seen as icons of Kali, the female destroyer. We miss in both situations the "grotesque" vision of estrangement and of passage across that we do find in Rusdhie. By doing so he curtáils the agony of direct confrontation and exercises his intervening authority by an act of disavowal, so as to deconstruct the rules that control the representation of the postcolonial "imagined" world. Instead of evoking death through a metaphor of regret and astute painful memory (as Arundhati Roy does) or to attend his transitions to the mood of revenge set by Bharati Mukherjee, Rushdie opts for a kind of "grotesque" heteroglossia, whose range moves away from the rigidity of "halal" to the free plasticity of Hinduism and whose multiplicity of relations deploys a universal language of narration and counter-misgenation. He devises a true "chutney" of style, simultaneously sweetish and sour, indigenous and cosmopolitan: a globalising script in which East and West meet at last.

NOTE

1. See also Bhabha: "Gayatri Spivak has usefully described the 'negotiation' of the postcolonial position 'in terms of reversing, displacing and seizing the apparatus of value-coding,' constituting a catachrestic space: words or concepts wrested from their proper meaning, 'a concept-metaphor without an adequate referent' that perverts its embedded context. Spivak continues, 'Claiming catachresis from a space that one cannot want to inhabit [the sentence, sententious] yet must criticize [from outside the sentence] is then, the deconstructive predicament of the postcolonial'" (183-84).

WORKS CITED

Bhabha, Homi. *The Location of Culture.* London and New York: Routledge, 1994.

Caldwell, R.C. *The Chutney Lyrics, A Collection of Comic Pieces* in *Verse on Indian Subjects.* Madras: Higgin Bothan, 1871.

Rushdie, Salman. *Midnight's Children.* 1980; rpt. New York: Penguin, 2000.

Bakhtin, M.M. *L'opera di Rabelais e la cultura popolare.* 1965; rpt. Torino: Einaudi, 1979.

Jameson, Fredric. "Third World Literature in the Era of Multinational Capitalism." *Social Text* (Fall 1986) 65-88.

Mukherjee, Bharati. *Jasmine.* New York: Grove Weidenfeld, 1989.

——. *The Tiger's Daughter.* 1971; rpt. Markham, Ont.: Penguin, 1987.

——. *Wife.* 1975; rpt. Markham, Ont.: Penguin, 1990.

11

Aldous Huxley's Early Journalism

GERD ROHMANN

Huxley's novels have always been characterised as novels of ideas with essayistic elements. At the same time, his 20 volumes of essays have been neglected. His early journalism is widely strewn in literary magazines and largely unknown despite its seminal effect on his later work which is deeply concerned with questions of the present and future situation of mankind. In a review of Conrad Aiken's *Scepticisms: Notes on Contemporary American Poetry* Aldous Huxley reveals that "[...] a critic really speaks only of himself and is only interesting in what he reveals about himself."[1] This could serve as the motto of my paper.

The Huxley bibliographies by Eschelbach/Schober[2] and Bass[3] comprehensively list his early journalism but looking through the five volumes of the 1919-1921 *Athenaeum* in the British Library, I found articles and reviews as well as two poems which were not listed and volume III of *The Athenaeum* from July 1920 to February 1921 was almost completely omitted. Robert S. Baker and James Sexton are editing Huxley's *Complete Essays,* the first volume of which appeared near the end of the year 2000. As I shall prove even this volume is not complete in reprinting Huxley's journalism. *The Complete Essays* rather reprint from previously published collections such as *On the Margin* (1923) and *Along the Road* (1925).

I would like to organise my paper as follows:

— French Literature

— Literature and Science

— Music
— Mysticism
— Education and Politics
— Dystopia-Utopia
— Poems

I. French Literature

Under John Middleton Murry's editorship the London *Athenaeum* was transformed into a "Journal of English and Foreign Literature, Science, the Fine Arts, Music and the Drama."[4] Huxley regularly contributed reviews and articles from April 1919 to February 1921. After the Great War a keen interest in French Literature arose in Britain and the contributions of Huxley together with the chief editor, T.S. Eliot and George Saintsbury met that interest.

Indeed, Aldous Huxley's very first review, dated April 11, 1919 deals with "Two French Novels" by minor authors. In his reviews, he placed an emphasis on three main topics: pacifism, war poetry and literary modernism. The first review signed A.L.H. is of May 16, and on Henri Barbusse's *Clarté,* a socialist and pacifist novel debunking modern war as "meaningless horror" (346). On November 14, an article "French War Poetry" (1202) follows on *Interrogation* by Pierre Drieu La Rochelle. This poetry of the trenches is compared to Sassoon's description of immediate horror. In the third volume of the *Athenaeum* 1920 (July into February 1921) which has not been carefully bibliographed, reviews of the French pacifists Georges Duhamel and Jules Remains appear under "Two Manifestations of Comedy" (94-96). Aldous Huxley's translation of Remain Holland's war satire *Liluli* started in 10 sequels in *The Nation* from September 20 and was finished in the November 29, 1919 edition.

This early journalism proves that Huxley is not only interested in French Literature, which deeply inspired his own work, but in pacifism. The immediate experience of the outcome of the First World War is so clearly evident that the hypothesis of Huxley turning pacifist only with his novel *Eyeless in Gaza* (1936) and because of his initiative in favour of the Peace Pledge Union can no more be justified.

In *The Athenaeum* of November 7, 1919, we find an article, signed A.L.H., which is titled "The Eighteenth-Century Method" (1164) and reviews Marcel Proust's second volume of *A la Recherche du temps perdu.* I quote the notorious comparison of M. Proust with "a diplodocus; [...] in weight of matter, as well as in weight of intelligence, pursuing the minute pea of social life in the Faubourg Saint-Germain and its upper-bourgeois and half-worldly fringes." It is more important to show Huxley's genius as a critic of literary modernism through his foreshadowing of James Joyce's *Ulysses.*

It is quite conceivable that Mr. James Joyce should some day write a book on the same theme as "Adolphe." He would present us, in place of Constant's clearly outlined hero, with a many-coloured medley of sensations, memories, desires, thoughts and feelings, leaving to our imagination the task of boiling them down into a consistent character. "Adolphe" or "Ulysses"—which is true?

After the introduction of the "Marginalia" page for Aldous Huxley, who wrote under the pen name Autolycus (the rogue in Shakespeare's *The Winter's Tale)* we also find a critical article on French readers, titled "Bibliophily." Huxley scourges the French mania of buying special editions expensively bound on precious paper: "To debase a book into an expensive object of luxury is as surety, [...], to kill the image of God, [...] as to burn it" (*The Athenaeum,* July 16, 1920: 81).

II. Literature and Science

Huxley's interest in building bridges between literature and science is not only the aim of his greatest and last essay, *Literature and Science* (1963) which is more a retort on the F.R. Leavis *vs.* C.P. Snow controversy which resulted in Snow's *The Two Cultures* (1959) but a life long endeavour. In an *Athenaeum* review dated June 27, 1919, Huxley calls Buffon's *Histoire Naturelle* not only a great antecedent of modern biology but "a monument of fine literature" (536). In a review of J.C. Squire's *The Birds and Other Poems* under the column "Poetry and Science" (*The Athenaeum,* August 22, 1919: 783). Huxley praises the marriage of science and poetry which is only too rare in English literature, not even the technically minded Victorian period could achieve it. The scientific poets are also his favourites: Fulke Greville, John Donne, William Blake.

On page 785 I discovered the following note:

> MR JULIAN HUXLEY has been elected to a fellowship at New College, Oxford, for purposes of research in biology. Mr Huxley, who is a frequent contributor on scientific subjects to THE ATHENAEUM, [...] won the Newdigate Prize for English Verse in 1908, and was placed in the First Class in 1909 in the Final Honour School of Natural Science.

Aldous Huxley's elder brother also spoke Italian well enough to serve as interpreter with the British Army in Italy.

For Aldous, the nineteenth-century French poet Jules Laforgue is the paragon of literature and science.

> [...] science and philosophy had been educated into him so deeply that they became a part of his inmost being, not a mere epidermis of acquired culture; [...]. It is surely of some poet like LAFORGUE, not scientifically didactic, but scientifically lyrical that Wordsworth is thinking when he says: "The Poet [...] will be ready to follow the steps of the Man of Science [...] he will be at his side, carrying sensation into the midst of the objects of the science itself." We believe that Wordsworth was right. (*The Athenaeum,* October 17, 1919: 1031)

There are also scientists who welcomed the opening of quantum and relativity theories from an obsolete positivistic materialism towards a more cognitive approach. Under an unbibliographed review by Aldous Huxley of a book on French poetry, I found a report on the relativity discussion at the Royal Society of Saturday, February 7, 1920 by J.W.N. Sullivan: "Whatever happens, Einstein's theory has come to stay for a good while yet, a fact that must rejoice those men of science who are also artists" (*The Athenaeum,* February 13, 1920: 213-14).

The union of the two cultures remains unsolved. An article in the job daily *First Executive* deals with a new M.Sc. course in Information Systems under the headline "Building bridges between creatives and techies" (*First Executive,* London, December 1, 2000).

III. Music

From February 18, 1922 to June 2, 1923 Huxley wrote 62 contributions on the criticism of music for *The Weekly Westminster Gazette.* His reports on concerts, mainly in London and in other English cities but also in Salzburg prove that he is a great expert. His attitude is conservative in favour of polyphony, against rhythm. Modern music for him is not characterised by "[...] the enormous richness and complexity, the endless intellectual potentialities [...] impossible to describe in words" (October 28, 1922: 294), but "[...] carried the cult of rhythm to extremes." Modern music, according to Huxley, also lacks the richness of melody of the old masters, however, "If the polyphonists had known as much about rhythm [...], their music would have been the finer" (December 2, 1922: 305).

It becomes very clear that his favourite composers are Johann Sebastian Bach, Wolfgang Amadeus Mozart, Ludwig van Beethoven and his teacher, Händel. Huxley is very fond of their great fugues and of their chamber music. As only 0.1 per cent of the London population are concert hall visitors (cf. January 20, 1923: 317). Huxley recommends music clubs, string quartets and gramophone records of the great and small works for home enjoyment. In an article on "Supplementing the Concerts" our music critic gets enthusiastic about the delights of excellently recorded classical music. The best voices, the best orchestras, the most complicated fugues and concertos can be carefully listened to, repeated and serve as a very welcome preparation for the highest enjoyment of live performances.

Huxley's most demanding novels, most of all *Point Counter Point,* are fictions of ideas.

Like his artistic mouthpiece Philip Quarles in *Point Counter Point* Huxley "never pretended to be a congenital novelist" (*PCP*: Penguin Edition, 299) he was a congenital essayist.[5]

The essay, like the musical structure and principle of the fugue, allows the introduction of always new and often contrasting topics, which take turns like polyphonous melodies. The voices achieve almost complete harmony only to fall apart again. If counterpoints collide structural highlights appear.

Huxley's description of the biological, medical, emotional and intellectual effects of Bach's Suite in B minor on Lord Tantamount's ears represents a musical analogy rated as world literature.

> The shaking air rattled Lord Edward's *membrana tympani*; [...]. The hairy endings of the auditory nerve shuddered [...] a vast number of obscure miracles were performed in the brain, and Lord Edward ecstatically whispered 'Bach!' (*PCP*, 38).

For Huxley a musical fugue does not only have a fascinating structure. It becomes his principle of organisation and creation for the essayistic concept of the novel of ideas. In the diary of the novelist in the novel,

> The musicalization of fiction [...] is on a large scale, in the construction. Meditate on Beethoven. The changes of moods, the abrupt transitions. (Magesty alternating with a joke, for example, in the first movement of the B flat major quartet. Comedy suddenly hinting at prodigious and tragic solemnities in the scherzo of the C sharp minor quartet.) [...] Those incredible Diabelli variations, for example. [...] A novelist modulates by reduplicating situations and characters. (*PCP*, 297-98, cf. Baker and Sexton, xviii)

Mozart's operas *Don Giovanni* and *Figaro* range, for Huxley, among the best examples of human genius, ever composed, closely followed by *Cost fan tutte* and *Seraglio.* They are like floating on the "[...] familiar sunny Aegean [...]" (September 9, 1922).

Not only Philip Quarles but Huxley's narrator is the roving conductor of a human fugue. Again and again, Beethoven comes into *Point Counter Point.* Before Spandrell invites his own killers he is convinced to have found the proof of God's existence in Beethoven's *Heiliger Dankgesang eines Genesenden an die Gottheit.*

> The artificial memory revolved, a needle travelled in its grooves and through a faint scratching and roaring that mimicked the noises of Beethoven's own deafness, the audible symbols of Beethoven's convictions and emotions

> quivered out into the air. [...] a counterpoint of serenities. [...] the rebirth was not into this world; the beauty was unearthly, the convalescent serenity was the peace of God. The interweaving of Lydian melodies was heaven. (*PCP*, 431)

The clash of Spandrell's meeting his fate and Beethoven's song of praise is, of course, highly ironic. It is interesting that Mark and Mary Rampion, the life-worshippers in the novel, dismiss the most prodigious music that has ever been written with the same words as Huxley reviews "Literary Music" in *The Weekly Westminster Gazette* of June 10, 1922. "[...]—the intellectual and spiritual qualities—are "inhuman")—this same inhumanity is found in the great fugues of Bach, in Palestrina, in Mozart's symphonies, in certain things of Brahms, [...]."

IV. Mysticism

In *The Nation* 27 (April 10, 1920: 52) I found under "The New Satire" an anonymous review of Aldous Huxley's short story collection *Limbo* which culminates in the statement:

> [...] at the back of all the stories in "Limbo" there is the homesickness of the soul born in an age that is dying in squalor for the clarity and coherence of some age of faith—at which, for very hunger, it needs must mock.

This is the lucid counter proof of the superficial common prejudice that the early Huxley was a cynic and a nihilist.

Already in 1919, Huxley reviews books on literature and mysticism. In Arthur E. Waite's *The Works of Thomas Vaughan* he praises the editor as "a leading student of mystical doctrine" (*The Athenaeum,* June 6, 1919: 443) in the introduction to the metaphysical poet. There is also a review of a translation, *Six Theosophic Points,* from the original work by Jacob Böhme (*The Athenaeum,* August 1, 1919: 699).

In his review of "A Wordsworth Anthology" Huxley defines the great English romantic poet's work as a "Bible of [...] pantheism [...]" and concentrates on the importance of emotions expressed in literature.

> Like [...] philosophers of a mystical tinge of thought, Wordsworth based his philosophy on his emotions [...].

> The mystical emotions have what may be termed a conduct value; they enable the man who feels them to live his life with a serenity and confidence unknown to other men [...]. (*The Athenaeum,* January 9, 1920: 47)

In a "Marginalia" contribution on "The Rewards of Literature" Huxley mentions Wordsworth again and his "Preface" to *Lyrical Ballads:*

> [...] the human mind is capable of being excited without the application of gross and violent stimulants; [...]. But it is also true that a human being may be so much elevated above his fellows that he will finally shrink, not merely from the gross and violent emotions, but from all the obvious and primary emotions of whatever sort. He will, in fact, become a highbrow [...]. Love and conviction must go into the work, and love and conviction are precisely the things that the highbrow cannot [...] put into it. (*The Athenaeum,* March 12, 1920: 339)

Huxley elaborated this insight into "The Philip Quarles Syndrome" in *Point Counter Point.* The novelist in the novel is incapable of writing a straightforward love story. He is regretfully caught in his own network of abstract ideas.

Most elucidating is a review of Paul Claudel's *La Messe Là-bas* and *L'Ours et la lune* under the headline "A Domesticated Poet" in *The Athenaeum,* August 22, 1919: 796. Claudel confessed that the reading of Rimbaud had launched him on his literary and religious career. Huxley writes of Rimbaud, the author of the poems collected in *Une Saison en enfer,* as a mystic "dans l'état sauvage:"

> [...] a tame mystic is not really a mystic at all. By definition the mystic is wild and unlike other men; he sees and feels the truth where other men arrive at it by reflection; [...].

Aldous Huxley then writes about Claudel what frequently has been written about himself:

> M. Claudel is not a mystic, but he is intellectually convinced of the truth and adequacy of mysticism; and having arrived by reflection at this belief, he feels that he himself would like to know the truth by immediate perception: he desires himself to be a seer [...] an

> experience which he himself has not known except through books and at second hand.
>
> Second-handedness, lack of immediate vision and the urgent emotion—these are the negative qualities which strike us in "La Messe Là-bas."
>
> A.C.H. [sic!]

Already in 1919, Huxley clearly preferred Blake to Pope:

> The mystical Swedenborgian with the enormous forehead and the great mad, staring eyes confronts the polite, spiteful little hunchback about town, and hates him at first sight.

This is his comment on a University of Cambridge lecture on "Pope" printed in *The Athenaeum,* September 12, 1919: 880.

V. Education and Politics

Right from the beginning of his early journalism, Huxley reviewed seven school books.

In an anonymous review on *The Essentials of English Teaching* (*The Athenaeum,* June 6, 1919: 444) Huxley supports the Members of the English Association with outlines for a comprehensive system of teaching because "Our native language is still, for the most part, taught by incompetents in an hour or two grudgingly spared from other studies."

Under "The Teaching of Appreciation" (*The Athenaeum,* September 12, 1919: 879, anon.) Huxley writes about a "[...] chaotic subject known in the schools as 'English.'"

Under the anonymous article "Miscellaneous English Schoolbooks" (*The Athenaeum,* September 12, 1919) we find his opinion on Sir James Yoxall's *The Patriotic Reader, for Schools in the British Empire*:

> Yoxall's patriotic reader makes us blush [...] he bids us do our duty. Our chief duty is to keep a large army and a large navy [...]. Someday, it is to be hoped, an educational subcommittee of the League of Nations will issue school-books for all the children in the world. (883)

The comment on Alice D. Greenwood's *English Literature for Secondary Schools* runs "It is a pity to tell children things that are not true" (883).

Editha Jenkinson's edition *The Malory Verse Book: A Collection of Contemporary Poetry for School and General Use* boasts of "[...] having carefully selected [poems] for their intrinsic beauty, charm of simplicity, and dignity of thought, [...] thoroughly representative of the finest, most expressive, contemporary English verse" (*The Athenaeum,* September 12, 1919: 915). Huxley's anonymous criticism proves his devastating harshness towards lies:

> [...] we find almost nothing in the book that is not minor poetry in the derogatory sense of the word. Contemporary English poetry may not be much to boast of, but why insult it superfluously by saying the present volume is a representative sample of it?

In regular anonymous contributions under the headline of "Ninety Years Ago" Huxley refers to a series of critical and biographical articles entitled "Shades of the Dead" which had been running in *The Athenaeum* of 1829. In the September 16 issue, Huxley finds a warm and eloquent panegyric on his favourite poet Robert Burns. A comparison of Burns with the professors and dilettanti of Edinburgh leads Huxley into an interesting digression on genius and education:

> Though education cannot produce genius, education can stifle it, and doubtless has in numberless cases stifled or perverted the genius which has come youthful and hopeful into the hands of Scotch professors [...]. Burns was just as much educated as the pupils of Dr Blair or of Dr Reid; but he was educated by realities, they by abstractions; and so admirable was the instruction given him by his father, so well had he learnt to attach importance to things instead of words, that his boyhood seems scarcely to have at all suffered [...]. (916)

From an anonymous review of Georges Deherme as "A Vehement Reactionary" we can conclude that Aldous Huxley in his early years expressed political sympathies with the French Socialists (*The Athenaeum,* October 31, 1919: 1134).

In an anonymous review on "Personal Satire in 'Gulliver'" (*The Athenaeum,* December 19, 1919: 1372) and in "Islands of the Blest" (December 26, 1919: 1395) Huxley expresses his views against imperialism in Ireland and in the South Seas:

> [...] one wonders why one is such a fool as to go on living in this dark, disgusting country [...] they wanted no clothes nor anything else from us, but only to stay in their own country; which made us wonder at their ingratitude.

VI. Dystopia-Utopia

In a very early review on *The Undying Fire* Huxley criticises H.G. Wells's belief in progress:

> [...] Satan is strong, but he is limited, and in the game with the creator we never doubt that the creator will win.
>
> [...] Mr Wells "most respectfully returned God the entrance ticket." (*The Athenaeum,* May 30, 1919: 398)

Under "All's Well that Ends Wells" Huxley's lifelong fight against the science fiction of progress was Hummorized.[6] In a "Marginalia" contribution one and a half years later Huxley quotes Mr Wells's ideas as "[...] the future world-state's organisation of scientific research and record [...] will be like an ocean liner beside the dug-out canoe [...]" (*The Athenaeum,* October 15, 1920: 522). I am not sure if Autolycus had anticipated the internet but in "Marginalia" no. 16, four months before, Huxley seems to imagine the brave new world:

> We foresee that, when the Eugenists gain control of the country, unprecedented intrigues will be set on foot. The poet with high connections will arrange for the procreation of an appreciative audience of not less than 20,000. [...] Immortality would be a matter of bargaining. [...] It already distresses many serious patriots that the only man of our time who seems secure of immortality should be a German-Jew. [...] We can breed for any belief whatever. Our future reputations lie in our loins. (*The Athenaeum,* June 4, 1920: 737)

or in our test tubes and hatcheries. And what is more, Julian Huxley contributed a leading article on the biology of "Eugenists and Eugenics" to *The Athenaeum,* December 31, 1920: 895-96. Above this article Aldous Huxley published a "Marginalia" on "Democracy and Literature" which concludes with a statement: "[...] a land without Reservations, is not a particularly cheerful home for artists." No one wants dictatorship and suppression to ensure the blossoming of literature but Huxley, again and again, protests against the neglect of the humanities in completely materialistic and egalitarian democratic systems.

VII. Poems

In *The Athenaeum* editions of February 6 and April 30, 1920 Huxley published two of his own poems, "A Sunset" and "The Birth of God." These are first publications because "A Sunset" was later added to the collections contained in *Leda* (London: Chatto & Windus, 1920, 1946, New York: Doran, 1920), *Rotunda: A Selection from the Works of Aldous Huxley* (London: Chatto & Windus, 1932: 1935), *Verses and A Comedy* (London: Chatto & Windus, 1946), *Modern British Poetry* (New York: Harcourt and Brace, no year) and "The Birth of God" was republished in *Leda* (London: Chatto & Windus, 1920, 1946, New York: Doran, 1920), *Verses and A Comedy* (London: Chatto & Windus, 1946). The first publications in *The Athenaeum* of February and April 1920 are not mentioned in Eschelbach/Schober's *Aldous Huxley: A Bibliography 1916-1959.*

"A Sunset" is a poem on lost love. It starts with an amber, green and rose sunset where a lonely cloud catches the last rays of the sun before black phantasmagories quench the light. The poet's memory evokes a vision of his last love, lonely before the fire like the cloud in the evening sky but, when the moon rises, the cloud and his love are gone and the poet feels left utterly alone.

"The Birth of God" is a sad poem with some glimpses of hope. The poet with his lost girlish love on his mind tries to find comfort in a cold and lonely night from the conviction that "[...] in privation the life of God began" (line 27). The poetic voice hopes that from the loss of his love a godhead shall be born to fill his emptiness. But again he despairs, ironically, with the statement "Shall I feed longing with what it hungers after, [...]" (line 32). However, the disillusioning force of his reason tells the poet to admit his own loneliness. Both poems are pessimistic in tone and "The Birth of God" cannot deceive us about Huxley's situation as a searcher in this period of life where longing for the immediate mystical experience was his overwhelming attitude.

John Middleton Murry, the chief editor of *The Athenaeum* reviewed *Leda* discouragingly a month later:

> [...] the reason why, being so clever, he [Huxley] has deceived himself is precisely that he is so clever.
>
> [...] As for two thirds of the shorter pieces, we think that he would have been well advised never to print them. (*The Athenaeum,* May 28, 1920: 700).

This attack was answered by Huxley in two ways.

First: a review "On Wit" about Paul Elmer More's book, *With the Wits* sounds like a rebuff of Murry's malice:

> Malice will not suppress genius, and it may conceivably rankle in the hide of the fool.
>
> Malice is certainly a very important factor in all wit; but malice without cleverness is of little avail.

Second: Aldous Huxley never again published a poem in *The Athenaeum:*

> In his two and a half years of journalistic grind, he:
> [...] must have felt like that billion minus one [spermatozoon which]
> Might have chanced to be
> Shakespeare, another Newton, a new Donne—
> But the One was Me.
>
> (in the "Fifth Philosopher's Song," *Leda,* 1920)

Huxley-Autolycus was the pedlar in *The Athenaeum,* Murry was the rogue, "[...] the best hated man of letters in the country" (*Dictionary of National Biography,* s.v. Middleton Murry). But Huxley lashed back terribly by modeling Burlap, the bullying hypocrite in *Point Counter Point* (1928), on Murry.

After the success of his first novel, *Crome Yellow* (1921), a contract with Chatto & Windus earned Aldous Huxley the freedom to write *Antic Hay* and a second creative stay in Italy (1923) with his French speaking Belgian wife Maria and their little son Matthew. Ten years after the beginning of Huxley's journalistic limbo, *The Nation* of October 19, 1929, which had made *The Athenaeum* its literary contribution since March 1921 and later stifled it, put *Do What You Will* on the front page, on top of a review list of six books by other authors, as:

> Essays which provide most subtle entertainment, [...] a special signed edition [...], which has been over-subscribed [...].

Not least due to the success *of Point Counter Point* (1928), the poor essayist and reviewer had become famous.

By Aldous Huxley's early journalism, however, it has been proved that

— his late Victorian colloquial style,

— his dislike of insipid simplicity,

— his satire of the hypocrisy of this world,

— the multiple personalities including the psycho-analytical novelist in his novels,

— the importance of music for the structure of his fiction,

— his authentic combination of scientific knowledge with the humanities,

— his search for new values due to his hunger for faith despite all clever doubt,

— his moral endeavours as an educator,

all this is cradled in his contributions to *The Athenaeum, The Nation* and *The Westminster Weekly Gazette,* in the full range of his early journalism.

NOTES AND REFERENCES

1. *The Athenaeum*. London, January 2, 1920: 10.
2. Claire John Eschelbach, Joyce Lee Schober (eds.). *Aldous Huxley: A Bibliography 1916-1949* (Berkley and Los Angeles: University of California Press, 1961).
3. Ebenezer E. Bass. *Aldous Huxley: An Annotated Bibliography of Criticism* (New York: Garland, 1981).
4. Robert S. Baker, James Sexton (eds.). *Aldous Huxley: Complete Essays,* vol. I, 1920-25 (Chicago: Ivan R. Dee, 2000), xvi.
5. Wemer von Koppenfels. "Themes & Variations: Aldous Huxley, Essayist," in: Bernfried Nugel (ed.). *Now More Than Ever: Proceedings of the Aldous Huxley Centenary Symposium Münster 1994* (Frankfurt: Lang, 1996: 45-54, 46).

6. Gorman Beauchamp. "All's Well That Ends Wells: The Anti-Wellesian Satire of *Brave New World,* in: Michael S. Cummings, Nicholas D. Smith (eds.) *Utopian Studies II* (Lanham: University Press of America, 1989), 110-17.

   cf. Ralph Pordzik, "Gelebte Zukunft: Aldous Huxley, Marge Piercy und dieAmbiguisierung der Utopie 1960-1980." in: Rüdiger Ahrens (ed.) *Anglistik* XI, 2 (2000), 74-89.

12

Glocalization of English in the Cyber Age: A Cultural-Linguistic Perspective

N.D.R. CHANDRA

1. Introduction: The Role of English in the Cyber Age

The Cyber age has an immense impact on the life-style of the people. The world has become a 'small village' with the expansion of the information technology and cyber revolution. English is still a 'window to the world' and it continues to be the language of opportunity, employment, science, technology, electronics and so on. However, a significant change is taking place in its use and expansion. It has been predicted that by 2010, the number of people who speak English as a second and foreign language will exceed the number of the native speakers. Secondly, it is interesting to note that the linguistic centre of English moved from England to elsewhere in the last 20 years and this has given rise to several varieties of English which Braj Kacharu calls "World Englishes."

2. The Major Factors Responsible for Expansion of English

The three factors which mainly contribute to the spread of English are: (a) English usage in Science, Technology and Commerce; (b) The ability of English to incorporate vocabulary from other languages; and (c) The acceptability of various English dialects and literature in postcolonial world. Out of these three, the first one is highly influenced by the process globalization and cyber revolution. The revolution is redefining the world ignoring geography and borders. In less than twenty years information processing once limited to the printed world has given way to computer and Internet or computer-mediated communication, which is closing the gap between spoken and written English. It encourages more informal conversation in language and tolerance for diversity and individual style has resulted internet English replacing the authority of language institutes and practices. Secondly, it has large vocabulary of which 80% is foreign borrowed from Spanish, French, Hebrew, Arabic, Hindi, Urdu, Bengali, *Chinese* and so on.

3. Cyber English

Cyber as a prefix first appeared in the word "Cybernetics," which was coined by Norbert Weiner derived it from the Greek for "Steersmen" and the idea of control is *central* to it. William Gibson is best known for using *Neuromancer,* but he had actually invented it years ago in a short story in the *Omni* magazine. The meaning of cyber has evolved over the past decades. Its original sense in "Neuromancer" was of electronic space as perceived by what we would now call "Virtual Reality." The brain and senses strictly linked with the world of computer and communications and so could experience it as an actual landscape. With explosive growth of interest in the internet, its popular sense shifted to a weakened one that refers to the intangible (and hence mysterious) electronic domain. More recently, still, it has moved towards becoming a loose synonym for 'electronic' (*Tol* April 2001, 16).

At present, people feel that the world has become a small village because one can talk to anyone, enter into any library, discuss on any academic problem, share the idea, seek any information, search the information which is not commonly available. This shows that one can access to any nook and corner of the world. This has been made possible due to the *invention* of internet, voice mail, E-mail, Cyber Cafe, etc. Recently, virtual university has come to existence—without walls and bricks. People are studying in the virtual classrooms. One need not travel to other countries and complete education staying at own place of residence. This was not possible earlier, which shows that *accessibility* has increased.

One with internet connection can get an access to any library whose membership is open. One can search the title of the books in any subjects, within a book contents can be searched, after selecting the topics, one can download it for reading, and if required one can either print all the pages or even a portion of the page. It also points out the increasing accessibility to library, classrooms, research organization, etc.

Net Speak or Basic Abbreviations and New Jargons

While working on computer and sending E-mails, one has to familiarize the abbreviations and basic net speaks like **BTW** = By The Way and **FAQ** = Frequently Asked Questions. Given below is a letter received by a lady.

Dear Aunt,

I hope **UR** fine. I went to the book fair = ***0*** to find so many titles! I bought *Lord of Flies.* Talk about ***F2F; BTW.*** Took up a summer job, *RU LoL* ? Sorry, I did not write earlier >:— 0? *TTFN.BCNU:>*

—*Ashok*

ABBREVIATIONS

1.	*BTW*	=	By the way
2.	*BCNU*	=	Be seeing you: (embarrassed)
3.	*BRB*	=	Be right back (used while chatting)
4.	B4	=	Before
5.	*FAQ*	=	Frequently asked questions
6.	*FY A*	=	For your action
7.	*FYI*	=	For your information
8.	*FlF*	=	Face to face
9.	*HRU*	=	How are you
10.	*IMO*	=	In my opinion
11.	*IMHO*	=	In my humble opinion
12.	*IMNSHO*	=	In my not so humble opinion
13.	*FWW*	=	For what its worth
14.	*LOL*	=	Laughing out loud
15.	/ ..... @	=	a rose
16.	= 0	=	surprised
17.	> :—0	=	angry
18.	: >	=	smile
19.	*TIA*	=	Thanks in advance
20.	*ROTFL*	=	Rolling on the floor laughing

21. *WTG* = Way to go
22. *TTFN* = Tata for now

It's learning a new language, isn't it? With precise, informal and intimate style. The purpose of the E-mail message and abbreviations are to communicate quickly and effectively within a short span of time. In fact, the cyber revolution is responsible for coining new words, phrases and expressions Monosyllabic and disyllabic words are being used more and more. The long letters are being avoided. The style is becoming informal day by day. New Jargons and netiquettes are increasing gradually. Thus the new forms of structures, symbols, instructions are coming up which have brought a significant change in the realm of communication and interpersonal relationships.

4. The Acceptability of Various English Dialects and Literature

Language is a product of culture. English throughout the world has many dialects such as British English, American English, Indian English, Canadian English, Australian English to name a few. There is no uniform standard pronunciation. But within this diversity, there is more or less unity of grammar and one set of vocabulary. Thus, each country that speaks the language can inject aspects of its own culture into usage and vocabulary (Hasman 2000 : 04). Further, English language is changing day by day with the changing needs of the people who come from different clime and culture. It is enriched not only in its form but also in contents as it comes in contact with different linguistic groups, their culture, tradition, and way of life, political system and social practice. It grows conceptually assimilating these different divergent social and cultural norms. Thus many distinctive forms identify the Englishes of the other countries of the inner circle; Australian English, New Zealand English, Canadian English, South African English, Caribbean English and within Britain, Irish, Scottish and Wales English. Among countries of the outer circle, several varieties have grown in distinctiveness in recent decades. There is one group in India, Pakistan, Bangladesh and Sri Lanka often collectively called South Asian English. There is another group in the former British Colonies in West Africa and further group in the former British Colonies in East Africa.

Other emerging varieties had been noted in the Caribbean and in part of South-East Asia, such as Singapore and so on. Thus, the spread of English around the world has demonstrated the winds of linguistic change in totally unpredictable ways, where the emergence of new varieties of English in different territories have taken place. The change has become a major talking point since the 1960's hence the term by which these varieties are often known as 'new Englishes.' The different dialects of English and American English provide the most-proved familiar example. These two varieties diverged amongst their spelling and pronunciation, syntax and grammatical structure, which are in fact the result of differences in the two cultures as Dylan Thomas puts it, 'separated by the barrier of a common language' (Crystal, 1997: 131).

5. Glocalization of English

These new Englishes are somewhat like the dialects which emerge because they give identity to the groups which own them. These differences are clearly noticeable in informal setting on the internet. The Indian author Raja Rao writing in 1963, was one who looked forward to the development of new 'Indian English':

> English is not really an alien language to us. It is the language of our intellectual makeup like Sanskrit and Persian was before—but not of our emotional makeup. We cannot write like the English. We should not. We cannot write only as Indians. We have grown to look at the large world as part of us. Our method of expression has to be a dialect which will some day prove to be as distinctive and colourful as the Irish or the American (Crystal 1997: 131-35).

And a similar view comes from the Nigerian novelist Chinua Achebe. Who says, "I feel that English will be able to carry the weight of a African experience. It will have to be a new English, still in full communion with its ancestral home but altered to suit its African surroundings."

Local varieties thus, express national identities and are a way of reducing the conflict between intelligibility and identity. Because a speaker from country 'A' is using English, there is an intelligibility bond with an English speaker of Country 'B' and this is reinforced by the existence of a common written language. On the other hand, because speaker 'A' is not using exactly the same way of speaking as speaker 'B' both parties retain their identities. It is another way of 'having your cake and eating it' (Crystal 1997: 134). This is in fact, glocalization of English language in the cyber age. In a way the internet, multimedia, international TV and other electronic devices are forming a tradition of linguistics in the context of global culture in general and local culture in particular. In the Cyber age, informal varieties, colloquial grammar and local phrases are growing up day by day.

It has been predicted that 'World Standard Spoken English' (WSSE) will emerge in future which will facilitate people.' Yet again to 'have their cake and eat it,' the concept of WSSE does not replace a national dialect: it supplements it. People who can use both are in a much more powerful position, than people who can use only one. They will have dialect in which they can continue to express their national identity and they have a dialect which can guarantee *international* intelligibility when they need it. The same dual tendencies can be seen on the internet, incidentally, which simultaneously presents us with a range of identifying personal varieties (local) and a corpus of universally intelligible standard of English (global).

6. The Future Tradition of English: Possibilities and Prospects

(i) English may emerge as a single world standard language. If so there will be a need and pressure for a global uniformity of this language. Hence, it will become a supranational variety which needs to be acquired by all the *people*. The *global* uniformity of English language could result in declining standards, language changes, and the loss of geolinguistic diversity (Hasman 2000: 04).

(ii) On the other hand, English is the vehicle for international communication and because it forms the basis for constructing cultural identities, many local varieties could instead develop. This trend may lead to fragmentation of the language and threaten the role of English as a lingua franca. However, there have always been major differences between varieties of English (Hasman 2000: 4).

(iii) A language shift, in which individuals change their linguistic allegiances, is another possibility. These shifts are slow and difficult to predict. But within the next 50 years substantial language shifts could occur as economic development affects more countries. Because of these shifts in allegiance, many languages may disappear. While languages such as English, German and French have been international languages because of their government's political powers, this is less likely to be the case in the 21st century where economics and demographics will have more influence on language. On the other hand, those remaining languages will rapidly get more native speakers. This includes English.

(iv) Internal Migration and Urbanization may restructure areas, thereby creating communities where English becomes the language of inter-ethnic Communication—a neutral language (Hasman 2000: 5) as in the case of Nagaland and metropolitan cities like Bombay, London and California.

(v) Universities using English as the medium of instruction will expand and rapidly create a generation of middle-class professionals. Economic development will only increase the middle class, a group that is more likely to learn and use English in jobs. In other words, there may be a gap between computer literate people and computer illiterate people.

7. The Major Challenges of the Future Tradition in English

When we talk about reinvigoration of curriculum in the present context, we encounter three major challenges for English:

1. The first is that we need a new history of the language which will be based on classical philology and modern linguistics. It will describe the major changes in discourses. Further, it would look as to how discourses were produced and reproduced through the major national systems of education and entertainment and consider how this discourse were challenged and invigorated both by local and global variation.
2. The second question is of value which poses either major challenge to the future of English. Students are looking more and more for a straight cash value

for the education that they purchase. While neither ignoring nor despising this growing emphasis of English must find ways of emphasizing the value of reading and writing which are not reducible to cash value (Batholomae 1997: 07).

3. The need for mutual intelligibility which is part of the argument in favour of global language, is only one side of the coin. The other side is the need for identity and people tend to underestimate the role of identity when they express anxieties about language injury and death. Language in fact, is a major means of showing where we belong and of distinguishing one social group from another, and all over the world we can see linguistic divergence rather than convergence. The need for natural or cultural identity, however are often seen as being opposed to those of about the need for mutual intelligibility. This is another challenge which is directly related. To glocalization of language in particular. For David Crystal it is misleading. It is perfectly possible to develop a situation in which intelligibility and identity harmoniously co-exist. This situation is the familiar one of bilingualism but bilingualism where one of the languages is the global language, providing access to the world community and the other regional language providing access to a local community. The two functions can be seen as complementary, responding for different needs. And it is because the functions are so different that a world of *linguist!c* diversity can in principle continue to exist in a world united by a common language (1997: 18-19). At the same time local 'varieties' of English have become medium of their expression.

8. Conclusion

Canon, Multiculturalism and Glocalization of English

Language originates from culture and there is always something about the intimate relationship between language, thought, individuality and social identity which generate strong emotion. In the Cyber age this strong bond is expressed in written and spoken form as well as in print and electronic media through the tradition of glocalization of English which satisfies the dictum, 'think globally and act locally.' Our younger generations, in fact need knowledge through a precise linguistic medium which should also reflect the ingredients of their culture. In fact, the need of the hour is to impart education forming a syllabus based on the canon of local, economic and global requirements.

In Multicultural countries identities such as nation, language, race and sex are *cultural* specific despite their similarities. Gates says that Multiculturalism is concerned with representations, not of difference as such, but *cultural* identities while Guiding Howe *declares* that the critic, the writer and the audience all are rooted in their biographies and *historical* circumstances. Art is neither anonymous nor universal: it springs from the particular of gender as well as class, race, age and cultural experience.

1. The paper puts a significant question that America is increasingly a multicultural country, and students have cultural courses that recognize and include the elements of Asiatic, African, American, *Indian,* Hispanic as *well* as European *cultures. This* new plan is *democratic* in the sense that it sees every body gets represented *to* some *extent.* Can multicultural literature be also canonized in *India?* Do we need an anthology that can do justice to the marginal, to the experience of working class, tribals, Dalits and women?
2. Secondly, when we talk about canon formation, *it* must *include* such names as Plato, Aristotle, Virgil and so on *down* the ages. Such literature apart from their entertaining value, provides how human beings behave, how they succeed and how they fail, how they justify their lives or how they fail to do so, we may enrich our *lives.* In short, such literature engages us in total human situation often much more deeply and powerfully than philosophy or even history does.
3. Thirdly, our young generation *is* looking for straight cash value. Can we prescribe some courses such as

media studies, journalism or computer assisted language learning (CALL) which can fulfil their economic needs to some extent?

It is therefore, suggested that the teachers and educationists should evolve a cultural literary canon considering our local, national, economic and global needs. In tact, our curricula should have judicious combination of literature of our own (*i.e.*, multicultural literature), literature of information and knowledge and world classics. Which will satisfy the needs, means and ends of our present generation of students. This sort of cultural linguistic and literary tradition will serve our purpose in the multicultural context of the cyber age. There should also be a judicious combination of print and electronic media. It is a fact that a small number of star teachers are replacing the large number of non-star teachers. Yet, the education needs to be imparted by a teacher only who can mediate between man and machine enhancing human values.

Appendix 'A'

ENGLISH CURRICULA DISSEMINATION

Knowledge	Information	Wisdom
Needs	Means	Ends
Local	Economy	Global
Local surroundings Regional & Social needs	Media studies, CALL Hypertext & so on	World classics

ACADEMIC ENVIRONMENT MEDIA

Print		Electronic
	Writer	
Teacher	Text	Reader (student)
	Society	
	Media	
Mediator	Text	Reader
L1	L2	L3
Standards fixed scholastic Grammatical language	Tension & Friction in language	Language of everyday *i.e.* Spoken (dialects etc.)

MEDIA & TEACHER DILUTES THE TENSION

- Yesterday's literature has become today's grammar.
- In fact, our Standard English should be a linguistic compromise between spoken form and literary language of the canonical texts in the cyber age.

WORKS CITED

Crystal, David. *English as A Global Language.* Wales: Wales University Press, 1997.

Hasman, Melvia. "The Role of English in the 21st Century" *Forum* 38.1, 2000: 2-5.

Kachru, Braj. *The Alchemy of English: Spread, Functions and Models of Non-Nature Englishes.* Delhi: Oxford University Press, 1986.

Riley, Brian T. *Socio-Linguistics: Language in Culture and Society.* New Delhi: Cosmo Publication, 2000.

Times of India, New Delhi, April, 2001: 16 (several issues of this daily have been consulted).

13

MULTICULTURALISMS: THE USA AND ROMANIA

MIHAELA MUDURE

> Motto: "[...] we could think about disorders of ethnicity as we think about disorders of identity. From the individual point of view, overassimilation would be one such disorder, where the self would completely yield to the cultural milieu. The opposite we could call overmarginalization, the refusal to identify, or to take in the offered cultural ailment [...]. We could talk about cultural narcissism or chauvinism, as a related disorder, and its opposite, cultural devaluation." (Mario Rendon, *Psychoanalysis and Ethnicity*)

The present paper is written from the perspective of comparative multiculturalism. We firmly believe that there is no monocultural society, that all societies are multicultural, namely characterized by ethnic and cultural diversity.

The problem is the way in which society manages this diversity and this is subject to a lot of theoretical and practical discussions all over the world. In the USA the term multiculturalism followed the melting pot terminology and the recognition of cultural pluralism. The term multiculturalism is new in Romania and it appeared after 1990 with the efforts to ensure conditions for ethnic minorities in higher education as well as with the efforts of the minorities to get recognition and empowerment by developing separate educational structures. The problem was: separate up to what level? Completely separate? Or separate within an institutional structure? And as issues of language and education are very emotionally loaded in this area of Europe this debate quickly became symbolic for separatism within society.

Nowadays in Romania there is a strong competition between the term interculturalism and multiculturalism. Sometimes this debate hides personal attacks under the pretense of theoretical debates, other times this debate hides a political double-speak on the cultural coherence of Romania as a political entity.

Interculturalism emphasizes the exchanges among/between cultures. Multiculturalism also recognizes exchanges between cultures but it also presupposes a hierarchy between cultures with regard to the language of the cultures existent in a country. Multiculturalism recognizes the prominent position of the official language. Multiculturalism considers the hierarchies between cultures not in terms of values but in terms of the necessity of the promotion by affirmative action policies of certain cultures (members of certain cultures) that have been subject to discrimination and in terms of the necessity to ensure a cohesion factor which is the language of the market while also ensuring conditions to valourize the languages of other cultures existent within the frame of a political entity. Multiculturalism presupposes the desire of minorities not to ghettoize but to participate in the life of the political entity where they live.

There is also the third position: all these discussions are irrelevant.[1] There is only one kind of cultural phenomenon all over the world. The real danger is the Americanization of the world, the acculturation of the world through the preeminence of the English language which sometimes results in unnecessary linguistic adoptions, changes in foods and drinks—the appearance of the fast foods, the CocaColization of lives—the uniformity of festivals because of the irresponsible adoption of American festivals—St Valentine, Halloween, or the costumes at graduation ceremonies.

Our perspective is comparative multiculturalism. This is how we have proceeded to a comparison between the position of the African-Americans in the USA and the position of the Gypsies in Romania and to a comparison between the Mexican-Americans and the Romanians with a view to wider evaluations and assessments. We have used the term *Gypsy* because our paper concentrates on the stereotypes about the Gypsies and on the Gypsies' adversarial relations within the Romanian society. Consequently, we are looking forward to the moment when the content of the present paper will be irrelevant or, at best, purely historical, the moment when the scholarly and neutral term *Roma* or even *Rroma* (which is meant to spare Romanian susceptibilities because of the closeness of the words *Roma* and *Romanian*) will be considered as the only normal ordinary denomination. As we are unfortunately very far from this stage we thought it more in tone with the content of the paper to use the term *Gypsy* as a rhetorical and stylistic device to stress the issues at stake.

The debate on the use of the term *Gypsy/Roma/Rroma* reiterates to a certain extent the debate on the use of the term *Black/Afro-American/African-American*. It is a fight between a name given to an ethnic group by outsiders and the autonym. The autonym is a name given by an ethnic group to itself. Although, apparently, it would seem normal that every ethnic group should be called by the name it prefers for itself, this is not always the case. Naming is a power relation. This often appears in areas where there was a conquering or subjugation movement of one population by another. It is often in colonial areas that the native people are not named by the names they themselves would prefer being used for themselves. This illustrates the adversarial relations and the power relations in the area. Many of these names given by outsiders are seen as inappropriate as they are imposed. When the peoples around the world seek political and cultural self-determination, they usually revive the use of their autonyms. According to Levinson (18-19), the widespread practice of ethnic groups to rename themselves is an important demonstration of these groups' self-determination as it symbolizes the end of a certain type of domination. Therefore, it is not surprising that this process often accompanies efforts to achieve political, legal, social and economic autonomy. This holds true for the Gypsies and the African-Americans as well. Their preference for a certain autonym shows a *form mentis* evolution.

The position of the Gypsies within the Romanian nation depends on the historical evolution of the Romanian nation. The Romanian nation, developed as a steady continuation of the ethnic idea, whereas the United States, for instance, has completely other founding myths: the enterprising colonizer, the Black slave and the enduring Native American, all of them taken rather as social categories, or as anthropological attitudes. The peculiar ethnicity (German, or Irish, or Yoruba, or Apache) of the ethnic groups participating in the American semiosis is no longer that important. In fact, it is redefined as Whiteness, Blackness or Native-American-ness.

When analyzing the position of the Gypsies or of the African-Americans we must also take into account the reality that ethnic groups are not God given, still, definitive and clearly distinct from one another. Ethnic groups are largely the result of ethnic relations and, ultimately, they are the result of economic and political relations. No group exists as such. But it is only in and through these usually conflicting or competitive relations with other groups that ethnic groups exist. The ethnic group appears thus as a modality of social organization meant to confer force and legitimacy to a group in the competition for power and resources. The Gypsies or the African-American population in the USA developed strategies firstly of survival and then of competition within the respective societies. These strategies influenced their evolution and assessment in society.

One of the first Romanian personalities to have been interested in the Gypsy component of the Romanian society was the Ion Budai Deleanu (1763-1820). He jokingly used the Gypsy stereotypes in his epic *The Gypsiad*. *The Gypsiad* is an ethnic poem where the wise man is expected to understand a lot beyond the surface content, according to the *Dedicating Epistle* at the beginning of the poem. Budai Deleanu was aware of the idea of a white Arabia at the mouth of the Danube, an idea already mentioned in Ptolemeus' *Geography*. This so-called Blackness is used in the epic. The white Gypsiness is the oxymoronic doublet of the Romanian people itself. Ion Budai Deleanu expressed a lot of sympathy for the manumission of the Gypsy slaves, an idea which was, in fact, very much in the air at the time.

During the 18th century, the idea of the Gypsy and Black slaves' manumission appeared in the famous Masonic Lodge of the Nine Muses. This Lodge whose member was Franklin and whose president was Brissot and the famous La Fayette focused, with sympathy, both on the Black slaves of America and on the Gypsy slaves of the Old World. Many of the important militants of the 1848 Revolution were Masons and they were particularly sensitive to this issue. In fact, the Masons also considered that they themselves were "symbolic slaves." Slavery got, therefore, a strange aura of transcendence which increased the general sympathy for the slaves of the time.

The Romanian intelligentsia in the 50s of the 19th century followed with great interest and easy to explain empathy the evolution of the Abolitionist movement in the USA. In 1853 *Uncle Tom's Cabin* was translated by Teodor Codrescu. It was only one year after it had been published in the USA and it enjoyed great success in the Romanian principalities.

One of the most consistent Romanian perspectives on the Gypsies was offered by Mihail Kogălniceanu during this very same period. As a student in Berlin, Kogălniceanu writes a presentation of the Gypsies at the request of Alexander Humboldt. On the one hand, Kogălniceanu complains about the momentary and biased interest in the 19th century slaves and, on the other hand, he is a Jeremiah of the "lack of civilization" of this "miserable" ethnic group, the Gypsies.[2]

Kogălniceanu also mentions other peculiarities of the Gypsy situation in Moldovia as compared to the situation of the African-American slaves in America. The master had no right over the slave's life or over his own property unless the slave did not have heirs. But if a slave ran away, the master had the right to follow the fugitive slaves (Kogălniceanu, 1837, 11). The Gypsy slaves were allowed to have a home, a garden, and a little store but they could not have a farm or an estate (Kogălniceanu, 1837, 12). In Wallachia the situation was almost the same. There could be no legitimate union between a free person and a slave. Slaves coming from other countries become free if they marry a free person (Kogălniceanu, 1837, 10-11). In another essay also dedicated to the Gypsies and published in 1891, Kogălniceanu mentioned that although the law designated the Gypsies as chattel, the owners indicated them as souls, which, still, did not mean a better treatment especially if the owner had few slaves.[3] The slave concubine of a free man became free and their children also became free persons.

Whereas in the USA the children of a slave were slaves as well regardless of the juridical condition of the other parent.

Another important difference between the Gypsies and the African-Americans is that not all Gypsies were sedentary. Some Gypsies were nomads while others were slaves on the estates of the upper classes or of the monasteries, or of the state.

We must also mention the Romanian perception of the Gypsies as potentially hypersexual (Kogălniceanu, 1837, 11). The attractiveness of the Gipsy flower girl has inspired many Romanian painters or writers and its appeal comes from the supposed hypersexuality of the ethnic group. This is a well-known stereotype about the marginalized groups. They are usually associated with nature and considered more potent or more sexually accessible than the "civilized" groups. The same holds true for the African-Americans. American literature is haunted by dreams of interracial sexuality.

As reluctance to work has always been a behavioural response to slavery, both Gipsies and African-Americans have a reputation of "laziness." Therefore, no wonder that punishments are very important in all the documents about the Gipsies. The punishments that used to be inflicted upon the Gipsies are impressively cruel. They are: the whip and the "falanga." When punished with the "falanga" the convict's ankles were tied up to a stick and he was beaten on the sole with a stick. Punishments inflicted upon the African-Americans are not less violent.

The Gypsies, says Kogălniceanu, are very gifted musicians of exquisite taste and refinement but every effort to integrate them, namely "to civilize" failed. Let us not forget that music has also been a possibility for artistic expression with the African-Americans. Aristocrats tried to civilize some young Gipsies but they ran away from the "benefits" of civilization very much like Huck Finn and probably for the same reasons (Kogălniceanu, 1837, 21).

If the Gypsy steals something, he does not steal big things but he usually steals clothes and food (Kogălniceanu, 1837, 22). This suggests a rather marginal way of life, at the limit of survival in order to avoid the strong reaction of the dominant communities. This is a characteristic of the Gypsy way of life in the 20th century as well.

In spite of his good intentions, Kogălniceanu brilliantly proves the famous saying about the way to Heaven being paved with good intentions. His approach to the Gipsies is from a superior and paternalistic position imbued with the ordinary stereotypes about the so-called "inferior" groups. The Gypsy women are easily accessible for sex (Kogălniceanu, 1837, 1). The Gypsies have vices; but if we succeed in unrooting them from their hearts, they will be extremely useful for Moldavia and Wallachia, mostly working like workers in the factories (Kogălniceanu, 1837, 25).[4]

But the great difference between the slaves from the USA and the slaves in Romania refers to the situation of these groups when slavery was abolished. Whereas in American culture there were gifted individuals from among the former slaves who contributed to the glorification of a prestigious past of the African-Americans, Romanian Gipsies had no such prestigious tradition. The few African-American slaves' revolts were glorified. Frederick Douglass and Booker T. Washington are among the first to have become spokesmen for their people in the American society. Frederick Douglass started from the principles of the US Constitution and the Bill of Rights. He laid claim to the principles of full citizenship enacted in these documents. Booker T. Washington stressed the Black community's necessary efforts in order to surpass the stigma and the moral and material consequences of slavery. According to Booker T. Washington, the African-Americans had to prove that they qualified for civil rights by making a success of themselves first in the economic arena. Douglass depicts slavery as hell on earth, Washington calls it a "school" that helped prepare the African-Americans for their role in the post-war economic order. Booker T. Washington reiterates Franklin's story of the self-made man in a specific context. He appropriated Franklin's archetypal American success story which was made possible through the well-known virtues of selflessness, industry, honesty, optimism. "Then, when we rid ourselves of the prejudice or racial feeling, and look facts in the face, the ten million Negroes inhabiting this country, who themselves or whose ancestors went through the school of American slavery, are in a stronger and more helpful condition, materially, intellectually, morally, and religiously, than is true of an equal number of black people in any other portion of the globe" (*Heath*, II, 989).

Washington was vigorously opposed by DuBois. DuBois's outlook has its roots in his belonging to a small New England community and in his formal education in history and sociology. He strongly believed in human progress and perfectibility. He also realized that the black people's organized collective action needed an institutional structure in order to be effective. He was the main organizer and coordinator of the National Association for the Advancement of Coloured People. DuBois's perspective is of much greater sophistication and it metaphorically expresses the Black otherness. It implies both the gift of second sight but also the pain of ambivalence. "After the Egyptian and Indian, the Greek and Roman, the Teuton and Mongolian, the Negro is a sort of seventh son, born with a veil, and gifted with a second-sight in this American world,—a world which yields him no true self-consciousness, but only lets him see himself through the revelation of the other world [...]. One ever feels his two-ness,—an American, a Nigger; two souls, two thoughts, two unreconciled strivings; two warring ideals in one dark body, whose dogged strength alone keeps it from being torn asunder" (*Heath*, II, 1013).

The different approaches to slavery by Frederick Douglass and Booker T. Washington, the intellectual arguments between DuBois and Washington as well as the active efforts of the American society (mostly in the North) to help the former slaves overcome the consequence of their oppression do not have any counterpart in Romania. In the US these debates were continued between Martin Luther King and Malcom X. The Romanian Gipsies did not have an intelligentsia at the level of the African-American community in the USA and it is only now that there are some (not very numerous, unfortunately) individuals that could be considered as Gipsy Romanian intelligentsia.

Secondly, in Romania, which was an agricultural country, the lack of rural property practically further marginalized the former slaves. Romanian slaves were manumitted but they were never put in possession of land. Consequently, most of them got on the roads or adopted a marginal way of life with the consequences that we know. On the contrary, in the USA the lack of property by the slaves could be overcome in a booming industrial society. The consequence was the Black exodus to the North after the manumission.

Historically, the Gipsies of the State were emancipated first and then the Gipsies of the monasteries. On January 1, 1844, Mihail Sturdza enacted legislation concerning this problem in Moldavia. In 1845 the same legislation was enacted by Alexandra Ghica in Wallachia. In 1848, the proclamation issued on June 11 mentioned the manumission of the Gipsies as a Christian deed. The slave owners would be forgiven by the Romanian people for the shameful act of having held humans in bondage and they would be compensated for their economic losses as consequence of the manumission (Kogălniceanu, 1891, 16).[5] The manumission of the slaves of the private slave owners occurred on December 10, 1855 in Moldavia and on February 8, 1856 in Wallachia. Hundreds of owners refused the compensations.

However, Kogălniceanu's naïve or blind enthusiasm that this generosity automatically led to the acceptance of the Gipsies by the Romanian society is either baffling or mere flattery for Charles I, the king of Romania,[6] or both. One hundred and fifty years later the Gypsy problem still exists.

In the USA as well, in spite of all the efforts of both the African-American community and of mostly Northern intellectuals, the African-American problem was not solved with the abolition of slavery. In 1963 Martin Luther King said about the African-Americans: "One hundred years later the life of the Negro is still sadly crippled by the manacles of segregation and the chains of discrimination. One hundred years later the Negro lives on a lonely island of poverty in the midst of a vast ocean of material prosperity. One hundred years later he is still languished in the corners of the American society and finds himself in exile in his own land" (*Heath*, II, 2483).

For 500 years the Romanians had slaves. In 1856 actually there was only a judicial emancipation. The former slaves were given no property. The problem is whether this manumission was brought about by the greater productivity in agriculture and, therefore, by the need for less labour force or by ideological criteria, a sort of belated continuation of the Enlightenment and the dawn of a Romantic form mentis. Actually, Kogălniceanu himself acknowledged this influence of the ideological humanist tendencies of the time.[7]

In any case the manumission of the Gipsies gave Romanians a happy conscience that was expressed in the text *Vasile Porojan* by Vasile Alecsandri. This text reflects the survival of prejudice under the mask of egalitarian ideology. Alecsandri, a boy of aristocratic descent, and Vasile Porojan, a Gypsy boy, can play together as children but they will separate as soon as socialization through education occurs. Alecsandri will go to college, Vasile Porojan will remain at home and become, at best, a baker's apprentice.

After their emancipation, the Gipsies only became a concern for the authorities almost a century later, in 1941. On April 6, 1941, after an inspection in Bucharest during a blackout, general Ion Antonescu, the then ruler of Romania, ordered that the Gipsies be driven out of Bucharest. The general had been extremely shocked by the crimes committed by the Gipsies during the blackout when most of the population was in shelters. Later on the idea came to deport the Gipsies to Transnistria, a territory east of the Nipper and under Romanian administration until 1944 as a consequence of an agreement between Hitler and Antonescu. The policy against the Gipsies is considered by all World War II historians as entirely Ion Antonescu's creation and it "perfectly" fitted the general xenophobic atmosphere of the time. This policy was never enacted in judicial documents wearing Ion Antonescu's signature. The steps against the Gipsies were transmitted orally to the police and the ministers involved. The deportation was made in great hurry and there were even cases when Romanians or Turkish families were taken to be Gypsy and deported. There were cases, abuses when families of Gypsy soldiers fighting on the Russian front—who were not to be deported—were also deported. On the other hand, as the rumour spread that the Gipsies would be given land in Transnistria, there were Gypsy families who demanded that they should be deported. Generally, nomad Gipsies or Gypsy people with a criminal record were deported. But there were also sedentary Gipsies affected by this order either by abuse or by the confusing oral directions given by authorities of the time. There is very little material about this painful episode in the modern history of Romania except for some references in the documents of Ion Antonescu's trial or the novel *Satra* by Zaharia Stancu, a novel inspired from a real episode. No moral or material compensations have ever been offered to the survivors of the Transnistria camps or to their heirs. In 1944, as the Russians were approaching Transnistria, the Gipsies were set free. They walked all the way back home to Romania.

During the industrialization process under the Communist regime groups of Gipsies were sometimes forcibly sedenterized but they were also given the modest facilities of the complexes of apartments built by the Communist regime. There was a first wave of sedenterization in 1957 and then a second one in 1962 following similar programmes in other Communist countries. As this process was under pressure, it often happened that the Gipsies did not appreciate their sedentary dwellings and often destroyed them, which increased the animosities between the majority and the Gypsy minority. After 1990, the weakening authority of the state, the corruption and the inefficiency of the judicial system which left unpunished criminal acts committed by members of the Gypsy community sometimes led to violent upsurges against this group, contrary to the solutions that should have been found under the rule of law.

Another important problem concerning the Gipsies after 1990 is restitution. In 1960 the then Militia confiscated the Gipsies' gold chains. In 1990 the Romanian administration inaugurated a restitution policy and returned all the gold that had been taken and officially recorded, but the Gipsies still claim the gold that was taken from them without any official record.[8]

The Gypsy problem is more acute than ever in the post-Communist Romania when the freedom of speech also means the free expression of prejudices. The study of Romanian newspapers is relevant in this respect and it proves the necessity of a politically correct language. It often happens that within a group of criminals newspapers distinguish the Gipsies specifically or that the spatial coordinates of a crime are presented like this: "In an area of inhabited by Gipsies [...]" (*National*, February 28, 1998). In spite of its limitations a politically correct language would limit the verbal abuse of the Gipsies.

Nowadays cultural conflicts also spring from the unlawfulness of the Gypsy practices. The Gypsy judgment, for instance, is not lawful. Therefore, the people who executed such sentences were themselves indicted because the Romanian penal code does not penalize crimes with such punishments as the mutilation of the nose or of the lobe of the ear which can be used in the Gypsy traditional system of justice (*National*, November 18, 1997). On the other hand, the defendants that have been punished according to Gypsy practices think they have already paid for their crimes should no longer be considered accountable in Romanian courts.

The non-existence of a group of Gypsy linguists and literary persons, ethnographers, folklore specialists, as the intelligentsia mostly linked to the ethnicity has led to the non-existence of a prestige tradition in Gypsy culture. Nowadays Romani is mostly a colloquial language (Zamfir, 22-23). It has not developed a written literature. Attempts are being made nowadays in this respect but they are still only a beginning.

The religious service for the Gipsies is performed in the language of the ethnic majority of the place. The importance of the church in the African-American community is undoubted. In *The Souls of the Black Folk* DuBois says: "In Philadelphia and in New York colour prescription led to a withdrawal of Negro communicants from white churches and the formation of a peculiar socio-religious institution among the Negroes known as the African Church—an organization still living and controlling in its various branches over a million of men" (*Heath*, II, 1020). In Romania the church is only starting to have a strong influence on the Gypsy community. However, the Pentecostal Church is already an example in this respect. It has developed among the Gipsy community and it succeeds in modifying their behaviour. The Pentecostal Church promotes non-violence, abstinence. The service is dynamic, with Gypsy music and dance something like the Hassidic experience, or the African Church described by DuBois. The use of Gypsy cultural elements in the church had led to its popularity and increasing influence.

A very difficult problem is the fact the Gipsy culture comprises a set of specific cultural patterns (oral and colloquial language, music, dances, oral literature) and also, as a defense stratagem, patterns associated with a marginal way of life, a sort of active adaptation through the acceptance of a negative situation imposed by poverty. The Gipsy have always lived in symbiosis with the majority population in Romania, but on its margins. The Gypsy way of life, their clothes, and dwelling are specific and frequently display stratagems to win self-esteem: the newly built Gipsy houses with empty but numerous towers and shiny roofs pagoda-like style, the importance of the car as an element of prestige, as well as the unorthodox naming policy of the children (Dollar, Dwarf, Stalin, names of fashionable sportsmen or political personalities). These stratagems have their counterpart with the African-Americans. The promotion of the typically African names or of Black English as a language of prestige in the USA are also efforts to increase the self-esteem of an ethnic group deeply affected by reification through slavery.

But the great problem of the Gipsy community in Romania is its lack of cohesion beyond the extended family. There have been and there are attempts to overcome this situation but still there are more attempts than results. Thus, in 1997, the SIS-Rrom was founded. The SIS-Rom is meant to prevent ethnic conflicts. It has three boards: the Internal Affairs Board, the Foreign Affairs Board, the Political Board and the Socio-Cultural Service. Still we are very far from any of the prestigious organizations of the Black community in the USA.

Other solutions envisaged by the Gypsy community may involve positive discrimination in higher education, business, army, police, administration. In order to find out the real proportion of this minority within the population of Romania (a very important element in order to charter further minority policies), Oprescu, for instance, recommends the possibility that a person could claim mixed ethnicity, for instance, Romanian Roma or Hungarian Roma. Oprescu also considers that the Roma communities themselves have to make efforts in order to surpass considerable traditionalism and especially the violence towards their own children and women.

Modernization is, therefore, a key issue for the Gipsy communities, which is not the case for the African-American community in the USA. Zamfir considers that any group that does not modernize its way of life automatically tends to become a chronically marginalized and disadvantaged group. Such groups then become a kind of social reservations which are maintained by the dominant community for a variety of reasons where "helplessness combines with vague abstract principles about minority rights quickly abandoned at the first conflict with that peculiar minority" (25). Such reservations can be tolerated or protected on condition that they be small. But if such communities grow in number, there inevitably arise tensions. This is very much the situation of the Gipsies in Romania whereas in the US the African-Americans do not have similar problems.

The Gipsies must modernize their own culture and stop identifying their cultural patterns with the traditional way of life. Actually, this is the beginning of a new tradition. The Gipsy problem is the problem of a modern way of life or of a traditional way of life. Reciprocal adjustment is necessary here: the self will of the minority and the support of the majority may pave the way for new and better realities. A new Gipsy tradition must be encouraged to develop. But the problem for the Gipsies is not to slip towards the deviant behaviour of the Mafia type in this modernizing process. Both the minority community and the mainstream society must envisage stratagems in this direction. This is a peculiar development of the Gipsy communities different from that of the African-Americans where the crime rate higher than in other ethnic groups has to do with unemployment and lack of education but not with the modernization process.

In their drive towards modernization we consider that the Gipsies slide towards the position of a middleman minority. According to Levinson (148-49), the middleman minority is a socio-economic category of ethnic or religious groups who occupy specialized economic niches in a society. The term is derived from the economic role played by the Jews in medieval Europe. The middlemen occupy economic niches that place them between those who produce goods and those who consume them. Middlemen are not natives to the host nation. They have strong patriarchal, extended families with a high tendency to marry within the group, they usually live in their own ethnic neighbourhoods, they tend to assimilate more slowly than other groups. The work the middlemen perform fills a status or an economic gap in the socio-economic structure of the society. The only nuance in the case of the Gipsies is their economic status. Middleman groups usually have very high saving rates and a material standard higher than the host population. We consider, that on the whole, the myth of the rich Gipsy is just a myth and rich Gipsies are a very minor segment of this ethnic group.

Under the Communist regime the economic niche necessary for the apparition of the middlemen was created by managerial and economic inefficiency. A product supply gap appeared and it was filled by the gray or black market. Nowadays the cheaper retail chains meet such demands and the Gipsies have lost a lot of their previous economic importance.

For centuries both the Gipsies and the African-Americans have held a mirror for the drawback of the majority, a negative Other on which to throw all their fears. Their problems have a common cause: slavery. But they evolved in different environments: a rural society, the Romanian society, vs. a highly industrialized society, the American one, dictatorships vs. democracy. Solutions, however, are strikingly similar: mutual efforts both by the minority and the majority. Failure to do this may have enormous material and human costs for the societies involved.

The second part of my comparison involves the Mexican-Americans and the Romanians. There is, of course, a great difference between these two groups in their position in society, namely, it is a minority vs. majority position but otherwise, there are also interesting similarities:

(1) *High awareness of their Latin origin*: The Mexican-Americans are "surrounded" by the Anglo culture, the Romanians are "surrounded" by peoples of other origins.

(2) *A special relation with their Latin heritage*: For the Romanians this is a source of empowerment and celebration, for the Mexican-Americans it is a source of ambiguity. The conquistador is, on the one hand, brave and valiant. On the other hand, he raped a culture. However, this ambiguous image does not create for the Mexican-Americans any special attachment to the Spanish language as spoken in Spain. On the contrary, the Latin heritage existent in the Romanian language has repeatedly been used as a source of empowerment. But in spite of differences and nuances, the Latin heritage is an important identity component both for the Mexican-Americans and the Romanians.

(3) *The frontera mentality*: The Romanians are a gateway between the West and the East. The Mexican-American are borderlands people between the USA and Mexico.

(4) *The highly emotionally charged myth of the separating river*: The Rio Grande for the Mexican-Americans and the Prut for the Romanians.

(5) *The attachment to the land and the importance to the land*: The we-have-been-here-for-so-long motto is common to both cultures. The Mexican-American talk about their mythical-historical roots in Aztlan, which shows their pre-eminence in the Southwest.[9] The Romanians talk about the continuity of the Romanian people on the same territory.

(6) *The prestige of programmatic documents which valourize the importance of the land*: The language and style of the 1848 Romanian nationalist programmes is strikingly similar to *El Plan de Aztlan*. The "rediscovery" of Aztlan at the Chicano National Liberation Youth Conference, in Denver, 1969 by Rudolfo "Corky" Gonzales catapulted the term to public attention (51).[10] The conferences held at Loyola University in Los

Angeles in the summer of 1966 led to a movement of young Mexican-American intellectuals in the urban areas. Later on in 1967 there were other conferences organized by such groups as United Mexican-American Students, Mexican-American Student Association, Mexican-American Student Confederation, Mexican-American Youth Organization. This led to the development of a parallel movement: Chicanissmo. The thrust of Chicanissmo is both economic and cultural. Chicanissmo and the Aztlan movement are both conscious raising movements similar to Romanian nationalist movements. One must not forget the similarity of the above mentioned Chicano programmatic documents with the programme of *Dacia literară* and the Romanians' efforts to encourage the beginnings of modern Romanian literature.

(7) *Mexican-American female myths (Malinche, La Lorona) or Romanian myths (Dochia, master Manole's wife or Stephen the Great's mother)*: all of them construct women as identical with the land, potentially treacherous, willing to sacrifice and prone to delayed gratification. An effort to create new female models is particularly relevant among the Mexican-American writers (Sandra Cisneros) and much less obvious in Romanian literature.

(8) *The relevance of the Pachuco type*: A Pachuco is a rural young Chicano man who moves to lower class urban areas. This is a new urban Romanian phenomenon. The Romanian Pachuco appears in such famous barrios as Manastur, in Cluj-Napoca, for instance, new neighbourhoods, the result of the industrialization age under the Communist regime.

In conclusion we reiterate that the aim of this comparison reaches far beyond the purely informational aspect. We think that such comparisons will lead to increased mutual understanding and a growing sense of relativity of ethnic and national values which regarded within the frame of only one culture seem categorical and ineluctable. Or survival in our complex and interdependent world creates the need for comparative approaches. The present paper is an effort in this direction.

NOTES

1. Cf. Claude Karnouh, “Un logos fără etos. Interculturalism Şi multiculturalism” *Tribuna*, nr 38, 18-24 septembrie, 1997, 7-9.
2. Kogălniceanu talks about “un intérêt qui, malheureusement, ne sera peut-être que passager, car voilà comme sont les Européens! Ils ferment des sociétés philantropiques pour l’abolition de l’esclavage en Amerique, tandis qu’au sein de leur continent, en Europe, il y a quatre cent mille Cigains qui sont esclaves, et deux cent mille autres qui sont converts des ténèbres de l’ignorance et de la barbarie! Et personne ne se donne la peine de civiliser tout un peuple (Kogălniceanu, 1837, IV).
3. “Legea ţării trata pe ţigani de lucru, vândut si cumpărat ca lucru, deşi prin deriziune individul se califica de suflet. Am alâtea suflete de ţigani, am vândut şi am cumparat atâtea suflete de ţigani, în realitate şi mai ales stapânii care aveau puţini ţigani îi tratau mai rău decât prescnpţiunile legii” (Kogălniceanu, 1891, 14).
4. In another essay dedicated to the Gipsies, an essay published in 1891. Kogălniceanu also mentions “the separation of the families, the bad treatment slaves were submitted to, which reminds us of the worst passages from the American abolitionist literature. Gipsies were taken in chains or obliged to wear an iron horn on their forehead and chained around their necks” (Kogălniceanu, 1837, 14).
5. “Poporul romn leapede de pe sine neomenia şi ruşinea de a ţine robi şi să declare libertatea ţiganilor particulari. Cei ce au suferit pncum ruşinea patului de a avea robi sunt iertaţi de poporul romn; iar patria, ca o mumă bună, din visteria sa va despăgubi pe oricine va reclama că a avut pagubă din această faptă crestinească” (Kogălniceanu, 1891, 16).
6. “Reforma emancipatoare a avut în curând efectele sale salutare: afară de ţiganii lăiesi care încă trăiesc în parte sub şatră, şi în afară de ursari care fac încă meseria de a domestici fiarele sălbatice, dar totuşi se dau lucrului câmpului, mai toţi astăzi din celălalte clase de ţigani s-au contopit în masa naţiunii şi ei nu se mai cunoscu decât prin faţa lor smolită şi asiatică şi prin vivacitatea imaginaţiei lor, altminteri noi îi găsim în toate clasele societăţii noastre” (Kogălniceanu, 1891, 17-18).
7. “De aceea povăţuiţi de spiritul secolului, de legile omeniei un număru de boieri bătrâni şi tineri au întreprins de a spăla patria lor de ruşinea sclaviei” (Kogălniceanu, 1891, 14-15).
8. Rudy Varga, a Gipsy goldsmith from Cluj is such a recent case, in Cluj. He claims 8.2 kg of gold confiscated by the Romanian police before 1999.
9. “We did not, in fact, come to the United States at all. The United States came to us. We have been in America a long time. Somewhere in the twelfth century Aztec ancestors left their homeland of Aztlan, and

migrated south to Anahuc, "the place by the waters," where they built their great city of Mexico-Tehochtitlan [...]. Aztlan was left far behind, somewhere "in the north," but it was never forgotten. Aztlan is now the name of our Mestizo nation, existing to the north of Mexico, within the borders of the United States Chicano poets sing it, and their flor y cant points toward a new yet very ancient way of life and social order, toward new yet very ancient gods (Luis Valdez, apud, Daniel Cooper Alarcon, Aztlan, 380).

10. The most important point of *El Plan de Aztlan* were:
    (a) the refusal of recognition of capricious frontiers—the northern land of Aztlan is Mexican-American land by ancestral birthright
    (b) the necessity for unity to transcend all internal differences in the Chicano community
    (c) the importance of a nationalist ideology
    (d) social, economic, cultural and political independence as the only road to total liberation from oppression, exploitation and racism
    (e) art as an aim to strengthen identity and maintain unity: "writers, poets, musicians, and artists" should "produce literature and art" that is appealing to our people and relates to our revolutionary culture.

WORKS CITED

Douglass, Frederick. *Narrative of the Life of Frederick Douglass, an American Slave Written Himself.* Ed. and introd. Houston A. Baker, Jr. Harmmondsworth: Penguin, 1982.

DuBois, W.E.B. *The Souls of Black Souls.* New York: Vintage, 1990.

Hawkins, Hugh (ed.). *Booker T. Washington and His Critics. Black Leadership in Crisis.* Lexington, Massachusetts, 1974.

Kogălniceanu, Mihail. *Autobiografie.* Bucureşti: Alcalay, no publishing date.

——. *Desrobirea Tiganilor. Stergerea privilegiilor boeresci. Emanciparea taranilor. Discurs rostitu in Academia Romana la 1 aprilie, 1891.* Bucureşti: Litotipografia Carol Grobl, 1891.

——. *Esquisse sur les moeurs et la langue de Cigains.* Berlin: Librairie de B. Behr, 1837.

Levinson, David. *Ethnic Relations. A Cross-Cultural Encyclopedia.* Santa Barbara: ABC-CLIO, 1994.

Liégeois, Jean-Pierre. *Roma, Gipsies, Travellers.* Strasbourg: Council of Europe Press, 1994.

Rotra, George. *Contributiuni la istoricul tiganilor din Romania.* "Bucureşti: FundaÛia Regele Carol I, 1939.

Washington, Booker T. *Up from Slavery: An Autobiography.* New York: Doubleday, 1901.

Zamfir, Elena and Cătălin Zamfir. *Tiganii între ignorare şi îngrijorare.* Bucureşti: Editura Alternative, 1993.

*

John Hope Franklin (ed.). *Three Negro Classics.* New York, Avon Books, 1965.

*

Antip, Felicia. *Tiganii şi drumul lor. Călătoria unei tinere "gagiu-pui" printre "oameni" in Adevărul literar şi artistic,* November 16, 1997.

Ciutac, Cătălina and Cătălin Ciutac. *Structura SRI-ului ţigănesc-SIS Rrom (Serviciul de Informaţii şi Siguranţă)* in *Naţional,* November 24, 1997.

Oprescu, Dan. *Despre romi* in *22*/February 10-16, 1998.

Popovici, Iaromira. "*Romii meseriaşii*" *din Meteor* in *Dilema* nr. 218/ March 28-April 3, 1997, 14.

——. *Poveştile Bulibaşei* in *Dilema* nr. 218/March 28-April 3, 1997, 14.

Someşfălean, Livia. *Istoricul ţiganilor din oraşul Cluj-Napoca* in *Adevărul de Cluj,* August 30, 1996.

Tache, Cătălin. *Am fost acolo, în Biserica ţiiganilor pocăiţi* in *Naţional,* October 21, 1997.

Naţional, November 18, 1997.

Naţional, February 28, 1998.

14

A Quest for Meaning: Deconstructing *The Tempest* as a Feminist Orientalist Discourse

SIVASISH BISWAS

Michel Foucault says: "The reader is of course free to make what he will of the book he has been kind enough to read. What right have I then to suggest that it should be used in one way rather than another?" (*Archaeology of Human Sciences*, Vintage, NY, 1973).

Readers interpret a text, because they try to understand and make some meaning, or order their experiences. Thus meaning is constantly created and recreated—it is a perpetual quest. This results in a negotiation between the author and the reader. The author is located in the ideological current of his time, and his work is a culture construct. Edward Said commented that literature is always embedded in historical consciousness. Reading a historical text by Shakespeare across four hundred years causes negotiation. History is not a set of facts, but a set of discursive practices. Thus, instead of a master narrative, there are a set of fragments which constitute alternate histories: the histories of the colonised, of the subalterns, of women, of the downtrodden and the oppressed. Thus, a continuous process of de-centring goes on, bringing the marginalised to the centre, subverting the text, and reading meaning into the silences of the text.

The Tempest was formerly read as a pastoral play, and thereafter as a Christian play of forgiveness and reconciliation. It is widely accepted as Shakespeare's most mature comedy—the product of his retirement to Stratford. Contemporary attitudes, however, see the play as a construct of England's patriarchal and imperialistic mindset, when political expansionism and creation of colonies with the necessary subjugation of the natives was accepted to be the right of the white man. Male dominance and dominance by white man progressed in tandem.

Prospero comes to the island, like Robinson Crusoe, and establishes his control over it: "was landed,/ To be the lord n't." (V, i, 160-61). It is nothing but a colony of the white man, who usurps the rights and authority of the native. He uses the "savage" Caliban to show him "The fresh springs, brine-pits, barren place and fertile" (I, ii, 340), and thereafter dominates over Caliban to the extent of subjugating him to the status of a slave, who is only fit for harsh labour, harsh abuse and harsh threats.

John Donne exposes a similar attitude in "The Sunne Rising": the spice and mines of the Indies must be possessed. "She is all States, and all Princes, I" [...]. It is the same gender construct and imperialist sentiment. British women writers found a relation between the European male and imperialists. Women were riches and the white man were princes. The colonies and the Orient always was the source of riches: "all the perfumes of Arabia [...]" (*Macbeth*, V, i, 49).

In post-colonial analysis of *The Tempest*, Caliban holds the centre-stage, and Sycorax dominates the discursive process by politics of absence. She cannot be erased from the Palimpsest, or overwriting. The feminine text is the under-text, while the dominant text is masculine. The under-text, where Sycorax is almost erased, has to be resurrected. She is the most potent silence of the text. Her presence governs the actions of Prospero, who seems to have a fixation of Sycorax, or Sycorax-syndrome. Even though she is dead, the magician (or wizard, *i.e.*, male of witch) Prospero seems to be shadow-boxing with a rival witch. There is gender bias even within blacks—the black man is seen while the black woman is not. The "other" is inferior on the basis of gender and race. Both Sycorax and Caliban are human—but black, and Oriental, for Sycorax was born in Algiers ("Argier" I, ii, 261). But Prospero denies them humanity and brands Sycorax immoral.

We can call Sycorax a character by re-contextualisation of Sycorax in the historical framework. Prospero has not met her, but is obsessed with her. He refers to her and her power even before leaving the island. She is present through memories: (a) in reference to Ariel; (b) as the mother of Caliban; Prospero invokes her to delegitimatise Caliban as a bastard, *i.e.*, "othering" Caliban, and therefore legitimatising himself; (c) Sycorax is the rival witch to Prospero, the magician (who has a rod, a book, and a cloak). In gender politics, "witch" connotes the wicked. Binary oppositions structure the way women are seen in patriarchal texts. The feminine stereotypes are Angel (Miranda) or Demon (Sycorax). There is polarity between two dead female figures—Sycorax (immoral) and Prospero's wife ("piece of virtue"—I, ii, 56). The only living female figure is Miranda who is angelic: Feminism rejects the essentialist figure of woman like Miranda as a male construct.

Prospero has an army of spirits who serve as slaves. They are good because they have conformed to the wishes of Prospero. But when Ariel demands freedom, Prospero threatens him with the punishment that Sycorax had meted out to him. Prospero postpones freeing Ariel till some fresh service is extracted. For the white man, all was "fair play" (V, i, 176).

Any modern reading of a text is a political reading. Feminists claim that the person is political. The primary power politics are of dominance and subjugation. The author has ideological presuppositions, because culture moulds man's mind. Thus, texts become sites for authorisation and legitimisation. Authority is vested in the male. Through the ages, the dominated fight back by interrogating the basis of power, and thus subverting the power. Meaning is structured through sets of binary and gender oppositions: man (heavenly, uranial, cultured), and woman (earthly, Teleorian, natural); coloniser, colonised; angel, demon; white (pure, good), black (corrupt, evil). Not only are there oppositions but hierarchisation and valourisation of one at the cost of the "other"—white is superior to black. In *As You Like It,* Rosalind says: "Such Ethiopian words, blacker in their effect [...]" (IV, iii, 39); Donne, too, associates blackness to evil (Second Holy Sonnet). Blackness is the main marker of Othello's inferiority *vis-à-vis* the whites. Truth is determined by people in power. Thus deviant, bad, inferior, mad, etc., are constructs of discursive practices that play on differences.

Thus, there is gender bias between the female witch and the male magician in *The Tempest*. Critics tend to overlook that there was a very strong local tradition of witches in England, who were accepted socially in ancient days. But history being a male domain, historians chose to background these witches. During the Renascence, between 1540 and 1645 (the data when anti-witch laws were repealed in England), almost a million witches were burnt to death in a virtual holocaust. Witch burning was perpetrated with the support of the clergy and the law.

The witch tradition figures prominently in *Macbeth* and *The Tempest*, both of which were written under the patronage of James I who ascended in 1603. Prior to that he was Prince of Scotland. Witch hunting was popular in Scotland. The Prince had promulgated a law against witchcraft with death penalty, the reason being that there was a storm at sea when he had gone to marry Ann of Denmark, and he was nearly drowned. He returned and blamed it on witches.

The Shakespeare biography by Halliday mentions an important socio-political event called the Enclosure Movement—in which people who had subsisted on common land were suddenly dispossessed and made beggars. Old communal life was transformed into new mercantile society. Old men and women were earlier looked after by the society and the clergy. Now those lands were distributed to the King's favourites as largesse. Even Shakespeare was a beneficiary, and there were riots on his land in 1615. By the enactment of "Poor Law"—giving alms was prohibited. A new class of bonded labourers evolved, of whom Dickens would write later. Witches were those who clung to old practices and demanded alms. The witches were wise women who had knowledge of medicines and who could foretell the future, as they did in *Macbeth*. By demanding alms, they became social irritants in male dominated society, and anger was vented on them. The witches were gender constructs: women going around alone were considered bad. Sycorax is such a construct, as are the three weird sisters in *Macbeth*, who had merely foretold the future on orders from Banquo and Macbeth, and are considered evil. Sycorax being single, and a woman, is considered a part of nature—free and licentious *vis-à-vis* Miranda who is angelic—who is supported by her father, and who conforms to the demands of the patriarchal framework, and thus is legitimate. *The Tempest* can be read as a discourse of patriarchal dominance and language of resistance.

Shakespeare juxtaposed the historical folk tradition of English witchcraft with contemporary colonial witchcraft. Due to dispossession of land, people lived in forest areas and practised witchcraft to eke out a marginalised existence. Because of takeover of land, and the introduction of cash crops, land passed on to settlers, and was alienated from original possessors. In old Oriental tribal societies—women were important, often central. Tribal societies are often matrilineal: Caliban knows no father—"This island's mine, by Sycorax my mother" (I, ii, 334). Transition to male dominated society happened because of the introduction of wage labour, and perception towards the hitherto beneficent witches changed, and they were killed or banished for doing things they did previously: Prospero says—"This damn'd witch Sycorax,/ For mischiefs manifold, and sorceries terrible/ To enter human hearing, from Argier,/ Thou know'st was banished" (I, ii, 263-66). It is notable that while witches were always female, the witch "diviners" or identifiers were always male, and they were invested with occult powers. So Prospero's witchcraft is legitimate, because it is male. In power politics, the power is seen to be wielded by man. *The Tempest*—far from being an ethereal fantasy of magic, is mythologicalisation; it is the struggle for power in gender strife. Prospero has an economic motive: dispossession of woman or her lineage from property. Formerly, women enjoyed property rights: ex. Chaucer's Wife of Bath. The widow was not marginalised in medieval times. But later, as in *Duchess of Malfi*, the attitude is that the widow should not remarry, and male society can dictate what a single female "should" do. Usurpation of female liberty is attempted. We may see tropes of possession and dispossession in *The Tempest*.

In 1609, English colonists going to Virginia were shipwrecked in a storm near the island of Bermudas, and a rivalry for supremacy followed. This was the actual circumstances which anticipated *The Tempest*, for it is fairly well accepted that Shakespeare had access to the "Bermuda Pamphlets" published in 1610.

Colonies, therefore, are to be possessed, and to be ruled. In the schema of male domination, women are relegated to the status of the colonised subjects, and are forced to conform. But witches being autonomous posed a threat to male dominance. In Oriental tribal societies, women enjoyed economic and sexual autonomy (freedom to choose partners and divorce). By trope of devil possession (a male construct), killing of witches was legitimised. James I declared in an Act in 1603 that a witch is one who had "traffic with spirits," thus, consorting the Devil. Reference may be made to the myth of "Incubus"—mothering children fathered by the Devil. So Caliban is illegitimised and bastardised. A woman is a commodity, or colony, to be possessed by man. If not possessed by man, she will be possessed by the Devil. So Caliban—assuredly the son of Sycorax and the Devil, is non-humanised, demonised and animalised: Prospero says, "Thou poisonous slave, got by the devil himself/ Upon thy wicked dam, come forth!" (I, ii, 321-22). And the anti-colonial subaltern answers back, "As wicked dew as e'er my mother brushed/ With raven's feather from unwholesome fen/ Drop on you both!" (I, ii, 323-25); and again, "All the charms/ Of Sycorax, toads, beetles, bats, light on you!" (I, ii, 341-42); and yet again, "You taught me language; and my profit on't/ Is, I know how to curse. The red plague rid you/ For learning me your language!" (I, ii, 365-67).

In Shakespearean drama, rebellion is defeated. When Caliban is invoking his mother's powers, Prospero does the same in a counter witchcraft ritual. He says, "I'll rack thee with old cramps,/ Fill all thy bones with aches, make thee roar,/ That beasts shall tremble at thy din" (I, ii, 371-73). The coloniser is apparently trying to establish control in order to civilise and promote justice, thereby legitimising his presence. God is on his side; it is his right to rule and dispossess the native. Thus, Caliban's attempts to regain his birthright are illegitimate. Caliban's condition is like the Red Indians in

America and the Aborigines in Australia who were considered "intruders," and who were driven out to the periphery.

It is interesting to take note of what Aristotle has to say in the *Politics*—"Men [...] who are much inferior to others as the body is to the soul [...] are slave by nature, and it is advantageous for them always to be under government" (*Politics*, 1254, a-b). Then the black cannibal must necessarily be the slave of the European gentleman.

In *The Tempest*, the trope of usurpation and the trope of gender discrimination can be discovered in the silences of the text. Binary oppositions structure the text, the basic being good vs. evil. The identity of evil is structured by demonising and otherising. The outcome is that evil is exorcised and wiped out being denied legitimacy. Female autonomy represented by erstwhile wise woman is erased and countered by a male construct of dependent possessed good woman. The "betrothal" process is a domestication of women. The Masque in Act IV was performed on a royal betrothal in the winter of 1612-13. Woman is made to fit into the role envisaged by the State or powers that be. Regulation of female sexuality as a State property is best seen in Miranda being married to Ferdinand, where their betrothal is nothing but stage-managed. But Sycorax represents unbridled sexuality: Caliban knows no father. Miranda is structured to conform, but Sycorax, albeit her absenteeism, is the rival who challenges. So her territory has to be usurped and her son delegitimised. Prospero hands over his daughter to Ferdinand in reward for obedience. Woman is a mercantile acquisition and thus Prospero and Ferdinand exchange property. But Caliban rebels against unnecessary forced labour, and is punished. Love between Ferdinand and Miranda is love sanctioned and under control: it is Art with direction, whereas Caliban's sexual attitude is unbridled and procreational. He laughs, "Thou didst prevent me; I had peopled else/ This isle with Calibans" (I, ii, 352-53). Even the mythological goddesses who are invoked conform to the male schema: Juno is the protectress of married women, and Iris is the goddess of fertility and plenty. But Venus is deliberately kept out because she is autonomous—the goddess of love or amorous desires which is not sanctioned.

At the end, Prospero attains his purpose: to regain and consolidate his power. All have submitted to him and his designs. His usurping brother Antonio is overthrown, and the rebellion of Caliban has been subjugated. Ferdinand has obeyed and conformed, so has Miranda, and their betrothal is achieved. Yet malcontent remains in Caliban, the "thing of darkness" (V, i, 275). Society is cleansed of evil and there is apparent harmony. But it is harmony with fissures. And attainment of sublimation remains a façade.

WORKS CITED

Aristotle, *Politics.*

Foucault, M. "Last Lecture" in *The Order of Things: An Archaeology of Human Sciences*. New York: Vintage, 1973.

Kermode, F. Introduction to *The Tempest.* London: Methuen and Co., 1954.

Shakespeare, W. *The Tempest,* Ed. F. Kermode. London: Methuen and Co. Ltd., 1954.

——. *Macbeth,* Ed. K. Muir. London: Methuen and Co. Ltd., 1962.

——. *Othello,* Ed. M.R. Ridley. London: Methuen and Co. Ltd., 1958.

——. *As You Like It, The Complete Works of Shakespeare.* London: Atlantis, 1980.

15

The Significance of Form and Function in Language Learning

SHAILENDRA KUMAR MUKUL

Language is a method of communication. It is a method of communicating ideas, emotions and desires by means of a system of arbitrarily produced symbols. All human beings learn language naturally. There may be some exceptions but these exceptions are only those who are prevented by some form of physical barrier. They may neither listen nor speak. It is a biological deficiency.

But learning a foreign language is a different case. People may learn a foreign language naturally if they have adequate environment for it. But where there is no adequate environment, they learn it in school and colleges or in language institutes. In learning a language the importance of both form and function has been realized.

In the past, grammar occupied a central position in language learning. It is still important because a very limited set of rules produce a good range of sentence-patterns. We can fit thousands of content words into these sentence patterns and express an enormous variety of meanings through them. For the foreign language teacher who is dealing with the students of homogeneous mother tongue, the knowledge of contrastive syntax is a very valuable. It guides the choice of teaching materials and determines appropriate remedial work. It helps the teacher foresee the difficulties which they experience with grammar. By knowing where difficulties are likely to lie, he can easily avert interference foreign-language students are prone to. The most traditional method of learning a foreign/

second language is the Grammar-Translation Method. This method is basically an adaptation of techniques used to teach classical languages like Latin and Greek. It aims at teaching rules of grammar and translation of sentences and passages into the target language. Text for translation offers quite a rich semantic framework for language learning. Learners acquire good reading knowledge of the foreign language. They are also almost accurate in their production of language if they have learned it carefully. The method focuses learners' attention on the written language; but they fail to acquire oral fluency and spontaneity. Moreover, translation is itself a specialized skill. Everyone does not want to be a translator. Nor is it true the best way of acquiring a foreign language is through translation. In this method there is emphasis on creating a framework in which rules can be applied. This emphasis may lead to stilted and unnatural use of language.

But the Grammar-Translation Method was attacked by a group of scholars and teachers in the latter half of the nineteenth century. The new method adopted by them is known as the Direct Method. This method regards speech is perceived as more universal than writing. Children learn their mother tongue through speech. It is more natural to acquire language orally. Translation is regarded as positive harm to the language acquisition because it allows interference from the mother tongue. Learning a foreign language means learning a new and independent system of language. It also means acquiring awareness of the culture of the target language. In this method all materials to be learned is first presented orally in the target language. Grammar is taught, not through direct rules, but by situation and association. Learners are requested to engage in practice and repetition till they acquire a certain grammatical pattern. The strong point of this method is that learners cultivate oral fluency and spontaneity. Its greatest weakness is that it fails to impart any real grammatical awareness. For want of real grammatical awareness learners face difficulty in tackling new material on their own.

An attempt was made to improve on the shortcomings of the Direct Method by devising more structured material for students. The new method is known as the Audio-Lingual Method which reached the height of its popularity in the early 1960s. It involves a systematic presentation of grammatical construction often in the form of drills. It is guided by a belief that the fluent use of a language is essentially a set of habits which can be developed with a lot of practice. Much of this practice involves hours spent in a language laboratory in repeating oral drills. During 1950s this approach was justified by a claim that foreign-language learning is basically a mechanical process of habit formation.

The Audio-Lingual Method believes in the separation of skills—listening, speaking, reading and writing (LSRW). It used certain practical techniques like mimicry, memorization, pattern practice and some performed in language labs. It lays emphasis on selection, gradation and presentation in a systematic manner. Items of grammar are graded, following the principle that simple forms should be taught before complex ones. The period between 1958 and 1964 is called by Stem the Golden Age of Audio-lingualism. By the end of the decade the Audio-lingual Method received a blow from Noam Chomsk who argued that language acquisition did not take place through habit formation. Human beings are endowed with the language acquisition device which helps them acquire language naturally.

But mere study of the form and structure of language does not help a learner use it in different situations. All the method discussed so far for language learning are concerned with language in its ideal system. But this ideal system is far from the problems of the practical use. People do not talk as consistently and uniformly as grammar books imply. They do not talk to produce grammatically correct sentences in isolation. The fact is that they utter for a variety of purposes in diverse situations. When they speak, they have something to communicate to other people. Language for them is a tool; and they use it with a purpose. They do not possess their language; but they employ it and do work with it. When we learn a new language or improve our mother tongue, we intend not to possess something but to do something. If we learn language with a view to possessing it, we cut a sorry figure in our actual life. Vocabulary remains in our mind but we fail to use it, fail to express ourselves.

If we possess something, it does not change. But we cannot learn language without changing it for our own purposes.

Change is no more than collective different ways in which individuals find it convenient to change their personal use of language. Individuals do not usually change in isolation. It takes to create an understood message; it really takes many to establish a convention. But the language cannot change unless we have something new to say. Language use and language change are one and same thing. Language change from speaker to speaker and from situation to situation. It also changes as each speaker matures. So the study of language, either of the mother tongue or of the foreign language, remains incomplete unless it is dynamic role in sericultural situations.

Mere linguistic competence does not enable a language learner to communicate with others in society. What he needs more than this is communicative competence. It is Dell Hymes who introduced the concept of communicative competence in the U.S.A. Later, many British applied linguists, such as D.A. Wilkins, Christopher Candlin and Christopher Brumfit recognized the functional and communicative aspects of language. The goal of language instruction has shifted to building learner's communicative competence. It is based on the view that the functions of language should be emphasized rather than the forms of language consisting of correct grammatical or phonological structure. It has become apparent that there is no straightforward relationship between grammatical categories and functions of language, such as between the category "interrogatives" and the function "asking questions." Native speakers can elicit information as much through statements as through questions. How often does one ask the way by means of an interrogative sentence? We just express our request for information simply by saying: "Excuse me, I am looking for station." There may be another example. When we feel cold and want to ask anybody to close windows, we may not use imperative sentences:

It is cold outside. Windows are still open.

Learning a language means not merely producing grammatically correct sentences but also using them appropriately. Learning to engage not merely in speech but in speech acts means mastering something more than mere structures of a language and, indeed, more than the language itself. In the final analysis it also means learning how to behave in a certain culture.

In learning a language the importance of both form and function has been realized. In order to speak a language correctly a learner needs its grammar, lexis and phonology. But mere correctness will not help him. He must know how to use it with different people in different situations. Knowing this aspect of a language means knowing not merely the form of a language but also its functions in society. Asking a teacher for a glass of water in his drawing room is entirely different from asking a servant for it:

Sir, I wanted to drink a glass of water.

Acquiring competence to communicate is much more than learning the morphology, syntax and phonology of a language.

16

Teaching of English: A Study in Indian Context

JAYDEEP SARANGI

> The telling has not been easy. One has to convey in a language that is not one's own the spirit of one's own. One has to convey various shades and omissions of a certain thought movement that looks maltreated in an alien language. I use the word 'alien,' yet English is not really an alien language to us. It is the language of our intellectual make-up—like Sanskrit or Parsian was before—but not of our emotional make-up. We can instinctively bilingual, many of us are Writing in our language and in English. We cannot write like the English. We should not. We cannot write only as Indians [...].
>
> [Raja Rao in Preface to *Kanthapura*]

In colonial India, language studies had been based on the literature (Kavya) and grammar (Vyakarna). The English Teaching was mainly teaching literary texts. 'Shakespeare' and 'Nesfield' became the 'two pillars of English Education in India.' The textual (literary) interpretations were supported by excessive teaching of grammar. Learning was preceded by oral practice—memorization, recitation and revelation. The 'Grammar-Translation' method was employed in Indian classrooms. And the method was effective and ready acceptance in India. In this method the communication skill was neglected. There was an undue emphasis upon knowing rules and exceptions.

It is an established fact that English Education in post-colonial India has been only a mere continuation of the colonial time. In a speech delivered on August 7, 1959 Prime Minister Nehru said:

> [...] for an indefinite period—I do not know how long—I should have, I would have English as an associate, additional language which can be used, not because of facilities and all that, but because I do not wish the people of non-Hindi areas to feel that certain doors of advance are closed to them because they are forced to correspond—the government, I mean in Hindi language. They can correspond in English [...].
>
> [from the speech delivered on August 7, 1959]

Language planning (in India) actually started in 1960s. 1960s saw two opposite streams of movements—'Angrezi hatao' and 'anti-Hindi movement.' In 1961, the conference of Chief Ministers recommended the three language scheme for school education:

(a) a regional language for example; Bengali, Tamil, Marathi etc.

(b) Hindi (when Hindi is not the L1).

(c) English or any European language.

This three-language formula was reiterated by the Kothari Commission (1966). The commission recommended that Hindi and English should both be link languages. English was also continued as the 'library language' and a channel of international communication. The commission further recommended English as the medium of instruction for higher education through Universities. The first English Language Teaching Institute (ELTI) was established in Allahabad in 1954. CIE (Central Institute of English) was established in Hyderabad in 1958. Now CIE is known as CIEFL (Central Institute of English and Foreign Languages). The Study Group observed (1971) that,

> English will be used in our country, as a 'source language' with a view to enriching our own languages [...] and as a link with the wider world of thought and discovery.

The "Syllabus Reform in English" (1978) talks about the aims and objectives of Teaching of English in College Education:

The aims and objective have to be formulated in the light of what we perceive our needs for English to be, at both the national and the individual levels.

At the national level, English must serve as our 'window on the world'—as the language in which nearly all contemporary knowledge is accessible. As the language of science and technology, English will be important for industrial and economic development. It will function as the language of development. Our scientists, technologists, engineers, doctors, etc., must be able not only to have access to professional literature in English but also to contribute to it, and to communicative with their counterparts in other parts of the world. The continuation of English seems important if our science and technology are to be truly international.

As the Associate official language, the *de facto* 'link language,' the language favoured by the UPSC, the legal and the banking systems, trade and commerce and defence, English will have important functions to serve internally—in addition to its role as our 'window on the world.'

English may continue to be the medium of instruction in several faculties at the college level.

Where the medium of instruction is to be some language other than English, the 'library language' function of English will have to be stressed.

At the individual level, English will still serve as 'the language of opportunity'; any individual seeking socio-economic advancement will find ability in English an asset.

It is clear, therefore, that English will have important function in communications of diverse types. The skills of communication, oral as well as written, both expressive and receptive, will continue to be at a premium, and teaching will have to try impart a certain competence in these skills.[1]

India is a vast and almost an endless country. Here, "English and Indian language co-exist in a diglottic relationship" (Parasher 1979a, 1980).[2] In India, learning English in addition to one's first language is becoming the order of the day. 'Second Language' familiarity is a matter of necessity and in a sense a matter of prestige and privilege. In most cases English co-exists with state-language of India. For example: in West Bengal the State-language is 'Bengali' whereas English is used as the 'second language.' English is the state-language in the states like Mizoram and Nagaland. There are tribal languages in both of these North-eastern states. English cannot be their native language. Generally, English is used as the 'Second Language' in India. "Second Language" stands for a cover term for any language other than the 'First Language' (FL) learned/acquired by a particular or a set of learners (a) irrespective of the type of learning conditions and (b) irrespective of the number of the other non-native languages possessed by the learner(s). 'Second Language' is abbreviated to L2 (whereas the 'first language' is abbreviated to L1). An L2, then, means, unless specified, a particular 'non-native language under discussion,' that is so-called 'Target Language' (TL). In the linguistically and culturally pluralistic Indian subcontinent English is used as the 'Second Language' which is acquired after one has learnt the First Language.

The Teaching of English in India involves a complex network of activities. It involves the political decision makers who take broad-based decisions, the Boards/University who frame the course, design the syllabus, who appoint teachers and administrative (academic) chairs and who frame a module for evaluation and other rules and regulation teaching as well as learning and at last the classroom teachers—the link between the entire programme and the target learners. The entire scheme of Teaching of English in India can be shown in the following Pyramid:

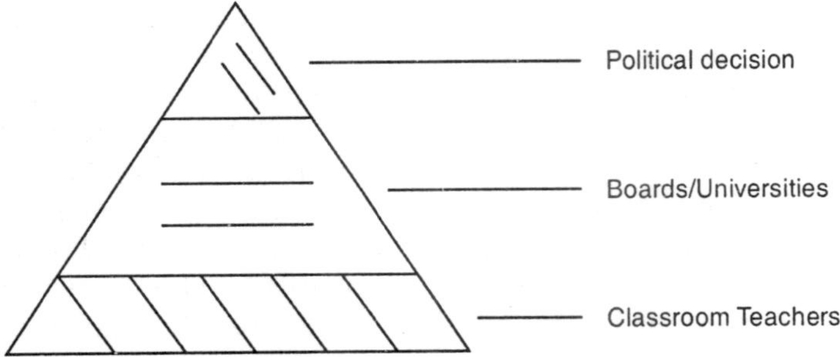

Learning of English in India continues to be governed by both academic consideration and extra-academic considerations. And we have an atmosphere in which we plead for the continuance of teaching/learning English on the basis of following factors:

1. English is a 'window on the world.' It is an established international link language.
2. English is the 'library language.' A large number of periodicals, journals and resource books are written in English.
3. It is the language of International Trade and Commerce.
4. In South India, people like to communicate in English. They seldom use Hindi as a medium of communication.
5. 'Indian Variety of English' is a socio-linguistic reality today. 'Indian Writings in English' (IWE) have earned recognition all over the world.
6. English is needed for studying abroad.
7. India is a land where different cultures and linguistic entities exit side by side. Therefore, English serve as a link language among the educated Indians.
8. English is a must for specialised jobs like translation, interpretation, broadcasting etc.

Through this paper I propose to make an attempt to identify the pedagogical issues and academic principles which underline the teaching of English in India. Such consideration can help us to understand the problems related to the teaching as well as learning of English in India.

'Academic factor' is a significant pedagogical issue. It includes syllabus, text, examination system etc. The syllabus should be objective-oriented. It must be focused and should have a gradation. If we examine the syllabus factor at the Secondary level we can trace out some of the weaknesses. The objective of teaching English at the Secondary level is to teach students to communicate in correct, acceptable English. The other aim of teaching English at this level is to read all kinds of material in English fluently. English Literature can be a tool to learn English language. Secondary level texts are often full of so-called literature staff. And literature is taught through series of lectures. Even after the introduction of 'Functional communicative syllabus' the system remains the same. The learning fail to build up a tie with texts in the syllabus. For example, *The Daffodils* by William Wordsworth is prescribed for the Secondary level in a state of India. The teaching find difficulties while teaching the students who even do not know William Wordsworth. The concept of Daffodils is difficult to communicate because both the teacher and learners have not seen the flower. The learners do not find their familiar world in British literature. Indian poetry in English can give them relief.

At the H.S. (+2) level, the major texts are from the British literature. And there is a big gulf between the Secondary level and Higher Secondary level. But the objective of teaching English at the H.S. level is same as the Secondary level. After H.S., learners opt for different streams.

At the Graduation and Post-graduation level the same tale continues. A large number of English Hons. Graduates and M.As. go for teaching jobs in schools, colleges and Universities. Considering the fact, 'English Language Teaching' should be included in their prescribed University syllabus. But sorry indeed, except only a few Universities have changed their module and duly have included 'Indian Writing in English' (IWE). But the modern dimension of English Language/ literature like Linguistic—Socio-linguistics, Psycho-linguistics, Neuro-linguistics, Stylistics, Comparative Literature, Commonwealth literature are yet to be included.

Tests are an integral part of any system. The teacher must ask himself the following questions before he starts testing the students:

(i) What is the purpose in testing these students?

(ii) What is the test expected to achieve?

(iii) What is being taught?

While framing the questions the teachers should make a list of question-types they are going to offer. The question must cover textual, inferential and extrapolative type. In India sometimes tests do not match the 'exit-behaviour' of the learns. Tests are mainly teacher-centred. Sometimes the examination paper contains only a few questions and admit no choice, students may be penalized unduly if they happen to be ill-prepared about some of the questions on the paper. A large number of short-answer questions covers the paper fully and gives a more valid and reliable result.

'Teacher—learner—classroom' can be chained together to constitute a pedagogical issue India is a multi-cultural and multi-language country. Here the classrooms are mixed classrooms. The learners come from different socio-linguistic backgrounds. The competence level of the learners are different. They are difficult to teach at a time. 'Peer teaching,' 'role play,' 'group activities' are rare in Indian classrooms. Through group activities learners can learn their own. A model of group activities in a classroom is shown below:

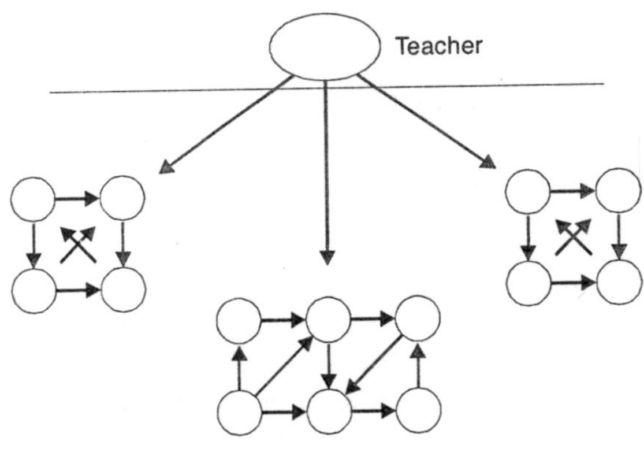

Learners

In Indian classrooms, lecturers speak, the class listens passively. The learners sometimes takes note. Normally lecturers are not interrupted or asked questions, but proceed at a uniform speed, and do not know whether they are being fully understood the subject or not. It is almost a monologue. But the lecturer's words must generate through process among the learners. Many lecturers are ineffective due to problems in delivery, pace and presentation. Indian classroom (upto graduation level) often do not allow projects, seminars, conferences etc.

'Language choice' is an important pedagogical issue. Frequent changes in language policy is not good for the learners as well as the teachers. Language choice involves broad zones, state policy and central policy. The state has freedom to make its own choice. 'Medium of instruction' is a vital area in Indian ELT situation. The learning may be monolingual, bilingual or multilingual. 'Pluralism' is the hall-mark of English Language Teaching (ELT) in India.

One of the major problems related to the teaching of English in India is that a large section of learners, in spite of being taught English for many years, fail to learn language—they cannot communicate in correct English, they cannot write acceptable English and cannot even comprehend conversation in English. Why does it happen? Does it means that Indian teachers of English cannot teach English well? Or does it means that fault lies somewhere else: in course designing, methodology of teaching, evaluation process and other pedagogical issues? We must be answerable to these valid and relevant questions.

Another related question in this connection may be—why learners (of Second Language) do not learn everything they are taught?

Some possible hypotheses may guide us to answer the question:

1. The incubation hypothesis, which was suggested by Lightbown.[3]
2. The input hypothesis of Krashen.[4]
3. The personal agenda hypothesis as suggested by John Schumann.[5]
4. The natural order hypothesis of Krashen.
5. The natural process hypothesis of Krashen.

The 'Identity hypothesis' asserts that the acquisition or availability of one language has little or no influence on the acquisition of another language. On the other hand 'Contrastive Analysis' is based on the hypothesis that the L1 habits of the learners are likely to adversely affect L2 habits "because it holds that all errors are made as a result of interference from the native language."[6] It is generally accepted that the conditions under which L2 is learnt are quite different from those of L1 learning. For the case of L2 learners, learners have passed through a language learning experience. And L2 learners try to use his L1 learning strategics (consciously or unconsciously). The transfer of training from L1 to L2 can be either positive or negative—positive as the two systems are similar and negative at points of their difference. But 'Contrastive Analysis' is not above criticism:

(i) C.A. cannot predict all the errors of the learners.

(ii) All the predictions do not come true.

(iii) It cannot explain in full even those errors which it predicts.

Newmark and Reibel (1968) challenged the very foundation of C.A. by saying that the errors which C.A. ascribes to L1 pull (interference) can be explained in an entirely different way. This error may be due to the learner's ignorance about the L2 system and not their interference.

The successive linguistic system that a learner constructs in the process of his way from L1 to L2 have been variously termed—"approximate system" (Nemser, 1971), "idiosyncratic" (Corder, 1971) and "interlanguage" (Selinker, 1969).

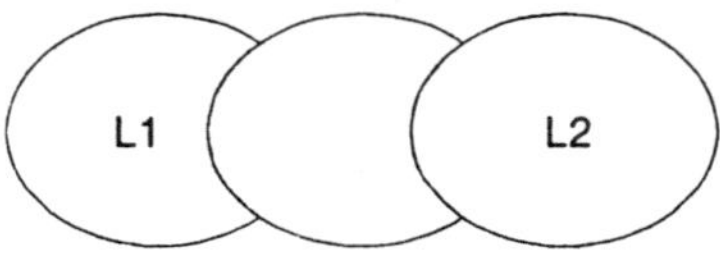

IL = Interlanguage

'Interlanguage' has same individualistic characteristics:

(i) IL has a different grammatical system which is neither L1 or L2.

(ii) IL has characteristics of both L1 & L2.

(iii) IL is the ' in-between stage' between L1 & L2.

(iv) Fossilizable linguistic phenomena—linguistics items, rules which speakers of a particular L1 (or Native Language) tend to keep in their IL relative to a particular TL. The factors like age of the learners, instructions they receive do not influence on IL system to a great extent.

Errors of the learners can be explained in two broad-based categories—interlingual (transfer) and intralingual. Intralingual errors can be of four types—Over-generalization, False concepts hypothesized, Incomplete application of rules, Ignorance of rule restriction.

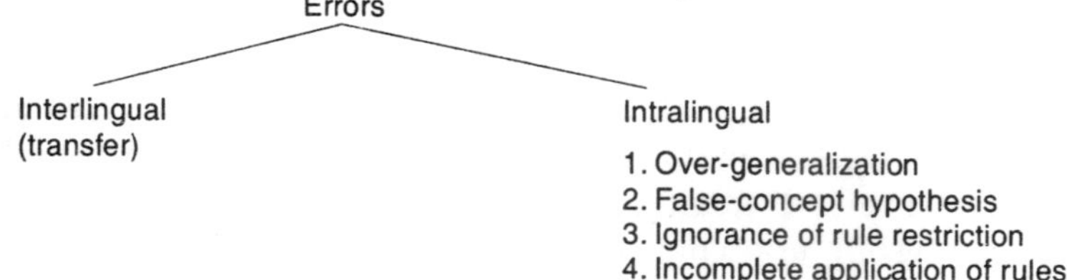

Interlingual errors are the errors based on language transfer. For example: in Bengali the syntax pattern is SOV, but English syntax pattern is SVO. When a Bengali learner writes 'He rice eats' means he simply transfers Bengali system into English.

Interlingual errors are development errors. These errors reflect the general characteristics of the rule learning, such as faulty generalization, incomplete application of rules, and failure to learn conditions under which rules apply.

Over-generalization in the use of "previously available strategics in new situations. In second language learners [...]."

Example

Teacher

	-Instruction-	Response from the student:
He walks quickly. He goes to school.	Change to Progressive Tense	He walking quickly. He is goes to school.

Ignorance of rule restriction involves in unnecessary application of rules where they do not apply.

Example

Teacher

	The response from the student:
He has to do it He needs to complete the innings.	He must to go home.

This is also a case of analogy. Sometimes errors occur due to analogy.

Take another example

Teacher

The response from the students:

I eat fish.

I eat rice. I eat water.

I eat mango.

Incomplete application of rules lead to systematic errors. Sometimes transformation rules, subject-verb agreement and other rules are difficult to understand. Therefore, students often go wrong applying the rules properly:

* When you came? → (1)

* Your name is what? → (2)

The actual sentences would be:

When did you come?

What is your name?

For sentence (1) Subject-auxiliary inversion rule was not followed.

For sentence (2) Wh-fronting rule was not followed.

False concept hypothesis leads to non-systematic errors. "There is a class of developmental errors which derive from faulty comprehension of distinction in the target language" (Richards).

Example Student

* I liking your idea.

* I am hoping to do so.

[Some verbs like 'like,' 'hope,' 'know' do not take(-ing) from.]

Human brain is uniquely suited to the acquisition and use of language. Brain is the most complicated organ of the body. It is hidden under the skull and consists of nearly 10 billion nerve cells (neurons) and billions of fibres that interconnect these neurons according to specific and selective patterns.

There are some specific areas of the brain we relate to the matters of language. The areas are: Broca's area, Wernick's area and supplementary motor area (invented by Paul Broca.

A French Surgeon) is "Crucially involved in the production of speech." Wernick's area is named after Carl Wernick, a German Doctor. Carl Wernick reported that damage to this part of the brain was found among patients who had speech comprehension problems. The motor movements involved in speech production is generally controlled in supplementary motor area. It is proved that the brain is involved in hearing a sound, understanding it and then saying it (as a response). The word is heard and comprehended via Wernick's area. This signal is then transferred to Broca's area where preparations are made to produce it. A signal is then sent to the motor area to physically articulate the sound.

The first stage in the comprehension process is the perception of the speech signal, and acoustic signal produced by the speaker. Physically, a sound is produced whenever there is a disturbance in the position of air molecules. Psycholinguists have found that speech perception and comprehension involves 'top down' (deductive or predictive) processing and 'button up' (inductive) processing.

A child learns his language through cultural transmission. The vast majority of people are not exposed to a second language until much later. "Moreover, foremost people, the ability to use their first language is rarely matched, even after years of study, by a comparable ability in the second language." There are some obvious problems people face in different stage of L2 acquisition/learning. Even in ideal acquisition/learning situation, very few adults seem to reach native-like proficiency in (L2). Joseph Conrad, the renowned novelist (who wrote *Heart of Darkness*) is an established name in English literature (For him, English was L2), but his English speech is largely influenced by Polish accent (Polish was his L1). The general belief is that during childhood (until puberty) there is a period when the human brain is most ready to 'receive' and learn languages. This period is known as 'critical period.' In most of the states in India, English education begins from class III or IV. Therefore, from neuro-linguistic point of view there is nothing wrong in the prevailing system.

The basic educational evaluations in India are 'summative.' Summative evaluation is designed to assess the total achievement of the learners during the end of a course. Is it valid and reliable? For summative evaluation the learners go on 'guessing question' and they rely on 'suggestion bank' formula. The learners cut short their syllabus and begin preparation only a few months before the examination. One test and that is at the end of an year may not judge the ability of the learners. On the contrary 'Formative evaluation' is the process of giving periodical tests which supply feedback to both the teachers and the students. This testing formula may be more valid and reliable.

Now things have changed—Teaching of English is possible even through Distance Education (DE). Distance Education was born out of pressing social compulsions, dynamics of change, new cultures and new objectives of the learners. It reflects a healthy evolution in the field of education, though in certain ways it may be considered a revolutionary development because it marks a significant break from the traditional, age-old face-to-face teaching system leading to the development of an innovative as well as effective multi-media teaching system. Modern Correspondence courses make English teaching/learning possible from home. There are some marked features of this new trend:

(i) It is self-paced.

(ii) Separation of the teachers and the students.

(iii) Learners are autonomous.

In course of time the focus of English Language Teaching has shifted from 'teaching' to 'learning.' The recent interest is more on 'what should be taught' than 'how things should be presented in the classroom situation.'

The majority of researchers and course designers pay more attention to the content of the language programme rather than the ways in which this content should be taught. 'Communicative methodology' is still unknown to a large mass. Keith Morrow in his *Principles of Communicative Methodology* divides English learning in two phases—learning the forms, and learning to use them or the application of forms. The classroom teacher is one who should choose the right path; because he is the real man in the teaching-learning situation. Nothing is sacrosanct for him. In a blending what percentage of forms should be blended with what percentage of application of forms is an open question to a classroom teacher.

NOTES AND REFERENCES

1. *Syllabus Reforms in English*, UGC, New Delhi, 1978.
2. Parasher, S.V., *Indian English, Certain Grammatical and Stylistic Features*, Published in *English World-wide*, 1983.
3. Lightbown, P.M., *Classroom Oriented Research in Second Language Acquisition*, 1983.
4. Krashen, S.D., *Second Language Acquisition and Second Language Learning*, 1981.
5. Schumann, F.M. & J.H. Schumann, *On TESOL '77*, 1977.
6. Chandra, S., *Aspects of Linguistics and English Teaching*. New Delhi: Doaba House, 1992.

17

Potentiality of Drama to Meet the Challenges of the National Curriculum

G.A. GHANSHYAM and SHIVAJI KUSHWAHA

Education is a sub-system of society, therefore, society exerts influence on education and is in turn influenced by education. A curriculum has to be sensitive and responsive to the society, it must reflect the needs and aspirations of the ultimate consumer of schooling, the learner.

Schools do not operate in vacuum and education cannot be decontextual. Keeping this fact in mind, National Curriculum Framework for School Education-2000 (NCFSE) has responded to the changing social needs and demands. The concerns that have been identified and emphasized in NCF document are:

- Education for a Cohesive Society.
- Strengthening National Identity and Preserving Cultural heritage.
- Education for Value Development.
- Common Core Components.
- Integrating Indigenous knowledge and India's contribution to Mankind.
- Meeting the Challenges of Information and Communication Technology.
- Linking Education with Life-Skills.
- The Child as a Constructor of Knowledge.
- Interface between Cognition, Emotion and Action.
- Culture Specific Pedagogies.

- Development of Aesthetic Sensibilities.
- Universalization of Elementary Education.
- Alternative and Open Schooling.
- Reducing the Curriculum Load.
- Empowering Teachers for Curriculum Development.
- Integrating Diverge Curricular Concerns.
- Relating Education to World of Work.
- Continuous and Comprehensive Education.

If these concerns are observed minutely, we find that most of these (first 12 out of 19 in the list mentioned above) are directly or indirectly influenced by language teaching. That is why the NCF lays great stress on the importance of language teaching. What I feel deep in my heart is that, to cater to the needs and concerns of the NCF, drama—which has been neglected hitherto in our ESL class must get its due place. Drama is a creative activity and as such fulfils the normal function of all creative activity; it provides a medium through which the individual can express his ideas—his reactions to the impressions he receives—and by expressing them, learn to evaluate them.

The potential of drama in ESL can be realized very well if we look at some of the concerns of the NCF more closely.

1. Education for a Cohesive Society

The curriculum emphasizes the importance of empathetic understanding of India's social life which is multi-cultural, multi-religious and multi-lingual but unified by an underlying common thread forming Indian culture which is a living process assimilating various strands of thoughts and life-styles. This induces the positive perceptions of social cohesion among school children which is need of the hour.

Drama in the class of ESL, can play very vital role in achieving social cohesion. Drama is a team-work; it will prepare the younger generation for 'Learning to live together.' The imbalance and disparities related with different locale, gender, caste and religion can be mitigated by drama.

2. Strengthening National Identity and Preserving Cultural Heritage

The development and progress of any nation very much depend on the intensity of pride the citizens feel about their nation and the way they retain their cultural heritage. The NCF emphasizes the importance of school curriculum in inculcating and nurturing a sense of pride of being an Indian.

Indian cultural heritage is one of the rich resources for strengthening national identity among our younger generations. There are a good number of drama which can enable our learners to have a conscious understanding of the growth of Indian civilization and also its contribution to the world civilization. If the children are engaged in the plays related with Indian freedom struggle, it will enhance among them the national spirit and the sense of national identity. Conscious efforts, through plays, can be made to acquaint the students with the events related to freedom struggle and the sacrifices made by the people in different parts of the country.

3. Education for Value Development

Contemporary Indian society has been sporadic eruption of communal violence. This is because of erosion of values and narrow understanding about religions. In this context the school curriculum has to contain components that communicate essential values in their totality.

> The role of language classes cannot be undermined, as they have the potential to restore and sustain the universal and eternal values. In language textbooks, we can introduce certain short plays which aim at inculcation of core universal values, such as, truth, righteous conduct, peace, love and non-violence, among school children. Our children must be aware that the essence of all religions is common, only practices differ. Care should be taken, while educating children about religions, through drama or any other co-scholastic activities, that no prejudice or narrow-minded perception are allowed. Education for value development helps an individual to evolve into a balanced personality, the collectivity which brings social cohesion.

4. Integrating Indigenous Knowledge and India's Contribution to Mankind

There is a tremendous treasure of indigenous knowledge that has contributed to world civilization, especially in the field of Philosophy, Medicine, Psychology, Economics, Political Science, Physical Science, etc. In recent times there has been a world-wide recognition of our indigenous knowledge.

Keeping in view the relevance and importance of indigenous knowledge, the NCF suggests:

- Innovative ways of preserving such knowledge.
- Analysis of indigenous knowledge and certain areas of modern science.
- Along with the contribution of other countries, the contribution of India to the world wisdom need to be emphasized.

5. Responding to the Impact of Globalization

The present century is remarkable for many challenges, especially in the context of liberalization, privatization and globalization. Of course, the phenomenon of glabalization may not drastically change education goals of reading, writing, arithmetic and skill development. However, due to globalization schools have to develop capacity of acquiring relevant knowledge among children that ensure them the efficacy. The important implication of globalization is emergence of learning societies. The challenges acted by globalization for the education as envisaged by NCF are:

- rethinking about the selection and delivery of educational content;
- integrating new sources of information;
- developing competence along knowledge;
- adapting curricula to the needs of the different socio-cultural groups;
- maintaining the national and social cohesion of the country;
- introduction of education towards active citizenship, human rights environmental issues;

- promotion of consensus on a common core of universal values.

Education should bring a balance between fast changing technology and our cultural traditions. Education, on the one hand, keep our children update to meet the global challenges and it should, on the other hand, develop a national consciousness to strengthen national identity, patriotism and nationalism tempered with the spirit of Vasudhaiva Kutumbakam (universal brotherbood). Though globalization and localization appears to be in binary opposition to each other, the NCF views these processes complementary to each other to enrich school curriculum. The repertoire of English literature has several plays which respond to the impact of globalization very well. The simplified version of these plays can be used very well to sensitize our learners to 'think globally but act locally.'

6. Linking Education with Life-Skills

The ultimate aim of education is to prepare children for life. But there is a gap between the content and living experience of the students. In order to mitigate this gap, the NCF opines that education need to be linked with different life-skills, the abilities for adaptive and positive behaviour. This linkage enables the students to deal effectively with the demands and challenges of everybody life. As life-skills are temporal and spatial in nature, they are required to be contextual. The core life-skills are problem-solving, critical thinking, communication, self-awareness, coping with stress, decision making, creative thinking, interpersonal relationships and empathy. Drama has all the potential to develop these life-skills among our children.

7. Interface between Cognition, Emotion and Action

All-round development of a child can be accomplished only when there is an interface between cognition, emotion and action. Emphasis is now, to be shifted from cognitive aspects to non-cognitive aspect by maintaining proper balance between them. The NCF suggests the nurturance of emotional intelligence by providing interpersonal and intra-personal development. Emotional literacy programmes may alter the level of success, self-esteem and well-being of a person.

Therefore, curriculum has to provide learning experiences which help in developing through, feelings and actions of learners. Multiple intelligence approach is recommended which helps learners to explore concepts and think about them on their own in many ways. Drama not only trains the imagination but it develops cognitive and kinesthetic abilities as well.

8. Culture Specific Pedagogies

The NCF clearly says, 'As India is a multi-cultural society, it is necessary to have culture specific pedagogy.' Cultural practices, such as, story telling, dramatics, puppetry, folk plays, etc. should become a strong basis of pedagogy.

Our myths, legends, fold-culture have always remained the unending source of the themes of Indian drama. Therefore, sensitizing our learners towards drama enables them to understand our culture.

9. Development of Aesthetic Sensibilities

In holistic education the ambit of learning is the total experience of the learner. Aesthetic approach attempts to balance the learning process of giving equal status to experience, imagination, creativity and intuition on one hand, and knowing, thinking, remembering and reasoning on the other. The potentiality of aesthetic experience is prevalent in any area in which the individual interact with the environment. Aesthetic approach to curriculum sensitizes the learner to gain new insights and understanding.

Drama, just as poems, sharpen the aesthetic sensibilities of a person. If the learners are given opportunities to take part in plays, they have better chances to develop balanced personalities.

Drama-teaching should get a respectable place in our classes for another practical purpose too. Now the oral aspect of language is duly emphasized in language education and oral examination in language is being made an integral part of the evaluation process. The NCF clearly states:

> Due stress is to be laid, in all language education programmes on the ability to use the language in speech and in writing for academic purposes, at work place and in community in general. (50)

The NCF has responded to the competing forces of modernity and traditionality, change and permanence, Universalism and Nationalism, globalization and localization which are at work simultaneously. Rama teaching in the language course materials will broaden learners' mental horizons, liberate them from prejudice, dogma and superstition and foster in them the desired personal and social values, an awareness of the pride in the artistic, literary and cultural tradition of the country and a deep understanding of the social psyche of the nation. It would ensure better mental health for the learners through exposure to finer human emotions, sentiments, mental conflicts and their resolutions. In drama, vague impressions and brought into sharp focus, puzzling impressions are understood, fragmentary ones are completed and alarming ones are faced so that fear is overcome. Imaginative observation is stimulated and our understanding of ourselves and the world around us is extended and deepened. Therefore, we must not deprive our students of the 'Music of Education' which Plato valued so highly.

WORKS CITED

Bright, J.A. and McGregor, G.P. *Teaching of English as a Second Language*. Singapore: ELBS and Longman Group Limited, 1982.

Doff, A. *Teach English—A Training Course for Teachers*. Cambridge: CUP, 1995.

Richards, Jack C. and Theodore S.R. *Approaches and Methods in Language Teaching*. Cambridge: CUP, 1995.

NCERT, *National Curriculum Framework for School Education*. New Delhi: NCERT.

18

PIDGINS AND CREOLES: A STUDY

SMITA JHA

Pidgins and Creoles, we know, are spoken mainly in what is commonly called the Third World countries. Their role and functions are closely connected with a variety of political issues involving social, economic and all-round national development as also the problems arising out of transition into a past-colonial society. What the earlier generations thought of Pidgin and Creole is abundantly clear from the very labels that were used for them, such a Broken or Mutilated English, Bastard Portuguese, Nigger French, Cookhouse lings and Collie language. It is only recently that the linguists could realize the importance of Pidgins and Creoles, for they are of the view that these two are not the deformed or distorted versions of other languages, but that they are new languages or media of expression in their own right. Their words or terms were taken largely from older languages during the periods of linguistic crisis to fulfil an urgent need for communication. This makes them appear to be the debased forms of older languages. However, if one examines them as linguistic systems, and tries to analyze their phonetic structure, syntax and word-formation, it becomes evident that these patterns or systems are aifferent indeed quite different, from those of the languages from which they drew their lexicon.

Although there have been several attempts at defining the term 'Pidgin,' it may broadly be defined as a reduced language that results from an extended contact between groups of people with no language in common, and it evolves when these people need some means of verbal communication, perhaps, for trade. However, no group learns the native language of any other group for specific reasons which may, among others, include lack of trust or of direct and adequate social contact between them. In other words, (i) Pidgins can and do develop in the course of time to a considerable degree of stability and complexity; (ii) in the case of Pidgins there is a tendency to confuse simplification (greater grammatical regularity) with impoverishment (lack of referential and non-referential power); and (iii) Pidgins are not mixed languages, and in this regard we find that, if at all, the mixed component of grammar is not syntax, but lexicon where syncretism of various types are common.

Pidgins are the examples of partially targeted or non-targeted second language learning, developing from simpler to more complex systems as and when communication requirements become more demanding. Pidgins, by definition, have no native speakers; they are social rather than individual acquisitions and solutions, and are characterized by the norms of acceptability. Moreover, implicit in this definition is the assumption that, speaking qualitatively, there are different stages in the development of a pidgin:

Jargon — Pre-Pidgin; multilingual idiolect; secondary hybrid

↓

Stable Pidgin — Pidgin; basilectal Pidgin; territory hybrid.

↓

Expanded Pidgin — Extended Pidgin

↓

Creole

The origins of Creole are not less complex than those of Pidgin. A Creole, we see, is traced back to a jargon or pidgin in respect of its ancestry; it is spoken natively by an entire speech community, mostly by those people whose forefathers were displaced geographically with the result that their ties with their original languages and sociocultural identity were substantially broken. Such social conditions were often the result of slavery. For instance, from the seventeenth to the nineteenth century Africans of divers ethno linguistic groups were brought by Europeans to the colonies in the New World to work together on sugar plantations. For the first generation of slaves in such a setting, the conditions were often suitable for the birth of a pidgin. Normally the Africans had no language in common except what they could learn of the Europeans; language, but access to their language was generally very restricted because of the social conditions of slavery. The children born in the New World were naturally exposed more to this pidgin than to any other means of communication, and they found it more useful than their parents' native languages. Since pidgin was a foreign language for the parents, they perhaps did not speak it very fluently; moreover, they had a limited vocabulary, and were, understandably, restricted in their syntactic alternatives. Furthermore each speaker's mother tongue influenced his or her use of the concerned pidgin in different ways, so that there was probably massive linguistic variation at a time when the new, younger speech community was being formed. Although it appears that the children were given highly variable and possibly chaotic and incomplete linguistic input, they somehow able to organize it into Creole which became their native language, and they could do so by virtue of an ability that may be described as the innate characteristic of our species. The process of creolization or nativization is different from that of pidginization; the former goes by expansion, while the latter by reduction. Creoles do have phonological rules which are not found in the case of early pidgins.

Most of the known Pidgins and Creoles arose only after the Western Europeans began setting up overseas colonies in the fifth century. There have been pidgins, among others, that are based on English, French, Dutch, Spanish, Arabic and Swahili. Pidgins have limited vocabulary, and speaking in terms of grammatical features, they typically enough, are found wanting in inflectional morphemes. That is to say their nouns have no endings to indicate plurality, and their verbs have no endings to indicate tense or subject agreement. Besides these, in the case of pidgins the verb forms are almost entirely missing and prepositions are often limited to a reduced set that alone serves multiple functions. In the course of a highly useful discussion of the Hawaii in Pidgin English it was noticed that the vocabulary of this pidgin comes primarily from English and that it syntax may and does vary in accordance with the original native language of the individual user. We may take due note of the following examples:

Pidgin form	English Gloss	Translation
Da pua pipl awl	The poor people	The poor people
Poteits it	Only potatoes eat	Eat only potatoes
Wok had dis pipl	Work hard these people	These people work hard

Although, as we find, pidgins are said to have limited uses as well as reduced vocabulary and grammar, they were used in highly expressive ways. Here is an example of Hawaii in Pidgin English, spoken by retired bus driver:

> Samtaim gud rod get, samtaim olsem ben gel, enguru ["angle"] get, no? eni kain sum olsem gud rod get, enguru get, mountin get—no? and, enikain, staumu get, naw deu get—olsem. Enibadi mi olsem, smawl taim

Literal Translation:

> Sometimes there's good road, sometimes there's like bends, corners, right? Everything's like that human life just like that. There's good road, there's sharp corner, there's mountain—right? All sorts of things, there's storm, nice days—it's like that for everybody, it was for me, too, when I was young.

It is quite interesting to see how a Pidgin, in spite of its limits and limitations, can be and is used as a vehicle of serious thought. Certain Pidgins have become well established, the most notable case in this regard being that of Tok Pisin, a Pidgin widely used in Papua New Guinea. Tok Pisin has a writing system, a literature, and even radio programmes.

When Pidgin is creolized, it registers considerable expansion of its vocabulary and grammar, and begins to acquire rules comparable in nature and complexity with those of any other language. Crowley and Rigsby have described an English-based Creoles spoken in the northern part of the Cape York Peninsula in Australia. Some typical words of this Creole are:

English	*Cape York Creole*
bad	nagud (from "no good")
diarrohea	beliran (from "belly run")
return	kambek (from "come back")
cold (illness)	koolsick (from "cold sick")

Among the grammatical features of this Creole found in several other Creoles as well, Crowley and Rigs by point to a system of marking verb tenses:

(a) Im bin ran.
"He ran." (bin has been used to mark the past tense).

(b) Im ran.
"He is running."

(c) Im go ran.
"He will run." (go is used to mark the future tense)

Within the noun system there is a kind of mechanism for distinguishing the singular from the plural:

(a) Wan dog! Bin singaut.
"A dog was barking."

(b) Plenti dog! Bin singaut.
"Some dogs were barking."

Wan, originally borrowed from the English word one, is generally equivalent to the indefinite article a, and plenty, a variation on the English word plenty, is generally equivalent to the English word some. It is worth noting that the word possession is expressed through the pre[positional] term blong which is evidently akin to the word belong:

(a) Stik blong olmaan
"The old man's stick."

(b) Dog blong maan
"the man's dog."

Certain morphemes, known as Concord particles, precede the verb of the sentence and agree with the subject. For example, when the subject is a third person noun, the concord particle is i

(a) Dog I singaut
"The dog is barking."

(b) Olman I kam I a
"The dog man is coming here."

Concord particles such as i perform the function of "agreement" with the subject, and thus are very similar to the English third person singular present tense, as in he/she runs versus I, you, we, they run. The difference is that concord inflectional suffix to the verb.

This evolutionary process has sometimes been described in terms of a broader "Creole Continuum." In his study of Guyanese Creole Bickertom notes that between the pure Creole (the basilect) and the local variety of Standard English (the acrolect) there is a series of mesolects: language varieties that form of continuum beginning at Creole and gradually moving towards Standard English, each successive mesolect approximating to Standard English more and more closely. The evolutionary process of pidginization and creolization may be summed up in the following manner:

(a) In the broadcast possible terms, many specialists accept a cyclic concept of the Pidgin/Creole evolution.

(b) The start is a kind of reduction process in both the inner and outer form (Pidginization), which leads to a non-standard linguistic system (Pidgin), different from any of the ingredients or source of substrata existing from before.

(c) The middle stage covers re-expansion (Creolization) to a less limited linguistic system (Creole).

(d) The end of the cycle is a stage in which the standard language exerts influence on the Creole (Decreolization), producing a result that can move up to a regional variety of the standard language.

(e) The process of decreolization is in evidence mostly in the New World varieties, though it is to be found in all those areas where the two types of language co-exist.

(f) The post-Creole Continuum situation may be illustrated in relation to Jamaica where between the 'pure' Creole and the Standard Jamaican English, there are several varieties of English in vogue, some of them being nearer the Creole end of the spectrum, while the others nearer the Standard English end.

(g) Negro Non-standard English (NNE) is a good example of the process of decreolization.

It is important and indeed useful to consider what Mulk Raj Anand, the internationally acknowledged Indian creative writer, in English, says about Pidgin-English in the Indian context. He discusses this problem in his paper entitled 'Pigeon-Indian: Some Notes on Indian-English Writing,' and comes straight to his thesis:

> [...] I believe that Indian-English writing has come to stay as a literature of India, because it is based on Indian-English language of the most vital character, like Irish English, American English, Welsh English, Australian English or Canadian English. It has the same advantage as those forms of English and similar disadvantages.

Dr Anand is of the view that 'Indian-English will last out, in spite of the denigration all-round.' Nevertheless, without any reference to linguistic purity or impurity, he differentiates, 'very loosely, between the highledy-piddledy spoken English in our country, from the imaginative use of the same language in the hands of the creative writers in 'Indian-English.' In this connection he says:

> I would like to define the two kinds of English by entitling the imaginative transformation of Indian-English as Pigeon-English and the 'anyhow' speech as Pidgin-English, without associating myself in the latter definition, with the British contempt implied in the word 'Pidgin.'

It is a common enough experience to hear and see such expressions as Helloji, Thank you ji, By God, Yaar, Have you finished your Khana? Or He is Jungli; and though, the British and a number of Indian linguists may find these expressions ludicrous, incongruous and lacking in good taste, and call Indian-English, Pidgin-English, the truth is that while in the case of speech these expressions are used habitually, almost spontaneously, in the case of writing they are used for the sake of authenticity and verisimilitude. This holds good also in the case of translation, transliteration and transcreation, such as, There is some black in the pulse, My head is eating circles. Go out and eat some air. Whatever you say is right to the sixteenth anna of the rupee, and eh gari ka injan hai, which we find in Indian English writing. 'There is,' says Anand, 'a psychological truth behind this kind of synthetic speech. It is this: even when Indians knew English grammar and have been used to speaking the alien tongue for a long time, they tend to feel and think in their own mother tongues. And often, the native speech enters the shell of the sentence in the foreign language through certain indigenous words. It include a sign of healthy linguistic climate that the so-called Pidgin-Indian English is being increasingly accepted all over the world with greater understanding and respect.

Pidgins, Creoles dialects are the necessary steps in the evolution of languages; some of them may die out, but others do evolve into languages.

WORKS CITED

Akmajian, Adrian. *Linguistics: An Introduction to Language and Communication.*

Albert, Voldman and Highfiold, Arnold. *The Process of Creolization.*

Damers, A. Richard & Harmish, M. Robert. *Decreolization: A Process of Pidgin and Creole.*

Holm, John. *Pidgins and Creoles: Theory and Structure,* Vol. I.

Naik, M.K. (ed.). *Aspects of Indian Writing in English* (Madras, 1979) 24.

Petere, Miihlhauster. *Pidgin and Creole Linguistics.*

Ramaine, Suzanne. *Pidgin and Creole Languages.*

Todd, Loreto. *Pidgins and Creoles.*

19

Stylistics in the Classroom: A Framework for Novel Criticism

HAREKRISHNA PRADHAN

Stylistics in the sense of linguistic interpretation of literary texts has already carved a niche for itself in pedagogical parlance. It may be pointed out that literary style is not a case of only the linguistic choices or deviations found in the text but the author's overall exploitation of the resources of language for his creative purposes. Literary style is thus the aggregate of all sorts of foregrounded structures either made use of or created in the text.

Repetition, parallelism and deviation lead to some degree of foregrounding in a sense. Stylistics in today's pedagogical domain is both formalist-cognitive and systemic-functional. On one hand, it recognizes the Chomskyan thesis that language is arbitrary, recursive and creative and on the other, it endorses the Hallidayan dictum that linguistic forms are 'socially constituted and contextually determined,' their meaning being untraceable in isolation from such a social semiotic. What is further stressed is that the reader with his knowledge of language in its widest sense which includes his literary and other experiences and with his creative imagination can retrace not merely the design but the meaning of the literary text as well.

My proposed model of Stylistics draws from the domains of various schools of Linguistics and Linguistic Criticism including Discourse Analysis, Pragmatics and Text Linguistics as well as Traditional rhetoric. It is an eleven-component framework as mentioned below:

1. Lexicalization
2. Figuration
3. Sound Patterning and Deviation
4. Group Structuration
5. Clausal Structuration
6. Syntactic Patterning and Deviation
7. Semantic Structuration and Deviation
8. The Speech Event
9. The Narrative Structure, Points of View, Modes and Focalization.
10. Allusions and Intertextuality
11. Typography

It is proposed to apply this model to a single text, namely, Orwell's *Nineteen Eighty-Four.*

1. Lexicalization

Lexicalization in the sense of the total vocabulary or lexical items in the text maps is the conceptual repertoire of the text. It is a fact that words carry some ideational or propositional meaning and the various lexical sets that might be established in the text's context give us a clue to its themes. For example, the political theme of *Nineteen Eighty-Four* can very well be guessed from the lexical set of such items as the ministry, freedom, democracy, party, justice etc. Further semantic fields along such categories as learned, literary, formal, informal, dialectal and registral might be explored in the text's context to explore certain significance of meaning, atmosphere and perspectives in the world of the novel. We may also look for neologisms, lexicalisations, overlexicalizations, underlexicalizations, collocations and formal scatters operating in the text.

1.1. Neologisms are the newly coined words which may serve some purpose in the text. For example, Orwellian neologisms such as doublethink, black-white, thought-crime, face-crime, spyhole, newspeak, duckspeak, oldspeak, minipax, miniluv, miniplenty etc. are expressive of deceit and dehumanization of the world of *Nineteen Eighty-Four.*

1.2. Overlexicalization involves the presence of many synonyms or near-synonyms for some area of experience. For example, words like tremor, helplessness, predicament, restless, uneasy, panic, cramp, unwell, fear, constricted, ache, painful, grimacing, helplessly, screaming, tremulous, cramped, expressionless, nervously, frightened, half-heartedly, quailed, pain, whimpering, grief, tears, mournful, fornication, doomed, shudder, sour, aching, grovelling, torment, shuddering, quivering, sleeplessness, gelatinous, fatigue, snivelling, stirred, agonizing, trembling, convulsive, humiliation, intolerable, etc. form more or less a synonymous group and indicate the theme of despair and disappointment in *Nineteen Eighty-Four.*

1.3. Underlexicalization in the sense of suppressing a term or of substituting a rich and complex expression for somewhat simple and naive word may sometimes prove very significant from the text point of view. For example, Swifts presentation of the Yahoos as animals rather than humans makes his satire quite caustic and sharp. In *Nineteen Eighty-Four* 'Ingsoc' is the word for English-Socialism and it negates altogether the complex feelings associated with the Socialist Movements. Words like ungood, doublegood, doubleplusgood to mean bad, very good and extremely good respectively are examples of underlexicalization and are indicative of reduction in the complexity of the system of value judgments.

1.4. Relexicalization involves the reorientation of the existing meanings of words and often points to inversion of meaning. For example, in *Nineteen Eighty-Four,* war, freedom and ignorance have lost their conventional meanings and mean the opposite of what they should mean: 'War is peace,' 'Freedom is slavery,' 'Ignorance is strength,' 'Loathing' and 'adoration' again do not contrast semantically but overlap and blur. Such relexicalizations might be presented to establish the inverted and perverse world of the set novel.

1.5. **Collocation and Formal Scatter.** While 'Collocation' refers to the relation between lexical elements within a syntactic unit, 'Formal Scatter' is a group of such a related lexical units. The word 'strong' might be said to collocate with argument but a group of such words as 'strong,' 'strength,' 'strongly,' 'strengthened,' 'argue,' 'argument,' etc. points to one Formal Scatter. In the world of *Nineteen Eighty-Four*, 'Winston Smith' collocates with 'smallish,' 'frail,' 'meagre,' 'heretic,' 'lunatic,' 'panic,' 'a feeling of positive dread,' 'the sense of nightmare,' 'suicidal impulse,' 'paralysing boredom' and 'the long-hoped-for bullet.' 'Goldstein' collocates with 'loans,' 'Jewish,' 'small,' 'goatee,' 'senile silliness,' 'thin nose,' 'brotherhood' and 'heresies.' 'Julia' collocates with 'solitary' and 'silly voice.' The characters Winston, Goldstein and Julia are alike in being lonely, helpless and silly in the world of *Nineteen Eighty-Four*. A formal scatter that may form around these characters would imply that metal agony and physical torture constitute the major themes of the novel and that the thoughtful individuals are the indiscriminate victims of the state interference. The simultaneous collocation of 'asiatic' and 'expressionless' with 'man' points to the fact that the masses in 'Oceania' are not allowed the minimum of liberty that forms the basis of pleasure and comfort in human life. Further, 'feminine' collocates with 'silly' and 'women' with 'stink,' 'swollen waddling,' 'bloody,' 'dislike' and 'hate.' These collocations establish the theme of misogyny and anti-feminism in the novel.

2. Figuration

If lexicalization is basically concerned with assigning literal or referential meaning to vocabulary, figuration has to do with conveying some connotation or implied meaning. Broadly one may talk of metaphoric figuration and symbolic figuration.

2.1. Metaphoric figuration includes both similes and metaphors of different kinds namely 'concretive,' 'animistic,' 'humanizing' or 'anthropomorphic' or 'personification,' 'pathetic fallacy' and 'synaesthetic.' Simile and metaphor are analysable in terms of three constituents: tenor, vehicle and grounds. It is the vehicle part from which the meaning is to be inferred.

The Similes in *Nineteen Eighty-Four* are expressive of mainly the cruelty, despair and dehumanization of a nightmarish world. For example, it has been presented in the context of The Proles: 'They are helpless like the animal.'

The Metaphors further imply how the people of Oceania are no more than beetles, swine, goats, sheep and even ants.

These dehumanizing metaphors convey the littleness, ugliness, loathesomeness, despair and unconscious blockheadedness off the Oceanic people.

2.2. **Symbolic Figuration.** A symbol, in contrast to a metaphor, is simply an image that evokes, suggests or represents an idea. In context of a novel, symbolism may draw themes together, illuminate certain features of character or thought.

The three main symbols in *Nineteen Eighty-Four* are: 'The Golden County,' 'The Paperweight' and 'The Proles.' 'The Golden County' with its reference to the old European pastoral landscape symbolises great beauty, peace and unity and contrasts with the world of death, decay and disintegration in the world of the novel. 'The Paperweight' in its soft beauty, its roundness, with the tiny frame of coral embedded in it, symbolises the fulfilment that Julia brings to Winston in the novel's world. 'The Proles' who constitute eighty-five per cent of the population in *Nineteen Eighty-Four* symbolise the warmth and hope of humanity from Winston's point of view.

3. Sound Patterning and Deviation

Sound patterns are formed when there is some form of echo between syllables in words that occur close to one another. In the context of the novel, we may consider such patterns as alliteration, phonesthesia and onomatopoeia.

Alliteration occurs when there is repetition of initial consonants or consonant clusters of nearby words. While phonesthesia refers to the set of words characterised by a recurring cluster of phonemes called a phonestheme. In English, phonesthemes are either initial consonant clusters *e.g.* gl- and fl- or rhymes *e.g.* -ash, -umbly, -atter, -itter that recur in one or two lexical classes. It may be seen that nouns or verbs like glace, glade, glance, glamour, glow, glimmer etc. involve something eye-catching because of the emission, reflection or passage of light. Verbs like flack, flag, flash, flit, lop, flux etc. are suggestive of a sudden or violent movement. Verbs like clash, crash, dash, flash, mash, smash, thrash etc. signify violent impact. Verbs like bum! ble, fumble, grumble, mumble, rumble etc. signify dull and untidy action. Verbs like batter, clatter, patter, scatter etc. signify a formless collation of iterated things, action, events etc. Itter words suggest 'bittiness' as in flitter, glitter, skitter, twitter etc. while –utter words suggest untidiness, ungainliness, imperfection as in clutter, flutter, sputter, stutter etc.

Onomatopoeic deliberately mimic the sounds they name. For example, words like hiss, moo, murmur, clatter etc. name the source of the sound they mimic. Again words containing hard sounds like the stop consonants might be said to convey something harsh while words containing soft sounds like the vowels might be said to convey some sort of musicality. Sound Patterning may serve a cohesive function, bonding the words together as a formulaic or fixed unit, and in the process enhancing the memorability of the unit, Patterning may also have the effect of emphasising some aspect of the text.

Alliteration is a pervasive feature in *Nineteen Eighty-Four.* We may specially cite the examples of 'big brother,' 'periodical panic,' 'senile silliness' and 'fact photograph' which point to the various aspects of the novel.

Two onomatopoeic expressions 'quacking' and 'stamping' stand out in the novel *Nineteen Eighty-Four.* 'Quacking' is the sound of the ducks and is suggestive of the pejorative toeing of the partyline of thought and activity on the part of the Oceanic people. 'Stamping' which associates with the sound of boots conveys the impression of suppression through physical torture in the world of *Nineteen Eighty-Four.*

4. Group Structuration

Group structuration might be seen in terms of the three important syntactic categories: Noun Phrase, Verb Phrase and Adverbial Phrase.

4.1. **The Noun Phrase.** The Noun Phrase typically consists of an obligatory noun as head with or without optional pre-modifiers and/or post-modifiers. Sometimes we have a noun phrase consisting of a definite article and an adjective *e.g.* the rich. The Noun Phrase typically functions as a subject, an object (direct or indirect), a complement (subject complement or object complement) or an adjunct in a sentence. The Noun Phrase may be abstract or concrete and if abstract, it may refer to an event, a perception, a process or a moral or social quality. It may be a proper name or a collective term.

If we look at the nominal groups in *Nineteen Eighty-Four,* we find that a proportionally a large number have Winston Smith or his hopes, beliefs, fears etc. as their heads. In as many as seventeen out of twenty-three chapters of the novel, Noun Phrases with Winston as head function as the subject in either the opening or the second sentence. The reader is implicitly urged to watch and appreciate the world of *Nineteen Eighty-Four* through the perception of Winston Smith alone. It is from Winston's point of view that a set of nominal groups like a sense of complete helplessness, the pain of coughing fit, a twinge of fear, a sharp cry of pain etc. reflects the solitude and agony of the individual in a totalitarian state.

4.2. **The Verb Phrase.** The Verb Phrase consists of a verb together with its obligatory objects and complements and its optional modifiers. The various features like finiteness, modality, tense, aspect, voice, contrast and presupposition are usually associated with this group structure.

It may be seen that the narrative of *Nineteen Eighty-Four* is in the past tense, even though the setting of the novel was published in 1949. The past tense narrative gives the novel a kind of very similitude, eliminating the element of fantasy. Winston Smith maintains his diary both in past tense and in present tense. The past tense is used to describe his past experiences while the present tense is used to present his current experiences and to convey his message to the future of mankind. The party slogans that one comes across in the novel are in present tense: finite, indicative and non-modal. The finiteness, indicativeness and non-modal nature of the present day slogans: 'War is piece,' 'Freedom is slavery,' and 'Ignorance is strength' suggest bureaucratic high-handedness.

4.3. **The Adverbial Phrase.** The Adverbial Phrase is any phrase that modifies the action of the sentence in respect of time, manner, place or circumstance. In the example: 'He finished his work lovingly and with great care before he left his workshop,' all the three expressions 'lovingly,' 'with great care' and 'before he left his workshop' are adverbial phrases, though only the first is a typical adverb. 'Down with Big Brother' which has been repeated a number of times constitutes the most significant adverbial group in *Nineteen Eighty-Four,* setting its tone. It is expressive of Winston's deep sense of anger, disgust, discontentment and disappointment with Big Brother, the Party, Ingsoc and all the inhuman practices that go with them. It is worth noting that this adverbial structure spreads, though dispersedly, throughout the novel, forms some sort of leitmotif and contributes to the artistry of the work.

5. Clausal Structuration

The clause may be defined as a grammatical unit containing a noun phrase, a verb phrase and an optional adverbial phrase, the noun phrase usually being the subject of the verb. It embodies in itself three sub-systems : the system of modality, the system of theme and the system of transitivity.

5.1. **Modality.** Modality is a system derived from the interpersonal function of the function of the language, expressing the speaker's assessment of probability. The modals like can, could, may, might, will, would, shall, should, need, dare, be + to, ought to and used to usually exhibit some distinctive grammatical properties and express some degree of certainty with which something is said. We usually distinguish from alethic, deontic and epistemic modality. Alethic modality is concerned with the degree of certainty of a proposition. For example, the modal 'must' in 'We must have a visitor today' expresses alethic modality if it means that the proposition is a reality. Deontic modality involves obligation and permission while epistemic modality is concerned with knowledge and belief. Of course the grammatical category of mood also represents the interpersonal element in the clause by assigning the speech roles to the speaker and his interlocutors. We have thus declarative mood of a sentence, imperative mood of a command or a suggestion, the interrogative mood of a question and the subjunctive mood of a wish.

All the four types of moods can be localized in *Nineteen Eighty-Four,* but the declarative mood overwhelms the other categories. The prominence of declarative mood in the novel is indicative of a clarity of vision and expression. This is to suggest that the novelist does not face any dilemma or ambiguity of tone and intention, and that the reader is there to judge and appreciate things for himself.

The concluding paragraph of the novel displays two clauses that are in the subjunctive mood and worthy of a close look:

> O cruel, needless misunderstanding!
> O stubborn, self-willed exile from
> the loving breast!

In the context of Winston's abysmal dejection and total surrender o the Party and the Big Brother, these two clauses of subjunctive mood keep the omniscient observer and Winston Smith on the same plane. This may again be taken as the cue for equating the novelist's point of view with that of Winston Smith.

A clause expressive of epistemic modality, though undertoned is if there is any hope, it lies with the proles. This structure is crucial to the understanding of the total impression of the text. It is suggested that in spite of the essentially dystopian view, the novel is not pessimistic in vision. There is a recognition of the fundamental worth, dignity and valour of mankind which ought reassert one day.

5.2. **Thematization.** Thematization assigns to the clause an information structure in the form of theme-rheme sequence, the theme being whatever the speaker puts first and the rheme being the rest. In principle, the theme is the take-off point of the clause and the speaker is free to select whatever theme he likes. Topicalization which involves placing some part of the sentence at the beginning so as to make it a topic is closely linked with this sub-system. For example,

> 'This text, I cannot recommend'

is a case of both topicalization and provision of marked theme, 'this text' being both topic and marked theme of the construction.

Thematization in most of the clausal structures of the novel moves in a distinctive pattern and reinforces the fact that Winston Smith is the focal point of the novel.

5.3. **Transitivity.** Transitivity is the grammar of the clause in its ideational or experiential aspect. It is a way of describing the relation between participants with attendant circumstances and processes in the construction of clauses—basically who/what does what to whom/what. Transitivity relations and the roles of participants depend upon the kind of process encoded in the main verb of the clause.

5.3.1. **Action Process Clause.** It has a process with roles such as an agent (someone or something performing the action) and the affected (someone or something receiving the action). For example,

The thief	broke	the window.
agent	process	affected

The agent may not always be the grammatical subject of the verb. In the passive form, the subject is the affected and it receives the focus while the agent may/may not be omitted:

The window	was broken	by the thief.
affected	process	agent

5.3.2. **Mental Process Clause.** It has a process with roles such as the senser and the phenomenon that is perceived by the senser.

The principal	understood	the problem.
senser	process	phenomenon

Your behaviour	pleased	me.
phenomenon	process	senser

5.3.3. **Verbal Process Clause.** It has participant roles such as sayer, message and recipient. For example,

I	told	him	it was time to sleep.
sayer	process	recipient	message

I	said	it was time to sleep.
sayer	process	message

5.3.3. **Relational Process Clause.** It has participant role such as carrier/animate and attribute or possessor and possessed. For example,

The sky	is	deep blue.
carrier	process	attribute

John	is	a teacher.
animate	process	attribute

She	has	little money.
possessor	process	possessed

Events and relationships of the real world are in fact filtered through and given linguistic shapes through these types of transitivity structures. The patterning of transitivity choices in a text can therefore reveal its predisposition to construct experience along certain lines rather than others. The analysis of transitivity will, no doubt, become a useful way of exploring the ideological dimension of texts.

Nineteen Eighty-Four opens with two meteorological relational clauses and one action-process clause with Winston being the only agent. Part one of the novel ends with an action-process clause where Winston is affected, the agent being words in the form of the three party slogans. The middle part of the novel like the first one opens with a meteorological clause and an action-process clause with Winston being the only agent. It may be deduced that Winston is perhaps a solitary person in the world of the novel. Further, the identical openings in part one and part two from the transitivity view are expressive of some symmetry in the novel. The third and final part of the novel opens with a mental-process clause of cognition and ends with another clause of reaction, Winston being the senser in both the cases. The fact that Winston is the sole senser in various mental-process clauses implies that the psychology of Winston is of vital importance to the meaning of the novel which may be seen as a study of totalitarianism in terms of Winston's perception, cognition and reaction.

6. Syntactic Patterning and Deviation

6.1. **Syntactic Patterning.** Syntax is the way in which the words are arranged to show relationships of meaning within sentences. Semantically a sentence can be a statement, a command, a question or an explanation. Structurally it may be 'simple' with one finite clause, 'complex' with a main clause with one or more sub-ordinate clauses and 'compound' with two or more coordinate clauses.

Nineteen Eighty-Four contains a variety of sentence pattern ranging from the most simple and short structures to very complex and intricate ones. There are simple and epigrammatic sentences, balanced and symmetric structures, juxtaposition of antithetical structures and sentences with clusters of nominals, verbals etc. All these patterns are semantically significant in the sense that they help the reader to build a comprehensive picture of the novel.

Let us look at the pattern of simple and epigrammatic sentences:

War is peace.
Freedom is slavery.
Ignorance is strength.
Big Brother is watching you.
God is power.
Two and two make five.

Other examples are:

Desire was thought crime.
The sexual act was rebellion.
Sanity was statistical.

Most of these sentences are in the nature of simple equations even though the two sides of the equation do not mean or represent the same thing and reflect the arrogance, austerity and high-handedness on the part of the authority in the world of *Nineteen Eighty-Four*.

6.2 **Syntactic Deviation.** Syntactic Deviation may be seen in terms of the violation of syntactic rules or formalities. This naturally leads to foregrounding and invites the reader's attention. We may cite two examples of syntactic deviations from Orwell's *Nineteen Eighty-Four*. The following structures might be seen as sentence of one word or a group of words without the formalities and intricacies of syntactic conventions:

> Ingsoc. The sacred principles of Ingsoc. Newspeak, doublethink, the mutability of the past.

Such structures though formally incomplete and unacceptable are nevertheless completely communicative and intelligible in the context of their appearance. They are indicative of the colloquial tone and the speaking voice that moves throughout the text. The text is also saved from the inclusion of more literate and artificial arrangements of grammatically acceptable sentences. Further, one would be tempted to infer that the language under totalitarian terror moves towards incoherence and silence. The following piece of instruction to

Winston from some anonymous source is another significant example of syntactic deviation:

> times 3.12.83 reporting 66 dayorder doubleplusungood refs unpersons rewrite fulllwise ubsub antefiling.

This official instruction does not use articles, prepositions, conjunctions, tense, modality and even punctuation marks. The formal relation between words, phrases, clauses and even between sentences has been suppressed.

There is no recognizable distinction between a verb and a noun. 'Refs' might be interpreted to mean either of the two. The adjectival 'doubleplusungood' shows how mathematical terms like 'double,' 'plus' are added to 'good' to eliminate the inclusion of a word like 'bad' which is of explicit negative connotation. There is a deliberate attempt in the language to get rid of the complexity and richness of thoughts and ideas. The word 'unperson' with a special meaning attached to it is suggestive of a heinous practice that the ruling bureaucracy takes recourse to for eliminating dissidence and unwanted personalities. Another peculiarity of the Newspeak instruction is that it is designed to be decoded and thus it involves a kind of censorship. The reader is told that a mistake has been committed but he never knows who has committed it. The reported errors has thus been glossed over and dehumanized in every subtle and foolproof manner.

7. Semantic Structuration and Deviation

7.1. **Semantic Structuration.** Semantic structures might be defined in terms of texts with cohesion and coherence. We may talk of several types of cohesive devices that make the sentences of a text hang together: conjunctive relations (with such motions as contrast, result and time), coreference (anaphoric relations looking backwards and cataphoric relations looking forwards for interpretation), substitution, ellipsis, repeated forms, lexical relationships (synonymy, antonymy, hyponymy and converseness) and comparison. Semantic structures have to be coherent in the sense that the concepts and relationships expressed should be relevant to each other and they must enable the reader to make plausible inferences about the underlying meaning. *Nineteen Eighty-Four* is a cohesive and coherent text in the sense that its various parts starting from the paragraphs and chapters through its three sections to the whole novel are organized in a neat and logical way. The connectivity has been maintained from the beginning to the end through various leitmotifs, and lexicogrammatical as well as structural devices.

7.2. **Semantic Deviation.** Semantic deviation might be seen in terms of the violation of logical and experiential facts and truths. All literary discourse is semantically deviant in the sense that it claims to refer to things in the world but we are not expected to take those claims seriously. Good literature should impress upon the readers that it is an imaginary work though it is based on and related to our life. Let us consider the opening sentence of *Nineteen Eighty-Four* (1949):

> It was a bright cold day in April and the clocks were striking thirteen.

In Britain, the idea of a bright cold day in April may not be remarkable but 'the clocks striking thirteen' is somewhat incomprehensible. It may be noted that clocks in public places in Britain strike thirteen. Again, though the novel was published in 1949, the title looks forward to a date in the future while the past tense in the first sentence refers backwards as if to events which have already happened. Readers would not interpret the first sentence as the beginning of a factual record of the events but appreciate Orwell's point that such events could conceivably come to pass.

8. The Speech Event

Dialogues or speech events often constitute an important part of the novel and hence the need for appreciating the same. The 'Speech Act Theory' developed by J.L. Austin comes handy for the purpose. It may be pointed out that in Speech Act analysis, the effect of utterances on the behaviour of speaker and hearer is studied, using a three-fold distinction. First in every speech, a communicative act takes place: the locutionary act. Secondly, the act might be seen to be performed as a result of the speaker making an utterance such as batting, promising, welcoming, warning etc. which are known as illocutionary act. Thirdly, if the act brings about certain effect on the listener such as 'his being amused, persuaded, warned etc.,' then it is known as a parlocutionary act. J.R. Searle, working on the theory, talks of five basic types of speech acts:

Representatives where the speaker is committed to the truth of a preposition (affirm, believe, deny etc.), directives in which the speaker tries to get the hearer to do something (ask, challenge, command, request etc.), commissives in which the speaker is committed to a certain course of action (promise, vow, guarantee), expressives where the speaker expresses an attitude about his state of affairs (apologise, congratulate, thank etc.) and declarations where the speaker alters the external status or conditions of an object or situation solely by making the utterance (I resign, you are fired etc.). Of course speech acts are successful only if they satisfy several conditions known as felicity conditions. For example, the person performing the speech act must have the authority to do so. The speech act must be performed in a sincere manner. We may look at the following speech event between Winston and O'Brien towards the end of the novel:

'Oceania is at war with Eastasia. Do you remember that now?' 'Yes.' 'Oceania has always been at war with Eastasia. Since the beginning of your life, since the beginning of the party, since the beginning of history, the war has continued without a break, always the same war. Do you remember that?' 'Yes.' 'Eleven years ago, you created a legend about three men who had been condemned to death for treachery. You pretended that you had seen a piece of paper which proved them innocent. No such piece of paper ever existed. You invented it and later you grew to believe in it. You remember now the very moment at which you first invented it. Do you remember that?' 'Yes' 'Just now I held up the fingers of my hand to you. You saw five fingers. Do you remember that?' 'Yes.'

This speech event is marked by the vigour and briskness of its moment. The language is one of quick fire police interrogation and brainwashing, and the tone is somewhat shrill and hysterical. O'Brien's queries are characterised by all the three major speech acts: locutionary, illocutionary and parlocutionary.

Winston's reactions are, on the other hand, supported by

only the locutionary and illocutionary speech acts. O'Brien performs the locutionary act of speaking, the illocutionary act of asking questions and the parlocutionary one of extracting the desired responses in the form of immediate affirmations. Winston, on the other hand, performs merely the locutionary act of interacting and the illocutionary act of submitting to the complete control of O'Brien over Winston and establishes the theme of unmitigated power and control in the overall context of the novel.

9. Narrative Structure, Points of View, Modes and Focalization

9.1. **Narrative Structure.** The novel as a narrative structure can be analysed into four components: setting, theme, plot and resolution. The setting has three subcomponents: the characters, a location and a time. The theme consists of an event and a goal. The plot consists of various episodes each with its goal and outcome. The resolution specifies how the plot comes to an end.

9.2. **Narrative Points of View.** The narrative point of view refers to the perspective from which the story is presented. It is customary to distinguish between the first person narrative point of view and the third person narrative point of view. The third person narrator remains outside the action of the tale while the first person narrator remains a character inside the story. Of course we may distinguish between the narrative told by the protagonist and that by a subsidiary character. Again we may distinguish between the third person omniscient narrator and the third person restricted narrator.

9.3. **Narrative Modes.** The whole narrative from the beginning to the end may be thought as a form of reporting on the part of the narrator. That is to say, a novel is a continuum of speech and thought presentation by the narrator. We may distinguish between direct mode, indirect mode, free direct mode and free indirect mode of presenting speech and thought. It may be pointed out that free direct speech/thought of a character is unfiltered by the narrator while indirect speech/thought is the most filtered by the narrator.

Direct speech/thought is less filtered than free indirect speech/thought. We may also talk of the 'narrator's representation of action' (NRA) which accounts for physical description and action in the narrative. Distinction may be made between actions by character, events or happenings caused by inanimate agents, states including internal states and character perceptions.

9.4. **Narrative Focalization.** Focalization refers to the way in which the text represents the relationship between experiences and what is experienced. The one who experiences is called the focalizer while what the focalizer experiences is called the focalized. Again we may distinguish between two types of focalization: external focalization, where an anonymous voice situated outside the novel functions as a focalizer and character focalization, where phenomena are presented as experienced by character within the story. We have thus external focalizer, first person character focalizer or third person focalizer in the narrative. The notion of focalization helps to reveal the way a text will shift from sentence to sentence in terms of who is experiencing what and how. Patterns of focalization are at once the expression and construction of the types of consciousness and self-consciousness.

The narrative of *Nineteen Eighty-Four* is very neatly structured, highly informative and modalizing. The opening passage gives a very precise setting by clearly stating the time and the weather. As the narrative progresses, the character of Winston Smith clearly develops and we feel that the plot develops round the theme of totalitarianism. It is the third person omniscient narrative point of view that operates in the novel. However, Winston Smith, the central character, is the focalizer while his consciousness has been focalized. Further, though the narrative moves along a linear dimension, it is tagged with two stretches of metalanguage: 'The Theory and Practice of Oligarchical Collectivism' and 'The Principles of Newspeak.' The first block of metalanguage expounds the principle of Ingsoc while the second block of metalanguage serves as a device to tempt and blackmail the people who do not feel at ease with the system. The two booklets within the book thus do not diffuse the narrative but helps the reader grasp the total meaning of the novel. As the two booklets might also be seen as serving towards the disintegration of the power structure operating in the world of *Nineteen Eighty-Four*, the novel might very well be seen as postmodernist in outlook.

10. Allusions and Intertextuality

Allusion refers to the implicit or explicit reference to other entities and might be helpful in comparison or contrast of theme in the text. Texts may allude to other texts through verbal references, epigraphs, names of characters and choice of titles. Intertextuality might be used in the sense of the various ways in which texts interact with other texts. It particularly focuses on the interdependence between texts rather than their discreteness or uniqueness. Intertextuality can be better perceived if the text is seen as a work in a particular genre.

Orwell's *Nineteen Eighty-Four* has alludes to Tragedy, Shakespeare, Byron, Milton and The Golden County and all these allusions being expressive of some form of beauty, dignity and exuberance contrast to the ugly prosaic and decayed world of the novel.

The intertextuality of the novel might be seen in terms of its being a work in the genre of scientific romance established by H.G. Wells. The novel may be compared with Wells's such work as *The Time Machine, The Island of Dr Moreau.* The scientific romance developed by H.G. Wells has within it a set of conventions which have been exploited by Orwell to combine political purpose with artistic instinct. It may be seen that Orwell's central character operates in a hostile setting which is similar to that *The Island of Dr Moreau.* There is much similarity between the character of O'Brien in *Nineteen Eighty-Four* and Dr Moreau in Wells's book. Again the scientific romance concentrates on the reactions of the hero to the strange life with which he finds he has to deal.

This is also true of *Nineteen Eighty-Four* and Winston's developing reactions to life in Oceania constitutes the main interest of the novel. Another point of similarity between Wells's book and Orwell's book is that the former novel talks of the tempering with brains on the part of the doctor to make them more rational while in *Nineteen Eighty-Four* there is a tempering with brains to annihilate ordinary logical common sense through reality control and the development of Newspeak. The novel can also be seen as a work in 'dystopian literature' and stands comparison to Zamyatin's We and Huxley's Brave New World.

11. Typography

This includes a wide range of printing conventions and devices like capitalization, abbreviation, italicization, division of words at the end of the lines, etc. These features are expressive of certain functions:

grammatical, semantic and/or stylistic.

Nineteen Eighty-Four displays a number of graphological deviations. For example, the Three Party slogans are in capital letters:

WAR IS PEACE

FREEDOM IS SLAVERY

IGNORANCE IS STRENGTH

So also is the caption beneath the picture in the Party poster:

BIG BROTHER IS WATCHING YOU

Winston himself express his discontent and disgust with the Party and its Controlling authority:

DOWN WITH BIG BROTHER

These graphological deviations not merely highlight and emphasize things which are significant from the semantic point of view of the novel, but point to things highly catchy and impressing. Besides capitalizations, one comes across numerous italics and small letters. The diary of Winston has been maintained in small italics. One also meets occasional italicized words and phrases that appear as neologisms or are intended to have some special significance in the context of the novel. The newspeak instruction and the black book appear in relatively small letters and make themselves distinct from the general narrative of the novel.

The typography has thus been exploited to simplify the complexities of the novel and make it easily intelligible even to an average reader. The graphological features support the reader's sense of critical understanding as and when he goes through the unique novel that *Nineteen Eighty-Four* is.

Stylistics can thus be very rewarding if the novel is seen as the manipulation of the potentialities of language both in its creative and socio-semiotic aspects. As the linguistic description of structures in text is objective and as there cannot be much divergence of social meanings of a cultural group, stylistic interpretation of text will more or less remains stable. Of course one with a better understanding of the socio-cultural and literary tradition can generate a richer interpretation of the literary text.

WORKS CITED

Allen, G. *Intertextuality*. London & New York: Routledge, 2000.

Carter, R. and Simpson, P. (eds.). *Language, Discourse and Literature*. London & New York: Routledge, 1989.

Flower, R. *Linguistic Criticism*. Oxford & New York: OUP, 1986.

Flower, R., Hodge, B., Kress, G. & Trew, A. *Language and Control*. London: Routledge & Kegan Paul, 1979.

Halliday, M.A.K. *Functional Grammar*. London: Edward Arnold, 1985.

Halliday, M.A.K. and Hasan, R. *Cohesion in English*. London: Longman, 1976.

Leech, G. *Semantics*. Harmondsworth: Penguin Books, 1984.

Leech, G.N. and Short, M. *Style in Fiction*. London: Longman, 1981.

Montegomary, M., Durant, A., Fabb, N., Furniss, T. and Mills, S. *Ways of Reading*. London & New York: Routledge, 1992.

Short, M. *Exploring the Language of Poems, Plays and Prose*. London & New York: Longman, 1996.

Weber, J.J. (ed.). *The Stylistics Reader*. London, New York, Sydney, Auckland: Arnold, 1996.

Contributors

Usha Manjunath. Lecturer, Management Group, Birla Institute of Technology and Science, Pilani, Rajasthan.

Kathyayani Venkatesh. M.Sc. CCC-SLP. Speech-Language Pathologist, Vineland School District, 14327, Vineland Road, Bakersfield, CA 933307, U.S.A.

Meenakshi Raman. Assistant Professor of English and Group Leader Languages Group, Birla Institute of Technology and Science, Pilani, Rajasthan.
E-mail: mraman@bits-pilani.ac.in

Mehmet Celik. Hacettepe University, Turkey.

Malavika Sharma. C/o Mr P.E. Sharma, Shree Nivas, Ajanta Path, Kalpataru By Lane, Beltola, Assam.

Krishna Mohan. Formerly Professor of English, Birla Institute of Technology and Science, Pilani, Rajasthan.

Meera Banerji. Visiting Professor, Birla Institute of Technology and Science, Pilani, Rajasthan.

Mimi Singh Sandhu. The Graduate School, College for Women, Jamshedpur, Bihar.

Pushp Lata. Lecturer, Languages Group, Birla Institute of Technology and Science, Pilani, Rajasthan.

Sangeeta Sharma. Birla Institute of Technology and Science, Pilani, Rajasthan.

Shih-Jen Huang. Fooyin Institute of Technology, Taiwan.

Hsiao-Fang Liu. Fooyin Institute of Technology, Taiwan.

Alessandro Monti. Deshi (Centre for the Study of Indian English), Department of Oriental Studies, University of Turin, Via Roero di Cortanze 5 10124 Torino, Italy.
E-mail: alessandromonti_prof@yahoo.com

Gerd Rohmann. FB 08 Anglistik/Romanistik, Universitat/ Gesamthochschule Kassel, Georg-Forster-Strasse 3, D-34125 Kassel, Germany.

N.D.R. Chandra. Reader and Head, Department of English, Nagaland Central University, Kohima, Nagaland.

Mihaela Mudure. Str. Pavolv nr. 18 B, ap. 5, 3400 Clij, Romania.

Sivasish Biswas. Senior Lecturer, Department of English, Karimganj College, Karimganj, Assam.

Shailendra Kumar Mukul. Department of English, L.S. College, Muzaffarpur, Bihar.

Jaydeep Sarangi. Lecturer in English, Seva-Bharti Mahavidyala, Kapgari, Midnapur, West Bengal and Guest Teacher, Vidyasagar University, West Bengal.

G.A. Ghanshyam. Deputy Registrar, Guru Ghasidas University, Bilaspur, Chhatisgarh.

Shivaji Kushwaha. Centre for English, Government College of Education, Bilaspur, Chhatisgarh.

Smita Jha. Department of English, L.S. College, B.R.A. Bihar University, Muzaffarpur, Bihar.

Harekrishna Pradhan. Reader in English, Rourkela College, Rourkela, Orissa.
E-mail: dr_hkpradhan@yahoo.co.in